ADOBE®
CAPTIVATE® 4
THE DEFINITIVE GUIDE

BRENDA HUETTNER

JONES AND BARTLETT PUBLISHERS
Sudbury, Massachusetts
BOSTON   TORONTO   LONDON   SINGAPORE

D0259626

World Headquarters
Jones and Bartlett Publishers
40 Tall Pine Drive
Sudbury, MA 01776
978-443-5000
info@jbpub.com
www.jbpub.com

Jones and Bartlett Publishers
Canada
6339 Ormindale Way
Mississauga, Ontario L5V 1J2
Canada

Jones and Bartlett Publishers
International
Barb House, Barb Mews
London W6 7PA
United Kingdom

Jones and Bartlett's books and products are available through most bookstores and online booksellers. To contact Jones and Bartlett Publishers directly, call 800-832-0034, fax 978-443-8000, or visit our website, www.jbpub.com.

Substantial discounts on bulk quantities of Jones and Bartlett's publications are available to corporations, professional associations, and other qualified organizations. For details and specific discount information, contact the special sales department at Jones and Bartlett via the above contact information or send an email to specialsales@jbpub.com.

Adobe, Captivate, Connect, Flash, Photoshop, and RoboHelp are trademarks or registered trademarks of Adobe Systems Incorporated in the United States and other countries.

Production Credits
Publisher: David Pallai
Acquisitions Editor: Timothy McEvoy
Editorial Assistant: Molly Whitman
Associate Production Editor: Tiffany Sliter
Associate Marketing Manager: Lindsay Ruggiero
V.P., Manufacturing and Inventory Control: Therese Connell
Composition: Northeast Compositors, Inc.
Cover Design: Scott Moden
Cover Image: © cystalfoto/ShutterStock, Inc.
Printing and Binding: Malloy, Inc.
Cover Printing: Malloy, Inc.

Library of Congress Cataloging-in-Publication Data
Huettner, Brenda.
 Adobe Captivate 4 : the definitive guide / Brenda Huettner.
 p. cm.
 Includes index.
 ISBN-13: 978-0-7637-8137-8 (pbk.)
 ISBN-10: 0-7637-8137-1
 1. Captivate (Electronic resource) 2. Computer animation. I. Title.
 TR897.7.H8384 2010
 006.6'96—dc22
 2009033349

6048
Printed in the United States of America
13 12 11 10 09 10 9 8 7 6 5 4 3 2 1

DEDICATION

For my daughter, Heidi, because I am always inspired by her determination, insight, and sense of style in all things.

About the Author

Brenda Huettner is a writer, speaker, and consultant with over twenty years of experience in the technical publications field. She has written manuals, help systems, procedures, proposals, and training material for a variety of corporate clients, and she has published several books on technical topics. She is a Fellow of the Society for Technical Communication and a Senior Member of the IEEE, serving on a variety of committees including the Professional Communication Society and the Engineering Management Council. She's also a member of the Usability Professionals Association. A regular presenter at conferences across the United States, Brenda speaks on documentation, management, and career issues. Brenda lives in Arizona with her husband and two children.

FOREWORD

I have known Brenda for many years, and we have met regularly at industry events all over the world, including in my home country, Germany, so I was thrilled when she told me about this book. It will quickly guide you through all the powerful features of Adobe® Captivate® software to develop engaging training products, without requiring any programming or Adobe® Flash® development skills.

My own background is in marketing. Before Captivate existed, I was tasked to develop online demonstrations of our software products. At the time, the available tools left me frustrated and annoyed with their limited functionality. If I moved my mouse to the wrong spot while recording, I wasted many hours recapturing the same tasks over and over until I got it right. For example, if I forgot to turn off my reminder window, it popped up while I was recording the screen. Since my reminders obviously have nothing to do with the demonstrated tasks, I had to painstakingly edit video segments to remove the little pop-ups, which resulted in missing pieces of the mouse moving over the screen. In addition to the recording and editing problems, I had to face access issues. The file formats I used were video formats that required special codecs, which were not always installed on all customers' machines. (If you don't know what a codec is, don't worry. Captivate does not need codecs. If you *do* know about codecs, you may have experienced browser and loading issues of your content, and as a result, frustrated users.) Some files were so large that they never loaded on viewers' browsers. As an author of marketing and basic training content, I was not satisfied with the process and needed a simpler, faster, and more effective way of developing content, which I helped develop into what became Captivate.

I have been the product manager of Captivate from the first release, originally titled RoboDemo (2002), to the current version. Over those few years, we have collected and received a lot of customer feedback that the development team has turned into new feature sets. The product has quickly grown from a simple demonstration tool to a very powerful software simulation application that has reached the leadership position for simulations in the e-learning industry. In a software simulation tool shootout at the Training 2005 Conference & Expo, Captivate won against nine other simulation tools. The audience evaluated the tool based on ease of use, interactivity of the output, quality of guidance and feedback, and most innovative approach; Captivate received the highest overall score with 33 points out of 40. Ease of use, including the ability to change the captured mouse path or update screenshots, combined with interactivity, learning guidance, and an innovative approach make Captivate a popular choice for rapid training development.

Instructional designers can easily use Captivate to create Flash-based training content and thereby benefit from the ubiquity of the Flash Player. Since no programming skills are required, all training professionals can quickly develop and update online training themselves. Our customer Safety-Kleen Systems is a great example. Their technical training manager, Frank Hanfland, told us that Captivate helped increase course production, reduced development cost, and increased employee productivity. Instead of one course per month, the training team now develops five courses per month, and costs were reduced more than $600,000. Nearly all instructional designers I have met have to face the same challenges: no time and no budget. As seen in Frank's case, Captivate can make a significant difference in responding to both of these challenges.

Cost savings and rapid development are not the only benefits offered by Captivate. The key to providing effective training is the ability for the learner to practice in a safe and simplified environment where corrective feedback is provided. My first recorded demonstrations for the Web were 45+ minutes long—and they were just that: demonstrations. Customers had to simply watch, which can become very boring (and typically does after 10 minutes). There were far too many steps shown in one large nonreusable, noninteractive segment. Captivate provides so much more flexibility than these video recordings I developed back then. As an author, you can take advantage of the experience I and thousands of other e-learning content developers have contributed. You can create small, reusable learning objects and then combine them in different ways using the viewer-controlled menu functions. Or you can deploy these objects through a learning management system, your online Help system, or Web-based support or Help Desk pages. You can add interactivity with branching to create realistic practice scenarios. Captivate supports many different interaction types, and its simulation recording modes even add the interactions automatically for you. No coding or scripting skills are required—Captivate is designed to empower the everyday user (like myself; I am definitely not a programmer) to create engaging learning content.

You will be surprised at the many different types of content you can create. This book guides you from learning the basics of creating your first demonstration all the way to using interactive features and creating e-learning content. Try out the different features today and let your creative juices flow. Captivate has so much power that you can use it for more than just demos or simulations.

Please share your engaging and interesting training scenarios with us and other users—we are always looking for great examples to include in our customer showcase. Now, let Brenda skillfully guide you through the features of Captivate and have fun!

Silke Fleischer
Senior Product Marketing Manager
Adobe Captivate
San Diego, California

ACKNOWLEDGMENTS

No man is an island, and no book can be brought to press without the effort and support of many people. I'd like to thank Silke Fleischer and Sandra Nakamura, who consistently came through with help, even at the last minute, as well as John Hedtke, who never wavered in his belief in my ability to write this book. I would also like to thank all the thoughtful, helpful people who devote their time and expertise to helping others in the online forums and in the Captivate community.

Brenda Huettner
bphuettner@p-ndesigns.com

INTRODUCTION

Adobe® Captivate® software allows you to create interactive Flash® movies quickly and easily with automatic recording functions, text captions, mouse tracking, and more. You can easily add e-learning capabilities with quizzing functions and branching, or create stand-alone movies that can run on a kiosk. Captivate 4 includes a variety of greatly enhanced functionality. Some of the features include:

- Panning while recording screens
- Project templates
- Design templates
- Variables
- Advanced Actions
- Text-to-speech functionality
- Customizable widgets
- Expanded output options
- Single SWF Output option
- Table of Contents on output
- Aggregator (allows you to combine multiple Captivate files into one output)
- Captivate Reviewer (allows for commenting directly on Captivate SWF output)
- Web-based Help System

HOW THIS BOOK IS ORGANIZED

This book covers Adobe® Captivate® software functionality in 14 chapters.

Chapter 1: Installing and Configuring Adobe® Captivate® Software

Chapter 1 reviews the system requirements for Captivate and describes how to set up the software. You can use this information for either a purchased copy of Captivate or the trial version that is available for download at www.adobe.com. This chapter also describes how to activate your software license if you've purchased a copy of Captivate.

Chapter 2: Getting Ready to Make Movies

This chapter covers some of the basics of designing movies. These are things you should consider before you begin any project, like creating a project plan and identifying the resources you'll need.

Chapter 3: Creating Your First Movie (Just the Basics!)

This chapter steps you through an entire movie from recording to publishing. It will give you a good understanding of movie basics.

Chapter 4: Recording a Movie

This chapter describes the various recording options, defines "full motion recording," and shows how to record a variety of movie types.

Chapter 5: Creating Movies without Recording

This chapter covers alternative ways of creating a movie. For example, you can start with a blank movie and add individual screenshots or images, create a movie of just questions, or import a Microsoft® PowerPoint® file.

Chapter 6: Working with Slides

This chapter covers the basics of how slides work, and it describes how to add, delete, and hide slides from view.

Chapter 7: Editing a Single Slide

This chapter describes the editing functions that apply to a single slide, such as how to work with the elements on a slide and how to change the timing of slide display. You'll also learn how to prevent changes to a slide and work with the slide background.

Chapter 8: Defining What the User Hears—Adding Audio

This chapter describes how to record audio within Captivate, either while recording or after recording. It also covers how to import and edit existing audio clips.

Chapter 9: Defining What the User Does—Adding Interactivity

This chapter describes how to add interactivity through elements such as click boxes, text entry boxes, and rollover images and captions. Use interactivity to create software simulations or simply to make your movies more engaging to viewers.

Chapter 10: Creating e-Learning Content

This chapter describes how to add quizzing functionality to your movies with a variety of question types. You can enter the correct answers and determine which slides display based on the viewer input. This chapter also discusses how to create question pools for random question display and how to store the answers that each viewer gives.

Chapter 11: Working with the Branching View

This chapter covers the functions available from the Branching view. This view lets you see the way the slides work together and view the various possible paths through your movie.

Chapter 12: Using Adobe® Captivate® Tools

This chapter describes the additional tools that come with Captivate, such as a spell checker, bandwidth analyzer, and notes for each slide. You'll also learn about Aggregator, a tool that allows you to combine multiple movies in a single menu, and you'll learn about Adobe Captivate Reviewer.

Chapter 13: Refining the Movie

This chapter shows you how to edit your movie as a whole by adding elements that cross all slides. For example, you can define the look and content of the playback controls or control the way the movie starts and ends. This chapter also describes movie-level functions such as saving or hiding movies.

Chapter 14: Generating Adobe® Captivate® Output

This chapter describes how to generate a variety of output types. In addition to standard .swf movie files, you can integrate with other packages, compress files on the fly, or export just the text to Microsoft® Word® documents.

Appendices

The Glossary defines the terminology used throughout this book. Additional Resources is a short list of websites that offer more information about Captivate, Flash, and general e-learning principles. The Captivate Shortcut Keys table lists the keyboard shortcuts available with the Captivate software.

CONVENTIONS USED IN THIS BOOK

Boldface text in a procedure indicates a button, link, or menu item that you should select. You can usually select these items with either the mouse or the keyboard.

- *Tip:* A tip provides a helpful hint or useful technique.
- *Note:* A note calls out specific information relevant to the current discussion.

CONTENTS

Chapter 14   Generating Adobe® Captivate® Output   413

Chapter **1** INSTALLING AND CONFIGURING ADOBE® CAPTIVATE® SOFTWARE

This chapter describes how to get your copy of Adobe® Captivate® software up and running. You'll also learn about activating and deactivating your software.

SYSTEM REQUIREMENTS

Before you begin installation, ensure that the system you'll be using has at least the following minimum configuration:

- Intel® Pentium® 4, Intel Centrino®, Intel Xeon®, or Intel Core™ Duo (or compatible) processor
- Microsoft® Windows® XP with Service Pack 2 (Service Pack 3 recommended) or Windows Vista® Home Premium, Business, Ultimate, or Enterprise with Service Pack 1 (certified for 32-bit editions)
- 512MB of RAM (1GB recommended)
- 1.5GB of available hard-disk space; additional free space required during installation (cannot install on flash-based storage devices)
- DVD-ROM drive
- 800x600 screen resolution (1,024x768 recommended)
- Internet connection for product activation
- Software and accessories for publishing and recording
- Microsoft® Internet Explorer® 6 or later
- Adobe® Flash® Player 7 or later

> **Note:** Flash Player must be installed before the Captivate software will start. If you don't have Flash installed, the Captivate installation will attempt to download a copy of Flash from the Internet for you.

> **Note:** If you're going to be recording sound for your movies, you'll also want a microphone, speakers, and a sound card.

INSTALLING THE SOFTWARE

The setup wizard for Captivate software makes most of the installation process automatic, so if you've used an installation wizard before, you can probably skip this section and go straight to the section called "Starting the Software." The steps you'll follow are the same whether you're installing a trial version or a fully licensed version of Captivate. If you have a software license, you'll also need to enter your serial number in order to activate the software. One Captivate license allows you to install the software on up to two systems.

If you're going to be installing a licensed version of the software at this time, make sure your Internet connection is up and running before you begin installation. This will make it easier to activate and register your software during the installation process.

To download a trial version of the Captivate software, open your Internet browser and follow these steps:

1. Navigate to the Captivate website: http://www.adobe.com/products/captivate.
2. Click **Download free trial**.
3. In the window that appears, you'll need to sign in to the Adobe site. If you do not have an Adobe password account, click **Create an Adobe account** and enter the required information (your name, requested login ID, password, etc.) If you already have an Adobe account, enter your ID and password, then click **Sign in**.
4. Once you've signed in, confirm your address and indicate which (if any) of the Adobe communications you'd like to receive. There may also be a short survey that you can take. This screen also includes links to the Adobe Terms of Service and Privacy policies. Click **Continue** to display the available trial downloads.

5. Select the appropriate Captivate version from the drop-down menu and click **Download**.

6. When the download is complete, open the executable file to begin the installation process. You will need to extract the .zip file and save it to your system.

7. Click **Next** to extract the files to the specified location. The installation welcome screen is displayed. Click **Next** to display the license agreement, and continue with Step 3 below to complete the installation process.

To install the Captivate software using a purchased copy of the software, close all other programs, then follow these steps:

1. Insert the CD into your computer's CD-ROM drive. The installation wizard should start automatically and should display a welcome message on your screen as shown in Figure 1-1. Click **Next** to display the license agreement, and skip to Step 3.

2. If nothing displays on your screen, you'll have to run the setup program manually. You can do this in either of two ways:

    ▪   Choose **Run** from your Start menu, click **Browse**, then type in your CD drive letter and a colon followed by the command **setup.exe**. For example, you might type D:setup.exe. Then click **OK**.

    ▪   Open your Windows Explorer by clicking **My Computer**, then browse to your CD-ROM drive and double-click the **setup.exe** icon.

    The license agreement screen is displayed.

FIGURE 1-1   **Extract the files.**

FIGURE 1-2   **The License Agreement screen.**

3.   You must agree to the terms of this agreement whether you are installing a licensed version or a trial version of Captivate software. Use the scroll bar to display the entire agreement. You may also choose from the drop-down list to display the agreement in another language.

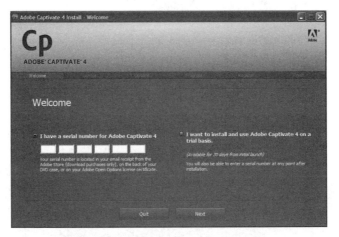

FIGURE 1-3   **The Software Setup screen.**

4. After you've read the agreement, click **Accept** to display the software setup screen. At this point, you'll have a fully functioning copy of Captivate whether you've purchased the system or are using the trial version. However, if you don't enter a serial number within 30 days, the software will stop working. To *activate* the product (as described in the next section), you must enter and verify your serial number and license.

5. If you want to just try out the software, click the **I want to install and use Adobe Captivate 4 on a trial basis** button. This will allow you full access to the Captivate product, but it can only be used for 30 days from the day you first launch Captivate. Otherwise, click the **I have a serial number for Adobe Captivate 4** button and type your serial number in the boxes provided. Enter four digits in each box.

6. Click **Next** to display the Installation Options window.

7. Choose the language for installation. You may change the storage location of the software by clicking the **Change...** button and entering a new path.

8. Click **Install** to begin the installation process. When the installation is finished, click **Exit** to close the installation window and to display the main Captivate window.

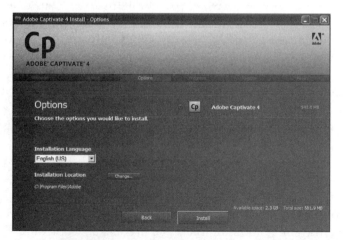

FIGURE 1-4 The Installation Options screen.

FIGURE 1-5   **The Software Setup screen.**

Starting the Software

1. Start the software by double-clicking the **Captivate** icon. If you entered a serial number while installing your Captivate software, the activation process occurred as part of installation, and your system opens directly to the main Captivate window. If you're using the trial version of Captivate, you'll be able to use the software for 30 days before you must enter a serial number. Each time you start Captivate during the trial period, you'll be given the opportunity to either continue the trial or enter a serial number.
2. Choose **I'd like to continue to use this product on a trial-basis** or enter a serial number.
3. Click **Next** to complete the activation process and display the main menu.

Deactivation

Each copy of Captivate software comes with an end-user license agreement that specifies the number of times you may install Captivate. For most people, the EULA specifies that you may have up to two installations, as long as you don't use them concurrently. For example, you may share one license between a home machine and a work machine, or between a desktop and a laptop PC.

If for any reason you need to change computers or significantly change your hardware configuration, you'll need to deactivate one of your licenses so that you'll be able to activate Captivate on the new system.

> **Note:** As soon as you deactivate your license, the software will stop working but will remain on your system. You may reactivate the software as long as you do not exceed the limit of active copies specified in your EULA.

The following steps require an active Internet connection.
To remove the license from your system, follow these steps:

1. From the Captivate main menu, click the **Help** menu, then choose **Deactivate** to display the deactivate license screen.
2. Click **Deactivate**. The Captivate license on your current system will be immediately disabled, and you'll be able to install and activate the software on another system.

SUMMARY

This chapter described the steps you'll need to take to get your Captivate software up and running. We also covered how to activate your software license so you can use Captivate past the 30-day trial period and how to deactivate your license when you want to move Captivate to a new computer.

The next chapter describes the planning stages that go into making a movie.

GETTING READY TO MAKE MOVIES

Chapter **2**

This chapter describes the steps you should take before beginning to use the Adobe® Captivate® software. Good planning and organization up front will help you to make better movies!

We'll assume that you already have good communication skills, including a good grasp of grammar and a full understanding of the topic or software you're going to be teaching or demonstrating. This chapter will discuss the factors you'll need to consider in order to create a fast-paced, exciting movie. We'll also review some basics of project planning and general preproduction issues.

WHAT MAKES A GOOD MOVIE?

Captivate movies can be used for a myriad of purposes, such as product demonstrations, tutorials, quizzes, assessments, training, and even simple slide shows. But like any tool, it can create poor output just as easily as great output.

A good movie delivers the information that the viewer needs in a way that the viewer can understand. It is timely, accurate, and helpful. It ISN'T boring, overly repetitious, or excessively long or complicated.

What Is Your Goal?

The very first thing you'll need to think about is the goal of your movie. If, for example, you are creating a demo to sell a product, you'll want to take a very different approach than if you're creating an e-learning course that students use to get a certain type of certification. One is "flashier" with perhaps more animation; the other requires significant consideration of things like minimum passing scores and integration with other learning systems.

You can use Captivate to create a complex, interactive movie that plays only the sections that are appropriate to each user and that tracks a variety of user input for grading and integration with a learning management system. You can also use Captivate to create a quick demonstration of a specific task that can be incorporated into standard online Help systems. Captivate has the flexibility to do these things and more, but this flexibility means that it's up to you to decide what you need and how to implement it. You'll also save time later if you make these decisions before you begin.

When you first create a Captivate movie, you'll need to specify how you're going to begin. There are many options, but the primary decision is whether you want to start by recording action on your screen (a Software Simulation) or you want to start by importing information (such as from an existing PowerPoint file or from a directory of existing images).

You'll also want to think about how interactive you want to make your movie. Prior versions of Captivate software used templates to predefine specific levels of interactivity (such as training simulations or assessments). Captivate 4 always starts with a Software Simulation, then allows you to incorporate a variety of interactive elements into your movie as you need them. You could create one scenario that simply demonstrates how something works, another that requires viewer interaction such as clicking areas on the screen or answering questions to move through the movie, and another that returns feedback to the user with success or failure captions, audio effects, and more. You can also create a simulation that includes quiz slides and a grading or assessment component, and may integrate with an external learning management system (LMS).

Elements of a Demonstration Movie

Use a demonstration-type movie when you don't expect the viewer to interact with the movie. For example, this is very useful as a component of online Help or product demos or sales tools. A demonstration could be run from a website or even a stand-alone kiosk. Demonstration movies generally use captions and animations to show where the action is happening on the screen, but they do not pause for the viewer's input at any point. A sample screen from a demonstration might look like this:

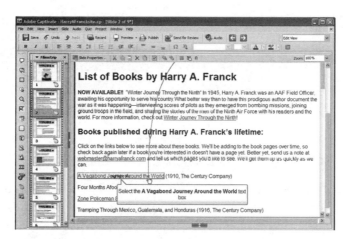

FIGURE 2-1   Demonstrations show how to do something.

The demonstration displays a text box that describes the action, and you can have an animation that shows a cursor moving to perform the action. You can even include audio that describes the action, or simply play a click noise to emphasize the action. The action (in this case, clicking on a text box) occurs within the movie without interaction from the viewer.

Elements of a Training Simulation

A training simulation builds on a demonstration movie by pausing at certain points to allow the viewer to interact with the movie. Like a demonstration, this type of movie can include text captions, highlight boxes, animations, and cursor movement. You can define a variety of parameters for each interaction, such as the number of attempts the viewer can make for each task, or different feedback messages that display depending on whether or not the viewer performs the correct task.

After the viewer performs a task, you can define which part of the movie to display next (the destination). For example, if the viewer can't successfully click a certain box, you may want to replay the part of the movie that described that box. Or, if the viewer performs a series of tasks correctly, you may want to skip ahead to a more advanced part of the movie. This sort of interactivity, combined with the multiple destination options, ensures that the viewer is performing the correct actions at each step in the movie.

A sample training simulation movie screen might look like Figure 2-2.

FIGURE 2-2   **Training simulations wait for viewer interaction.**

The simulation displays instructions in a text box and highlights the area the viewer is supposed to click. If the viewer actually clicks in the correct area, a "success caption" displays (in this case, the text "Good Job!!") and the movie can then continue.

If, for example, the viewer clicked on a different area (such as the Zone Policeman 88 link), then you could have a "failure caption" display, allow another try, or go back and restart the movie.

Elements of Simulation with Quizzing

An assessment simulation incorporates the interactivity of a training simulation and adds true e-learning functionality. As the viewer works through the movie, interacting as you've defined, you can track and store the results of each interaction. Like a training simulation, you can specify different destinations depending on whether the user performs the correct action. In addition, you can insert questions at any point, in a variety of formats (such as multiple choice, true/false, short answer, and more), and you can specify destinations and feedback based on the answers the viewer gives.

You can manage the results of all the interactions for the whole movie and specify how the results will be delivered to you. For example, you may just want a text file e-mailed to you, or you may want all answers integrated into an existing learning management system (LMS). Captivate can produce output in formats compatible with several e-learning standards. If you're integrating with an existing system, you can specify whether you want to track results for each interaction or send just a summary of interactions throughout the movie.

You can also create questions that are not scored, such as questions that ask for comments or suggestions, or ask the viewer to enter subjective ratings for various things. You can even have those results e-mailed to you.

A sample screen from an assessment simulation might look like Figure 2-3.

FIGURE 2-3   e-learning simulations add questions and tracking functionality.

For each question slide, the movie pauses while the viewer enters appropriate answers. In the example in Figure 2-3, you can see a matching question where the viewer is to match up the countries with the books that discuss them. This particular viewer got it wrong—you can see the "retry" caption on the slide. Depending on your goals, you may decide not to allow retries, or you may allow unlimited retries. The viewer can submit the answers, go back to check on the instructions in the previous parts of the movie, or skip this question altogether by clicking the **Skip** button. When you create an assessment simulation, you'll have full control over which buttons appear at which points in the movie.

Elements of a Branching Simulation

Simulations with branching present a student (in our case, the viewer) with a situation or problem that must be solved, and with a selection of options from which to choose at various points throughout the learning experience. In Captivate, you can create this type of learning using the branching functionality to display a list of options, and then you can display different slides based on which option the viewer chooses.

This type of simulation typically has multiple options or branches for each question slide. Each branch may have many questions and branches of its own, creating a fairly complex "tree" of possible paths through your movie. Captivate has tools to help create and manage the display of these various paths.

FIGURE 2-4   **Simulations can make use of branching.**

Elements of Slide Design

As you create your movie, much of your slide design will be determined by the screens that you capture as you move through the software you're demonstrating or simulating. However, you should also ensure that the elements you add are well designed and consistent throughout your movie. For example, if you display a failure message in red on one slide, it should be in red on all slides.

When you create questions, make sure they all use the same font and that the font you choose is easy to read.

A style guide for your movie can be a helpful tool to maintain consistency. There are lots of books on style guides and design, so we won't go into detail here. However, these are some elements you'll want to consider:

- *Backgrounds:* Although Captivate allows you to use any image as a background, whether you've got a screen shot or another image or just text on a slide, use discretion when designing your slide backgrounds. A busy background distracts from the point you're trying to make.
- *Text font, size, and color:* These may vary by type of text, but they should remain consistent for all similar text types.
- *Text phrasing and tense:* Generally, use a command only when you are inserting an interactive element and want to tell the viewer to do something. If the caption is not for an interactive element, use a statement. For example, if the viewer sees "Click this button to advance to the next slide," he or she is likely to try to click the button. If it is simply a demonstration, consider using a phrase such as "This button advances to the next slide."
- *Timing issues:* You don't want to have one slide go by too fast and another too slowly.
- *Spelling and grammar:* Make a list of words that are unique to your product or software or industry, and use them consistently. And by all means, use the Captivate spell checker (see Chapter 10)!
- *Animation:* Though this can enliven a movie, too much animation becomes distracting. If your words are flying all over the place, the viewer will be watching the animation and not reading your important message.
- *Color scheme:* Make sure that the colors you pick for text boxes and highlight boxes show up well on your background or on your screen shots. For example, viewers may not be able to see a light blue highlight box if it is highlighting a blue button.

Planning Is Everything

Okay, this isn't a new concept. Before you even start the Captivate software, you need to begin planning exactly what you want your viewers to take away from the experience. These are some of the questions you'll need to consider:

- Who will be watching this movie?
- What is the audience's current skill level?
- What hardware and software will they be using?
- What do they need to know *right now*?
- How much interactivity do they need?
- What determines success or failure?
- Will their progress or results be tracked, and if so, how?
- When does the finished product need to be delivered?

A comprehensive plan that answers all of these questions will serve as a guideline for the entire project and ensure that you end up with a movie that meets your audience's needs.

Elements of a Project Plan

There are lots of resources that discuss good project planning. Basically, a good plan will have the following minimum components:

- Executive summary
- Overview
- Audience
- Technical information
- Task list
- Schedule
- Script and/or storyboard

Executive Summary

The executive summary is a brief description of the scope and purpose of the project. Keep this short and sweet—it should never be more than one page long.

Overview

Here's where you can get into detail that you left out of the executive summary. Include the scope, purpose, and goals for the finished project, and summarize the rest of the sections in the plan.

Audience

The more information you have about the people who will be viewing this movie, the more accurately you can fulfill their needs. You're likely to have more than one audience category. For example, you may be creating a tutorial that shows novice users how to perform a task, but this same tutorial may also be used by instructors, by expert users who perform the task only occasionally, or by managers checking up on their employees. For each potential viewer type, you should consider these elements:

- What they are doing (the specific task they're trying to accomplish)
- Their skill level (with the product, with movies, and with computer systems in general)
- The environment in which they're likely to be working

Technical Information

The technical information describes what the project will look like when it is completed and what hardware or software you expect the viewers to have. This includes any standards or style guides you may have and the graphic look-and-feel you want, as well as specific output type. Captivate software has a wide variety of output options, including these:

- Flash files (.swf)
- Executable files (.exe)
- Stand-alone files for Windows, Linux, and Mac
- Handouts (Microsoft Word files, i.e., .doc)

You'll want to specify the level of interactivity. Will you include quizzes? Scoring? Interactive demos that require user input? You should also specify additional effects you'll use, such as audio, animations, or other customizations. Will you use a narrator? Will there be sound effects?

Task List

You know what you're doing and what it takes to make it happen, but there may be other people in your company who are not aware of the specific steps required to create this project. List all the tasks that need to be accomplished and who will accomplish each one of them. Make sure you include all of the stakeholders in your project, including the writer, editor, reviewer, tester, approver, and any other personnel who may need to participate. This is particularly important if you're going to be asking for time from people in other departments—such as a QA department or a usability group.

Note: Although you may include names at this point, be aware that things could change. This document is a tool that will need to be updated frequently throughout your project.

The tasks will vary for each project, but a good starting list of tasks is the following:

- Create plan
- Review plan
- Revise plan
- Approve plan
- Learn product or topic
- Create script/storyboard
- Review script/storyboard
- Revise script/storyboard
- Approve script/storyboard
- Create movie files
- Create auxiliary files (animations, sound, etc.)
- Create sample output file
- Review sample output file
- Revise as needed
- Integrate with other software
- Final approval
- Project review and wrap-up

Be very specific with the tasks, particularly those that you expect to be accomplished by other groups. If you expect the usability department to run a test on your movie, say so here so that there are no surprises later. Similarly, list the people you'll need for technical reviews. Often you'll want to include informational review passes by various levels of management, even though you may not expect feedback from them.

Though the exact names may change as the project goes forward, you are more likely to get the support you need if you get buy-in from everyone up front.

Schedule

The schedule is simply your estimate of the amount of time you think needs to be allocated for each of the tasks in your list, along with an approximate completion date for each. Particularly for larger projects, make sure you take into account holidays, vacations, staff meetings, and other nonproductive times. You'll also need to include a statement of assumptions that lists factors that could delay your project (such as slow reviewer turnaround, changes to code-freeze dates, or other issues).

Be aware that any schedule you set will change, and the larger the project, the more likely it is that something will go wrong. Some things are simply out of your control, such as when the software screens will be ready for you to capture or how fast the technical reviewers turn around and approve your output. The best you can do is to track the actual schedule against your estimates and adjust the next project accordingly. As you go through subsequent projects, you'll be able to come up with increasingly accurate data, and this will help you make better estimates on future projects.

Scripts and Storyboards

If you're writing a manual, you start with an outline. If you're building a house, you need architectural drawings. When you create a Captivate movie, you can use either a script or storyboards to plan the content.

- Scripts, like in Hollywood, are a printout of the text that will be in the movie. In this case, you may also include directions such as "user clicks the **Next** button" or whatever is appropriate to your project. The more detail you include in your script, the smoother your project will go. Scripts can also be useful in the review process if you need to get input or sign-off before actually creating a movie.

■ Storyboards are a graphic representation of your movie, usually consisting of a series of screenshots that represent the major components of the movie. The storyboards may be rough sketches on paper or more of a prototype done electronically, depending on your skills and available time.

Obviously, the script will have to describe some of the graphics, and storyboards will have some text. Both approaches are used to organize your content and, most importantly, to get sign-off or approval before you invest a lot of effort into the final movies.

As you plan out the movie, you'll want to think about the components. In addition to screen shots, lessons, and questions (if you have any), make sure you plan for the extra elements that complete the movie. For example, you may want to include these elements:

■ Title page
■ Credits page
■ Copyright page
■ Opening/closing graphic or splash screen
■ Introductory material, such as prerequisites and/or assumptions you've made about the audience's experience and skill level. This section often includes discussion of special navigation features you may have in the movie.
■ The body of your movie (demonstration, simulation, or assessment slides)
■ Feedback mechanism, which can be as simple as including an e-mail address or contact information at the end of the movie, or as complex as creating text boxes for viewer input and having their content e-mailed to you
■ Ending, such as a final slide that lets the viewer know the movie is over

Planning Paths through Your Movie

As you build your Captivate movie, there are numerous places where you can pause the movie to await viewer interaction. For each place you pause you can specify where the movie will resume based on the viewer's input. For example, you may want to replay the introductory portions of the movie if the viewer didn't answer the first set of questions correctly. Or you may want to allow the viewer to skip some sections if they get a pretest type of questioning correct. These paths through the movie are sometimes called branching or contingency branching.

As you think about your questions and interactive components, it's often helpful to create a diagram of potential paths through your movie. For example, a very basic flowchart showing three lessons might look like Figure 2-5.

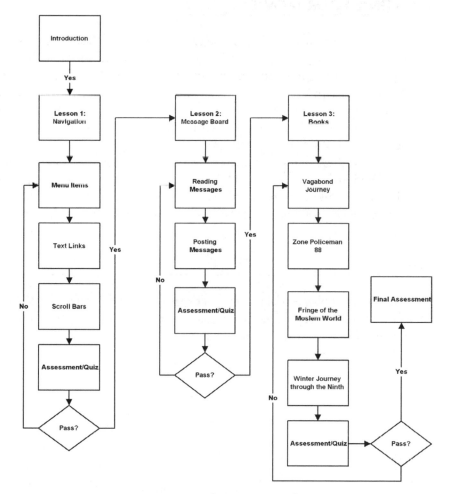

FIGURE 2-5 Plan out your paths.

The decisions—marked on Figure 2-5 with Pass? and Yes and No paths—can be easily entered in Captivate by specifying different locations depending on whether or not the viewer correctly answers the assessment or question. Note that you can also use this type of branching for any type of interactive element such as buttons (repeat the lesson if they click on the **Repeat** button) or text entry boxes (where the viewer types "Repeat" to go back or "Continue" to go ahead).

EVALUATING YOUR MOVIE

As a final step in your movie-making process, you should always check to see whether or not you met the goal or goals you set in the first step. If you were simply including a demonstration in a Help system, you'll need to use methods outside of Captivate to track its success. For example, you may want to check with your call center to see if the movie helped reduce support calls for that particular function. For movies with more interactivity and assessment options, you can look at statistics like the percentage of viewers who answer each question, the percentage of correct answers, or the overall scores for the whole movie.

Obviously, you can go back and edit this movie to make it better. You should also document the lessons you learn from each movie so that when you plan the next project, you'll have a good base of experience from which to work.

SUMMARY

This chapter reviewed a number of the things you'll need to think about to create a useful movie that meets your goals. The following chapter steps through the basics of making a simple movie in a very short time.

Chapter 3

CREATING YOUR FIRST MOVIE (JUST THE BASICS!)

Adobe® Captivate® software is powerful and flexible, and you can make your movies as intricate and interactive as you want. However, you will always start with a basic movie. This chapter describes how to make a basic Captivate movie using the auto-record feature. Follow along and create a demonstration from start to finish!

OVERVIEW

Captivate allows you to capture the movement of your cursor and the resulting screen images with just a few keystrokes. To make the simplest form of movie—one that you can modify and enhance later—there are only a few basic steps:

1. Decide what you're going to record (discussed in more detail in Chapter 2).
2. Turn on the Captivate recording function and then perform the tasks to create the elements you want to include in the movie.
3. Preview the movie and make changes as necessary.
4. Publish the movie for others to use.

For the rest of this book, we'll be creating movies about the website dedicated to Harry A. Franck, a well-known travel author from the early part of last century.

RECORDING WITH CAPTIVATE

To create your first movie, you'll need to decide what the movie will be about. For this example, we'll create a demonstration that shows how to navigate the various pages within a website. Before you begin, ensure that the website or whatever application you'll be recording is open and ready to go. If you want to follow along with our example, open up the website http://www.harryafranck.com in your preferred Internet browser.

1. Start the Captivate software by double-clicking the **Captivate** icon.

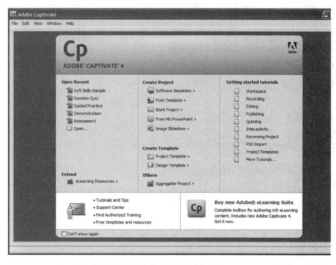

FIGURE 3-1   Start Captivate.

2. Under the **Create Project** column, click **Software Simulation** to display the New Project options.
3. With the first option (Application) under the Record tab selected (this is the default), choose the application that you'll be recording from the drop-down list under Select Application. All open applications on your system will display in this list. As you can see in Figure 3-2, for this example we'll be recording the Mozilla Firefox browser with the Harry A. Franck site selected.

FIGURE 3-2   **Choose the type of project.**

4.   We're going to be creating a demonstration for an application (the browser), so the default selection of Snap Recording Rectangle to **Custom Size** is fine. You'll still get a chance to set your window size in the next step. Click **OK** to display a red outline and the recording option icons as shown in Figure 3-3. Anything within this outline will be recorded to the movie file.

FIGURE 3-3   **Specify the area to record.**

5.   The red outline indicates the portion of the screen that will be recorded. You can move or resize the recording outline by clicking and dragging the

square "handles" at the corners and sides of the rectangle. When you've outlined the area you want to record, click the round red **Record** button at the top-left corner of the recording rectangle.

6. Perform the tasks you want included in the movie. If you've got your audio set up and turned on, Captivate will play a clicking noise, sort of like a camera shutter, each time it captures a screen. This generally occurs whenever you move or click the mouse, change focus to or from a window, type text, or press keys on the keyboard, such as the volume mute button. For this example, be sure to use the scroll bar to display additional material, click on an internal text link, and use the top navigation buttons to return to the main page.

7. When you've finished all the tasks, press the **End** button on your keyboard to stop recording and display the save options.

TIP

Take your time when recording a movie, making sure that each screen is fully loaded and appears the way you want it to before you go on to the next task. You'll make a better movie if you proceed slowly while recording.

Save Project Files

Project Name :	untitled
Project Location :	C:\Documents and Settings\ Browse...
Demonstration :	untitled_demo
Assessment :	
Training :	
Custom :	
Project to Open :	Demonstration
Re-recording Script :	

Learn more...   OK   Cancel

FIGURE 3-4   **Specify a name for your movie project file.**

Captivate displays a status message as it converts the stored images to .swf files and then displays the movie on the storyboard window.

FIGURE 3-5   **The captured screens display in the storyboard window.**

PREVIEWING AND EDITING MOVIES

Once you've completed recording a movie, Captivate displays the movie in the storyboard window. From here, you can preview the movie or make changes as necessary (including adding interactivity as described in Chapter 9).

There are five basic components of the storyboard window.

- *Menu:* Located at the top of the screen, the menu bar allows you to access the various Captivate functions that apply to the entire movie (such as Save or Publish).
- *Slide Tasks:* On the left side of the screen, the Slide Tasks area lists the functions that you can perform on individual segments within your movie. Note that the Edit and Branching tabs (just above the Slide Tasks list) give you access to even more functions.

- *Slideshow:* The largest area of the screen, this area shows a "thumbnail" icon for each captured screen. You can select multiple slides for easier, faster edits, or you can make changes to individual slides from here.
- *Information:* This area displays information about the movie, such as size and run-time length.
- *Comments:* Located at the bottom of the screen, this area displays notes about the selected slide.

Note: You can adjust the size of thumbnails through the Thumbnail Size command on the View menu.

Previewing Your Movie

Once you've recorded your actions, Captivate stores each captured screen and the actions associated with it as a slide. You can preview the movie at any time to see what it will look like. Captivate will generate an .swf file and then play it on your screen.

To preview a movie:

1. With the movie in Storyboard view, press the **F4** key or choose **Project** from the **Preview** menu.
2. The preview window includes some movie control buttons on the right side of the window. You can use these controls to play, pause, stop, or fast forward the movie preview, just as you would a VCR.

As you watch, you'll notice a variety of elements that Captivate has automatically added to the movie for you:

- Each slide is given a default display time.
- A sound plays that represents each mouse click.
- Some areas are surrounded by a highlight box.
- Captions with default text are added in some places.
- Controls for playback are on the top and side of the captured screen.

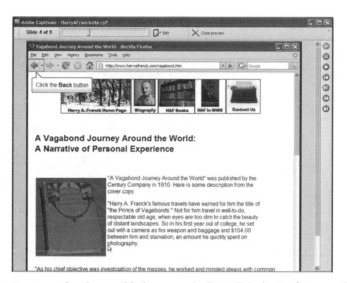

FIGURE 3-6   **Some text has been added automatically: "Click the Back Button" in this example.**

3.   When the preview is complete, you can use the controls on the right of the screen to view it again or to step backward through the preview.

4.   When you're finished watching the preview, click the **Close preview** button.

For this sample movie, Captivate added some text to the link we clicked. However, it isn't exactly the phrasing we want to use. We can easily edit this slide later in Edit view. In addition, we notice that some of the slides are not displayed long enough for the viewer to be able to read all of the text. But this is easy to fix, and can be done right from the Storyboard view, so we'll do that first.

Editing Multiple Slides from the Storyboard View

To edit the movie from the Storyboard view, follow these steps:

1.   Select the slides you want to edit by clicking once on the first slide, then holding down the **Shift** key and clicking on the last of the slides you want to change. The selected slides are highlighted.

TIP

If you double-click on a slide, you'll automatically open the slide in Edit view. While there are times you'll want to do this, for now you want to remain in Storyboard view. Simply click the Storyboard tab on the left side of the screen to return to Storyboard view.

FIGURE 3-7 **Select the slides you want to edit.**

2. Choose one of the Slide Tasks functions on the left side of the screen by clicking on it. For our example, we'll click **Properties**.

FIGURE 3-8   **Enter the Display Time in the Slide Properties window.**

3. In the Display Time box, type the time, in seconds, that you want each slide to remain on the screen.
4. Click **OK** to close the Slide Properties window.
5. Click **Save** at the top of the Captivate screen.

TIP

You could skip these last two steps, but it's better to save frequently. You never know when you might be interrupted!

---

6. Enter a name for the movie—in our case, we're calling it **HarryFranck_ demonstration**—and then click **Save**. Captivate automatically appends the suffix .cp (for Captivate project).

Editing a Single Slide from the Edit View

To make changes to a single slide, you'll want to go to the Edit view. This view has some of the same functionality as the Storyboard view, plus more. To make changes in the Edit view, follow these steps:

1. Open the slide you want to edit in Edit view in either of two ways:
   - Select the slide you want to change by clicking on it once, then choose **Edit View** from the drop-down menu in the upper right of the window.
   - Double-click the slide you want to edit.

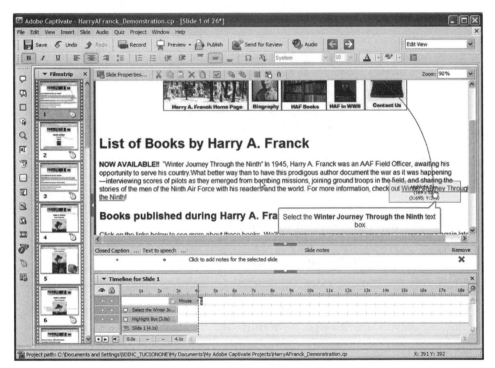

FIGURE 3-9   View a slide in Edit view.

2. Take a moment to locate the different areas of the Edit view and the elements that are on the slide we're viewing. The default Edit view is kind of busy, but you can rearrange the components as you like later. The upper

right of the view displays the selected slide. Note that the full slide may not be visible, but there are slider controls on the right and the bottom of the slide that you can use to move the display. Just below the slide is the comment section that shows you information about captions and other notes attached to the slide. Below the comments is a "timeline." This shows you exactly how long each element on the slide appears on the screen. For this example, you can see there are three components:

- A mouse track showing that the mouse movement comes up from the bottom of the screen to stop on a link.
- A text box that says "Select the **Winter Journey Through the Ninth** text box."
- A highlight box that outlines the text of the link that was clicked.

3. Double-click on the element, either in the timeline or on the slide itself, to display the properties for that element. In our example, we want to change the text in the text box. Double-clicking on the text box itself displays the Text Caption window.

FIGURE 3-10 Change the text in the Text Caption window.

4.   Make changes to the text as necessary. Note that you can change the font, size, color, and other attributes just as you would in standard word processing packages: Simply select the text you want to change; then select the new attributes for the selected text. For this example, we're changing the wording to "Click the **Winter Journey Through the Ninth** link."

5.   Click **OK** when you are done to close the Text Caption window and return to the Edit view display.

6.   Click **Save** to save your changes.

Note: Sometimes you'll need to adjust the size of a text caption after editing text. To do this, drag the appropriate caption handle to resize the caption.

PUBLISHING MOVIES

Once you've made whatever edits you need to make, you must publish the movie to convert it from a Captivate project file (.cp) to an actual Flash movie file (.swf). The Captivate publishing function can also create additional files that can be used to view the Flash movie. For example, if you publish to a Web page, you may set the publish feature to automatically create the .html file that plays your Flash movie. If you publish to a stand-alone .exe file, Captivate will create the .exe file that contains your movie. For more details on publishing options, see Chapter 12.

For this example, we're going to publish a Flash file designed for viewing on a Web page.

1.   From the open movie, in either Storyboard or Edit view, click the **Publish** icon to display the publishing options.

FIGURE 3-11   **The Publish options window.**

2. Click the **Flash (SWF)** icon to create a Flash movie.
3. Captivate enters a default name for the output movie that is the same as the name of the saved project. You can change this by typing a new name in the Project Title text box.
4. Captivate will store the output you publish in a new folder in the folder with your current Captivate project files. You can change this by typing a new location in the Folder text box.
5. Under Output Options, ensure that the **Export HTML** box is checked. Captivate will create an .html file that automatically plays the published movie.
6. Click **Publish**. Captivate generates the movie, much as it did in the preview window. It also creates the HTML file necessary to publish your file on a Web page and displays a message when it is complete. Captivate will prompt you if a new folder needs to be created.

FIGURE 3-12   **Publish the movie, then view the output.**

7.   Click **View Output** to see exactly what the movie will look like. For our HTML example, the movie will play in your default browser. Note that the movie playback controls appear at the bottom of your movie.

FIGURE 3-13   **The playback controls display at the bottom of the movie.**

8.   The controls allow the viewer to play, back up, stop, or view the movie from any point, just as the preview controls worked, similar to a VCR. The playback controls also include an icon with the letter *i* (for information). This is where you can include information about the movie, your company, or yourself. Click the *i* icon to display the default information. To customize the information in this box or to change the look of all of the playback controls, see Chapter 11.

PROJECT CREATED BY   ☒

Brenda Huettner
P-N Designs
bphuettner@p-ndesigns.com
http://vagabond.blogsome.com
copyright 2009

ADOBE° CAPTIVATE° 4

FIGURE 3-14   **Display the movie information window.**

9.   When the movie is finished, you can use the playback controls to view the movie again, or you can simply close the browser window.

Your movie is stored in the folder you specified as an .swf file. There's also another file in that folder, with the same name as your movie but the extension .htm. This is your HTML output. Although this isn't a book on writing HTML, you can see that the coding is fairly simple. It calls the Flash player and points to the .swf file you created.

```
<!-- Copyright [2008] Adobe Systems Incorporated.  All rights reserved -->
<!-- saved from url=(0013)about:internet -->
<!DOCTYPE HTML PUBLIC "-//W3C//DTD HTML 4.01 Transitional//EN"
"http://www.w3.org/TR/html4/loose.dtd">
<html>
<head>
<meta http-equiv="Content-Type" content="text/html; charset=utf-8">
<title>HarryAFranck_Demonstration</title>
<script src="standard.js" type="text/javascript"></script>
</head>
<body   bgcolor="#F5F4F1">
<center>

    <div id="CaptivateContent"> 
    </div>
    <script type="text/javascript">
        var so = new SWFObject("HarryAFranck_Demonstration.swf",
"Captivate", "921", "717", "8", "#CCCCCC");
        so.addParam("quality", "high");
        so.addParam("name", "Captivate");
        so.addParam("id", "Captivate");
        so.addParam("wmode", "window");
        so.addParam("bgcolor","#F5F4F1");
        so.addParam("menu", "false");
        so.addVariable("variable1", "value1");
        so.setAttribute("redirectUrl", "http://www.adobe.com/
shockwave/download/download.cgi?P1_Prod_Version=ShockwaveFlash");
        so.write("CaptivateContent");
    </script>


    <script type="text/javascript">
        document.getElementById('Captivate').focus();
        document.Captivate.focus();
    </script>
</center>
</body>
</html>
```

SUMMARY

This chapter showed you how to create a simple demonstration movie, make a few minor edits, and publish the movie for viewing on the web. The rest of this book goes into more detail about the many additional features and functions in Captivate, starting with the next chapter about choosing recording options.

RECORDING A MOVIE

Chapter **4**

When you begin an Adobe® Captivate® project, you'll generally record some actions on your computer, then go back and make changes or add interactivity. Although recording can be simple, you have a lot of options throughout the recording process. This chapter will cover these recording options and describe how to ensure that you capture the screens you'll need for your movie. To create a movie without recording screens, see the following chapter.

PREPARING TO RECORD A NEW MOVIE

When you begin a Captivate project, you'll start by specifying the type of project you want to create using the Software Simulation options. The Software Simulation captures a series of screens as you perform tasks on your desktop, allowing you to set a variety of recording options as you go. Whichever options you choose, you'll still be able to edit the files to create the exact type of movie you want.

Before You Record

Be aware that Captivate will capture everything that is on your screen within the designated recording area. Before you begin recording, you may want to check for some of the elements that may detract from the point of your movie.

- *Open programs:* If you're going to be recording the full screen or if your recording area includes the bottom taskbar, you may want to ensure that all extraneous software packages are closed. Also, be aware that if you have other programs running, such as an e-mail client or instant messaging software, any notifications or pop-up windows that happen to display while you're recording will be captured in the Captivate movie. Close programs to remove their icons from the taskbar.

- *Background:* Don't use a multicolored, textured, or an otherwise busy background. This can detract from your movie and make it hard to see mouse movement over the background.

- *Icons:* If your recording area is full screen or allows for space between program application windows, your movie will include any icons that are on your desktop. Make sure that you are displaying only those icons that belong in your movie.

- *Copyrights:* Ensure that you have permission to use whatever screen images or audio you plan to capture.

TIP

If you run through the tasks in your movie a couple of times before you begin recording, you'll become more comfortable with the script or storyboards, and you can identify and hopefully resolve any problems that occur without storing error messages as part of your movie.

Specifying the Recording Area

When you begin recording a new movie, you'll need to specify which part of the screen you want to record (the recording area). Follow these steps:

1. Start the program you want to record, then start the Captivate software. The first screen you'll see is the Captivate main menu.

FIGURE 4-1   Start with the main menu.

2.   Click **Software Simulation** under **Create Project** to open the New Project window. You can also open the New Project window from the **File** menu within the software by choosing **New** and then **Project**.

FIGURE 4-2   Choose the project type.

3.   To begin recording a project, you need to specify the amount of area on your screen that you want to record.

- *Application:* This option identifies all of your open windows and automatically sets the recording area to fit the application window or region that you specify. From the Record tab, you can choose **Application Window** to specify an open application window, **Application Region** to specify part of an open application window, or **Custom Size** to specify an area that may cross open application windows.
- *Screen Area:* Click **Custom Size** on the application window or click **Screen Area** on the left side of the window. This option displays a list of preset window sizes (or specify a custom size of your own) regardless of the open windows. Anything that occurs within the specified area will be recorded.

Choose what you want to record, and then click **OK** to display your own computer screen with the recording area options. If you choose **Full screen**, the entire screen will be recorded. If you choose any other option, you'll see the default recording area outlined in red.

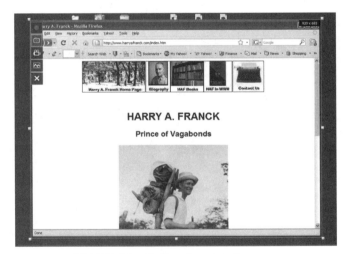

FIGURE 4-3   Define the recording area.

4. You can modify the recording area by clicking and dragging any of the square "handles" on the sides and corners of the red recording area box or by clicking anywhere within the red box and dragging it to a new location.

The size of the movie area will be displayed in the control box in the center of your screen.

5. The Project Recording controls display on the upper-left corner of the recording area.

TABLE 4-1 Settings for the movie recording area.

Icon	Title	Description
	Record in selected mode	Click this icon to begin recording based on the settings specified by the windows accessed through the other project recording icons. The default is to use the most recent settings.
	Automatic Recording	Click this icon to define the settings elements that the system will store as you record your movie. Available options are shown in Table 4-2.
	Full Motion Recording	When you scroll through your screens or use drag-and-drop functions while recording, Captivate automatically creates mini-movies that are embedded in the slide. You can also force full-motion recording by clicking the F9 key to begin and the F10 key to return to standard recording. This icon allows you to set the panning and audio functions that are in effect during full-motion recording.
	Manual Recording	When recording, Captivate captures each new screen based on your clicks. Manual recording allows you to specify additional screens that you want to capture and store as slides. This icon allows you to set the panning and audio functions that are in effect during manual recording.
	Cancel	Click this icon to close the recording window without recording anything.

6. Panning is a feature that allows you to move the recording rectangle around on your screen. This allows you to show various components of a screen without capturing the whole screen. If you're going to use panning in your movie, you must specify the type of panning before you begin recording.

Click the icon for the recording type (Automatic, Full Motion, or Manual) and choose from the Panning drop-down list:

- *No Panning:* The recording area remains in the same position on your screen.
- *Automatic Panning:* The recording area will always be centered on your cursor. As you move the cursor around on the screen, the recording area moves with it.
- *Manual Panning:* You can move the recording area while recording by clicking on the red outline and dragging it to a new location on the screen.

7.   If you want to record audio while you're capturing your movie file, click the icon for the recording type (Automatic, Full Motion, or Manual) and choose the input method for your audio from the drop-down list (No Narration, CD player, microphone, line-in, or wave out mix). See Chapter 8 for more information about audio options.

8.   Click the **Automatic Recording** icon to set the recording mode. The mode determines which features will be automatically included in your project.

FIGURE 4-4   **Choose Automatic Recording modes.**

Choose any (or all) of the three predefined modes, or use the custom mode settings. If you choose more than one mode, Captivate will create a separate project file for each mode while you're recoding.

TABLE 4-2 Recording modes.

Choose this mode:	To use these default settings:
Demonstration	Tracks mouse movement, automatically creates captions and highlight boxes.
Assessment	Automatically creates click boxes with a failure caption and text entry boxes for text fields with a failure caption. Captions and mouse movement are not included.
Training	Creates click boxes with hint and failure captions and text entry boxes for text fields with a failure caption. Captions and mouse movement are not included.
Custom	Allows you to choose which of the available elements (such as captions, mouse movement, highlight boxes, click boxes, and text entry boxes) will be included in the project file.

TIP

Recording multiple modes saves time and ensures that your files use the same base slides. However, because each mode saves a full copy of all the slides and other components, it can also use up system resources very quickly. This may limit the size of the movie you can make.

For any of the three movie recording types or four recording modes, you may modify additional settings, as described in the following section.

Modifying the Recording Settings

You can change the way that Captivate records your movies and the keys that activate the Captivate recording functions. You'll probably only need to set these options occasionally—subsequent movies will use the most recent settings you specified.

1. Open the recording Preferences window in either of the following ways:

   ▪ Set the recording area of the movie as described in the previous section, click the **Automatic Recording** icon, then click the **Settings** button.

▪ From the **Edit** menu, choose **Preferences**, then click **Recording** in the left-hand navigation panel of the Preferences window.

FIGURE 4-5   **Set general recording options.**

2. Specify the following options by clicking the boxes to check or uncheck each option. Note that this sets the default options for the captured screens—they can all be changed at any time. Available options are:

TABLE 4-3 Recording settings.

Check this option:	To do this:
Narration	Record audio while you're recording the visual portion of the movie. You must have a microphone set up for this to work.
Actions in real time	This feature causes Captivate to record at the same rate you perform actions. So, for example, if it takes you 10 seconds to move the mouse across the screen and click a button, the resulting slide will take 10 seconds to display that action. Without this option selected, Captivate adjusts the time for mouse movements and other actions based on default settings.

TABLE 4-3 Recording settings (continued).

Check this option:	To do this:
Camera sounds	Captivate can play a sound whenever it captures a screen. The sound, sort of like that of a camera shutter, is merely a tool to help you identify when the screens are captured. The sound will not be part of the finished movie.
Keystrokes	When you type on the keyboard, this setting will cause Captivate to store the keystrokes (but not capture a full screen for each character typed). The finished movie will display all the keystrokes without the overhead of a full screen per letter.
Hear keyboard tap sounds	If you have Keystrokes turned on, you can have Captivate play a sound file for each key it stores. The sound file sounds like a keyboard key being tapped, and is merely a recording tool—you will have the option later of adding mouse click sounds to your movie whether or not this feature is turned on.
Hide recording window	Remove the red recording area lines from the screen. This does not change the area that is recorded; it only hides the indication of the outline of the recording area. This option also temporarily removes the Captivate icon from the Windows taskbar (usually displayed across the bottom of your screen).
Hide task icon	Temporarily removes the Captivate icon from the Windows taskbar (usually displayed across the bottom of your screen).
Hide system tray icon	Temporarily removes the Captivate icon from the Windows system tray (in the lower-right corner of your screen).
Move new windows inside recording area	When the application you are recording launches new windows or dialog boxes, they are placed inside the recording area to the extent possible. In cases where new windows are larger than the recording area, some of the area on the right and bottom of the new window or dialog box may be missed.
Capture interim screenshot	This option is enabled by default. When you disable this option, screenshots in the demonstration mode might not get recorded as intended.
	Select this option when you do not want the focus to be set until the user performs the specified action. This option is especially useful in the assessment mode when you do not want the focus to automatically shift to the next area of action. The change in focus provides the user with the hint to perform the next action.

TABLE 4-3 Recording settings (continued).

Check this option:	To do this:
Automatically use full motion recording for drag-and-drop actions	Specify that you want Captivate to automatically use FMR mode when recording drag-and-drop actions. If you do not select this option, you must manually specify when you want to start FMR mode.
Automatically use full motion recording for mouse-wheel actions	Specify that you want Captivate to automatically use FMR mode when recording mouse movements.

3. Click **OK** to save your changes or **Cancel** to close the window without saving your changes.

4. Click the **FMR Settings** button or choose **Full Motion Recording** from the categories on the left side of the screen to define when you want to use the Full Motion Recording options.

FIGURE 4-6 Set the Full Motion Recording options.

5. From the Full Motion Recording screen, specify when you want to use the Full Motion feature. This feature automatically records more screens during drag-and-drop or mouse actions to give you a smoother movie. The extra screens are stored in one slide and indicated on the slide by a movie icon.

> **TIP**
>
> Full Motion Recording delivers a very smooth movie, but also requires extra resources such as disk space and memory. Use this feature sparingly for the most efficient movies.

TABLE 4-4 Full Motion movie options.

Check this option:	To do this:
Show mouse	Display the mouse during drag-and-drop Full Motion animations.
Disable hardware acceleration	Increase the resources available for Full Motion capture by turning off the hardware acceleration. If you check this option, you'll see a flicker on your monitor as the hardware resets, but this flicker will not appear in the finished movie.
Working folder	Click the **Browse** button to find and enter the name of the folder where the Full Motion video will be saved.
SWF Conversion	Choose **16 Bit** for a smaller file size or **32 Bit** for a greater range of color options.
FMR Mode	Specify the quality you want for the FMR recordings. The higher the setting (like Video), the higher the quality and more resources required. The lower the setting (like Safe), the lower the quality but smaller the file.

6. Click **OK** to save your changes or **Cancel** to close the window without saving your changes.
7. Choose **Keys** from the categories on the left side of the screen to define the keystrokes you'll use to control the recording process.

FIGURE 4-7   **Set Keys options to control movie recording.**

Note: Throughout this book, we'll use the default keystrokes to indicate recording stop and start instructions.

8. To change any of the recording keys, click in a text box and press the key combination you want to use (such as Alt+F2 or Ctrl+F4). You cannot use the Escape, Enter, Tab, Spacebar, F1, or Backspace keys, since these have other meanings within Captivate. You cannot use the Shift key unless it is in combination with either Alt or Ctrl (such as Shift+Ctrl+F3).

TIP

If you change the recording keys, make sure you write down the new keystrokes, particularly if you change the "end recording" keystroke.

9. Click **OK** to save your changes or **Cancel** to close the window without saving your changes.

10. Choose **Mode(s)** from the categories on the left side of the screen to define the components that will be automatically added while recording. You can set different components for each of the available recording modes.

FIGURE 4-8   Set Mode(s) options to determine which elements will be captured.

11. Specify the recording mode for which you want to set options by choosing from the drop-down list. Depending on which mode you choose, some of the displayed options may be inactive.

12. Click to select each of the available options, or click a check mark to deselect an option. Remember that even if you don't choose them here, you can always add options later. If at any time you want to return to the default options, click the **Restore defaults** button.

TABLE 4-5 Mode(s) options.

For this type of element:	Specify these options:
Captions	Captions are the instructions that the system automatically adds when you perform an action, such as "Click the File Menu." Select **Add text captions** to specify that you want captions for the selected recording mode. If the application you're recording uses tool tips (small text boxes that display when you move the cursor over certain areas of the screen), you can have Captivate automatically convert these tool tips to rollover captions.
Mouse	If you select **Show mouse location and movement**, Captivate will be able to simulate the mouse movement on the final movie. If you select **Add highlight boxes on click**, Captivate will insert a partially transparent shaded box that displays over each link or button that you click while recording.
Click Boxes	A click box defines an area on the screen that a viewer can click to cause something to happen (such as moving to the next slide in a movie). If you activate this option, Captivate will automatically create a click box the size and shape of active links, buttons, or menu items that you click while recording. When the movie is played, the viewer must click in the click box to continue the movie. You also may select which types of click box captions will be automatically generated:
	■ Hint captions display on the finished movie when the viewer moves the cursor over the click box. A typical hint caption might be "Try clicking on the File menu."
	■ Failure captions display when the viewer clicks somewhere outside of the click box. This type of caption might say "Not quite; try again!"
	■ Success captions display when the viewer clicks in the click box. They might say "Congratulations" or "Good Job!"
	Click box options also allow you to specify how many incorrect clicks you'll let the viewer make before moving on to the next slide. Select the **Limit attempts to** box and enter a number to limit the number of times the viewer can click outside the click box. If you don't want the movie to continue unless the viewer clicks correctly, simply ensure that this option isn't selected.
	The final click box option allows you to determine whether or not the cursor will change shape when the viewer moves it over the click box.

TABLE 4-5 Mode(s) options (continued).

For this type of element:	Specify these options:
Text Entry Boxes	Text entry boxes allow the viewer to actually type into the box. Captivate will compare the typed text to your predefined answers to determine whether or not the typed text is "correct." Like click boxes, you have a variety of options based on whether or not the text is entered correctly.
	■ Hint captions display on the finished movie when the viewer moves the cursor over the text entry box. A typical hint caption might be "Type the answer here."
	■ Failure captions display when the viewer types incorrect text. This type of caption might say "Not quite; try again!"
	■ Success captions display when the viewer types the correct text. They might say "Congratulations" or "Good Job!"
	Text entry box options also allow you to specify how many times you'll let the viewer type incorrectly before moving on to the next slide. Select the **Limit attempts to** box and enter a number to limit the number of times the viewer can type the text. If you don't want the movie to continue unless the viewer types correctly, simply ensure that this option isn't selected.

13. Click **OK** to save your changes or **Cancel** to close the window without saving your changes.
14. Repeat steps 12–13 for each mode you want to change.
15. Choose **Defaults** from the categories on the left side of the screen to define the appearance of the automatically generated captions and highlight boxes.

FIGURE 4-9   Set Defaults options to specify caption and highlight box appearance.

Choose from the drop-down list for each type of caption to specify the appearance of the box that outlines each caption.

Specify the font face, the size, the color, and the justification of the text within each caption type. Remember that this area is defining the default appearance of each caption type; you'll be able to customize them later if desired.

Choose the colors, width, and transparency for the highlight boxes. Like the captions, highlight boxes may be edited individually later.

Click **OK** to save your changes or **Cancel** to close the window without saving your changes.

Once you've set all the recording options, click **OK** to return to the recording control box. From there, you can begin recording your movie as described in the following section.

RECORDING ACTIONS ON YOUR SCREEN

Once you've defined the area of the screen you want to record, turn on the Captivate recording function, then simply perform the tasks you want included in your movie. Although this is a simple process, there are a few things you can do to ensure that the process goes smoothly.

Starting and Stopping the Recording Process

When you've set the recording area and specified the recording options, the recording area should be indicated by a red outline (unless you're recording the full screen) and the control box should be displayed.

FIGURE 4-10   Start recording.

When you're ready to start recording, follow these steps:

1. Click the **Record** icon.
2. Begin to perform the actions you want to record. If auto capture is on, Captivate will automatically capture the screen (and play a camera shutter sound) whenever you do the following:

    - Click the mouse
    - Change focus from one window to another
    - Press any key on the keyboard
    - Click the mouse while it is in the recording area

While you're recording, Captivate will also automatically insert the following components (based on your option settings):

- *Click boxes:* These are areas that the viewer will click in during playback.
- *Highlight boxes:* These are areas of particular interest that are highlighted.
- *Captions:* Text instructions, such as "Click here."
- *Pointer movement:* The mouse movement itself is not captured unless you are recording in Full Motion mode. Most of the time, Captivate will record the beginning and ending positions of the mouse, then animate just the pointer for the finished movie (rather than record the screen at every intermediate pointer location).

3. If you want to capture a specific screen while recording, press the **Print Screen** key (or whatever you've set as the manual recording key). You can repeat this as often as you like. Remember, though, that the more screens you capture, the larger your finished movie will be.

4. If you need to temporarily pause recording for any reason, press the **Pause/Break** key on your keyboard. You can then press the same **Pause/Break** key to resume recording when you are ready.

5. When you've finished with all the tasks you want to record, press the **End** key to display the save options.

FIGURE 4-11   Specify filenames.

6. Enter a name for the project. Notice that if you've specified that you want to capture more than one type of project, Captivate allows you to enter a unique name for each type. The default project names use the project name as the base name and add indicators for the project type (such as HarryAFranck_demo and HarryAFranck_training).

7. If you're making more than one project type, specify the type that you want to display first in the Storyboard view by choosing it from the drop-down list.

8. Click **OK** when you've specified all the names you want. The screens you've captured will appear as slides in the Captivate project.

High-Resolution Recording

Captivate allows you to create realistic movies and maintain relatively small file sizes because it does not use full animation for every action. Instead, Captivate captures a single screen, and then stores information to create the animated elements (such as typing or pointer movement) separately. Rather than store 30 copies of the same screen per second (or whatever your setting is), Captivate only captures a new frame when the screen changes. This keeps the disk space, file size, and memory resources fairly low.

However, there are several instances when you may want to capture a higher number of frames, such as when you're scrolling down a window. For these instances, Captivate will automatically switch to Full Motion Recording mode and actually capture a higher number of frames per second than normal recording.

By default, Full Motion Recording mode starts automatically whenever you drag and drop an icon or image or draw within a graphics program. You can change the default at any time.

TABLE 4-6 Full-motion controls.

To cause this:	Do this:
Manually start Full Motion Recording while recording a movie.	Press F9.
Manually end Full Motion Recording while recording a movie.	Press F10.
Stop the Full Motion Recording from automatically starting on drag-and-drop or drawing actions.	When setting recording options in the preferences window, deselect the Automatically use full motion recording for drag and drop actions option.

Once you've captured an action in Full Motion, it will appear on your Storyboard view as a movie within a single slide, represented by a movie camera icon. You can edit this slide as you would any other, treating the Full Motion movie clip as you would any other element on the slide (see Chapter 6). You can also double-click on the Movie icon to display the Full Motion animation properties.

FIGURE 4-12   **The movie camera icon indicates Full Motion Recording within a slide.**

SUMMARY

This chapter described how to create new movies and some basic recording functions. The next chapter will describe how to create different types of movies without recording screen actions.

CREATING MOVIES WITHOUT RECORDING

Chapter **5**

The previous chapter described how to create a movie by recording the keystrokes and screen images as you perform tasks on your computer system. Sometimes, however, it is more efficient to create movies in ways other than recording screen actions. This chapter describes how to use the Adobe® Captivate® templates, as well as how to create blank movies, movies from image files, and movies from Microsoft® PowerPoint® files.

USING THE CAPTIVATE TEMPLATES

The Captivate templates help you create a wide variety of movie types, such as business presentations or movies designed for mobile applications, or training for soft skills. Each template contains design elements, such as color and size, as well as sample content slides based on the type of template (such as an Agenda slide in a business presentation, or a Quiz Review slide in training material). When you create a movie from a template, Captivate automatically creates the appropriate slides, which you can then edit as needed.

To use a Captivate template, follow these steps:

1. Start the Captivate software. The first screen you'll see will be the Captivate main menu.

2. Under **Create Project**, choose **From Template** and then **Project Templates** to view the available templates. This folder (usually starting with C:\Program Files\Adobe\Adobe Captivate 4\Templates) will contain

the templates that are shipped with Captivate, as well as any templates that you've created.

FIGURE 5-1 **Choose a template from the available categories.**

3.   Choose the template you wish to use from the displayed list. For this example, we've clicked the **Simulation** folder and then selected the Modern_790x545.cptl template. Captivate opens a new project in Storyboard view based on the selected template.

FIGURE 5-2 This template creates a simulation project with a modern design.

4.   Some of the slides created by the template contain content that you can edit, while others are simply placeholders where you will enter additional slides. In this case, the first slide includes directions and is not intended to be part of the finished movie (note the "hidden" symbol crossing out the number at the bottom of the slide). Like all movies, you can edit a slide by double-clicking on it.

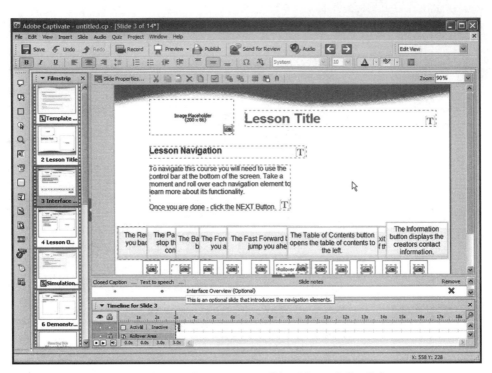

FIGURE 5-3   **The template creates a slide with predefined elements.**

5.   In this case, the template created a slide with a title, some image placeholders, several rollover areas with associated sample text boxes, and more. To use this slide in your movie, you would simply verify or edit the text, and add in whatever graphics apply to your application. See Chapter 7 for more details on editing a single slide.

6.   When you've made all the necessary changes, be sure to save your movie. Click the **Save** icon, choose **Save** from the **File** menu, or press **Ctrl+S**. Enter a new name for this movie, then click **OK** to save.

For more information about editing templates (or creating your own), see Chapter 12.

CREATING OTHER TYPES OF MOVIES

Creating a Blank Movie

A blank project consists of one blank slide and all of the movie settings. This can then be used as a template to ensure that all movies use the same settings. Or you might create a blank movie with the intention of recording slides later. To create a blank project, follow these steps:

1. Start the Captivate software. The first screen you'll see will be the Captivate main menu.

2. Under **Create Project**, choose **Blank Project** to view the available options.

FIGURE 5-4   **Choose to create a blank project.**

3. Choose from the list of predefined movie window sizes, or enter a custom size. Predefined sizes range from very small (for mobile devices) to full screen.

> **Note:** Remember that the larger the movie size, the larger your movie file will be. Also, keep your audience in mind. If they do not have high-resolution monitors, they may not be able to view the larger movies.

4. Click **OK** to see your single blank slide in Storyboard view. You can now edit or add slides as needed.

5.   When you've made all the necessary changes, be sure to save your movie. Click the **Save** icon, choose **Save** from the **File** menu, or press **Ctrl+S**. Enter a new name for this movie, then click **OK** to save.

Creating a Project from PowerPoint Slides

As you've seen by now, Captivate movies are based on slide images that the software automates in a variety of ways. If you have a set of PowerPoint slides, you can use them as the basis of a movie by importing the slides into Captivate.

1.   Start the Captivate software. The first screen you'll see will be the Captivate main menu.
2.   Under **Create Project**, select **From MS PowerPoint** to display the browser window.
3.   Choose the PowerPoint file you want to import, and then click **Open** to display the PowerPoint slides in a Captivate conversion window.

FIGURE 5-5   Specify PowerPoint conversion options.

4. Specify a name and size for the movie. You can choose to specify exact dimensions, or let Captivate choose the dimensions that best match the aspect ratio (the relationship between height and width) of the existing presentation slides.

5. The Slides Preview area of this window displays all the slides from the specified presentation, with the default that all slides have the **Include** check box selected. If there are slides that you don't want to import into the movie, simply click the **Include** check box to deselect it. You can also use the **Select All** or **Clear All** buttons to specify which slides you want to include.

6. Specify whether you want slides to advance on a mouse click or automatically by choosing from the drop-down menu. If you choose to advance slides by mouse click, Captivate will automatically insert a click box over each of the slides. If you choose to advance slides automatically, Captivate will use the PowerPoint timings to determine how long each slide is displayed.

7. Click **Linked** if you want to maintain the link between the Captivate project and the original PowerPoint file. If selected, this option allows you to edit the original PowerPoint file from within the Captivate project. This is handy if you need to maintain both files, but can sometimes slow down the Captivate editing process.

TIP

The linking feature will not work with older versions of PowerPoint; the slides must be at least PowerPoint 2007 to link to the Captivate project.

---

8. When you've finished entering the options, click **OK** to convert the presentation to a Captivate project and display the project in Storyboard view. You can now edit or add slides as needed.

FIGURE 5-6   Each PowerPoint slide becomes a Captivate slide.

9. When you've made all the necessary changes, be sure to save your movie. Click the **Save** icon, choose **Save** from the **File** menu, or press **Ctrl+S**. Enter a new name for this movie, then click **OK** to save.

Creating an Image Movie

If you have a series of images, you can create a slide-show type of movie by simply importing the images. Each image will become a Captivate slide. Valid image formats include JPG, JPEG, GIF, PNG, BMP, ICO, EMF, and WMF. You can also import PowerPoint template files (.pot) into an image movie.

> **TIP**
>
> Although you can add images to this movie later, it's easiest if all of your images are in the same folder. That way, you can import them all at once when you create the movie.

To create an image movie, follow these steps:

1. Start the Captivate software. The first screen you'll see is the Captivate main menu.
2. Under **Create Project**, select **Image Slideshow** to open the New Project window.

FIGURE 5-7   **Choose to create an image project.**

3. Choose from the list of predefined movie window sizes or enter a custom size, and then click **Browse** to display a browser window.

TIP

Remember that the larger the movie size, the larger your movie file will be. Also, keep your audience in mind. If they do not have high-resolution monitors, they may not be able to view the larger movies.

---

4. Select the images you want included in this movie from the browser window, and then click **OK** to import the images into your movie project.
5. If an image is larger than the movie size you specified, it is displayed in the Resize/Crop Image window.

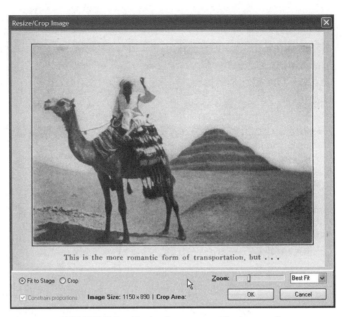

FIGURE 5-8   **Resize images to fit the movie.**

6. Choose whether you want to crop the image or resize it to make it fit by selecting the appropriate option.

-   *Fit to Stage:* Resizes the image until the largest dimension fits within the designated space. This may mean that you'll end up with blank white spaces on either side of the image. You'll lose some resolution, as tiny elements get more difficult to see. If you choose this option, you may also set the zoom. You may let the system choose the best fit or you may specify a zoom factor by moving the Zoom slider or choosing from the drop-down list.

-   *Crop:* Displays the image with an overlay that indicates the movie size. Move the red outline to the portion of the image that you want included in your movie. You can also resize the red outline if needed. Click the **Constrain proportions** option to ensure that the cropped image has the same proportions as the finished movie.

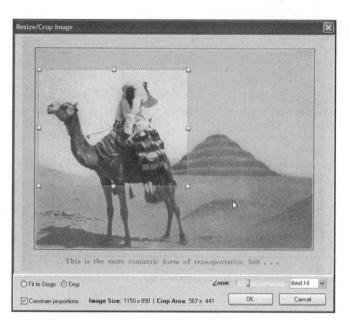

FIGURE 5-9 **Crop the image to fit the movie.**

Click **OK** to store the resized image in your movie.

7. Images appear as individual slides in the movie project file. You can add elements, import more images, even record additional actions, just as you would in any other movie.

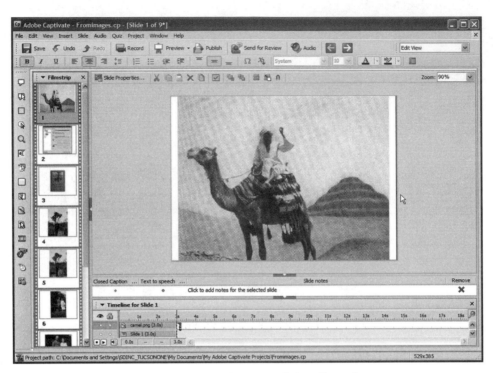

FIGURE 5-10   **An image movie in Edit mode.**

SUMMARY

This chapter described the various ways you create movies that don't necessarily start with capturing screen actions. The following chapter describes how to modify your slides for further customization.

WORKING WITH SLIDES

Chapter **6**

Adobe® Captivate® software allows you to customize exactly how the finished movie looks. You can rearrange or delete slides, edit the way the elements on the slide look, or change the way the mouse moves. You can adjust the speed the movie plays and how the viewer navigates through your movie. This chapter discusses how to add different types of slides and how to delete slides from your movie.

SLIDE BASICS

Each time you capture a screen, Captivate stores it as a slide. Each slide has its own properties, such as transitions and timing, and may also have additional components, such as captions or highlight boxes. When you publish and then play the movie, the timing of the slide components and the transition from slide to slide work together to create a seamless series of actions.

When you view your movie in Storyboard view, each slide is shown in miniature, with small icons representing the different components of the slide. If you've used the automatic features of Captivate, you'll see a variety of elements associated with each slide (such as captions or highlight boxes). Each slide also has associated properties, such as the length of time it will be displayed or the way you want to transition to the next slide.

> **TIP**
>
> Do not confuse slides with "frames." A regular movie such as you see in theaters is composed of a series of frames. Each frame displays for a fraction of a second, with tiny changes between frames that look like movement when the movie is played. In Captivate movies, a slide is more like the background on which other things happen. Slides typically remain on the screen for many seconds, and the elements on them that move (such as a mouse) are stored as separate animation instructions.

In Edit view, the full slide is shown with the actual components. For example, the mouse path will be displayed, not just the icon representing mouse movement. The Edit view also includes some icons for slides surrounding the current slide.

We've already seen that some slides can also contain high-resolution mini-movies (when you record click-and-drag actions). You can also add other types of multimedia elements described later in this book:

- Working with animations is described in Chapter 7.
- Adding sound to your movie is described in Chapter 8.
- Adding interactivity is described in Chapter 9.

Viewing Slides

There are two primary modes for viewing your slides:

- *Storyboard view:* Shows all of your slides, with icons that indicate the elements associated with each slide.
- *Edit view:* Shows a single slide and all the elements on it. Edit view can also display a "filmstrip" view of the other slides in the movie. The filmstrip displays icons representing the slides in the movie, but in a single line on the edge of the currently selected slide.

A third view, Branching, is discussed in more detail in Chapter 11.

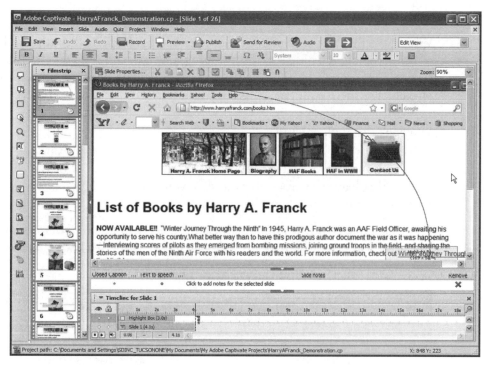

FIGURE 6-1   Viewing a movie in Edit view.

To display a slide in Edit view, do one of the following:

- From Storyboard view, click on a slide to select it, then choose **Edit View** from the drop-down list in the upper-right corner of the view.
- From Storyboard view, double-click on a slide.
- From Branching view, click on a slide to select it, then choose **Edit View** from the drop-down list in the upper-right corner of the view.
- From Branching view, double-click on a slide.
- From Branching view, right-click on a slide, then select **Edit Slide** from the context menu.
- From Edit view, use the filmstrip scroll bar to display the slide you want to edit, then click on that slide.
- From the Edit view menu bar, click the right-facing arrow at the top of the screen to display the next slide in sequence, or click the left-facing arrow to display the previous slide.

Changing the Edit View Display

When you first open Edit view, there are toolbars across the top and bottom of the screen and a filmstrip representing multiple slides down one side of the screen. You can modify which toolbars appear and where they display. You can also change the size of the icons (or "thumbnails") within the filmstrip.

Changing the Toolbar Display

You can turn the toolbars on and off as often as you like. For example, you may want to leave the toolbars you use most frequently open all of the time, even though that leaves less room for the slide you're editing. You can also move the toolbars around as you like.

1. Click the **Window** menu to display the list of open components, and click **Toolbars** to display the list of available toolbars. A check mark indicates which elements or toolbars are currently displayed.

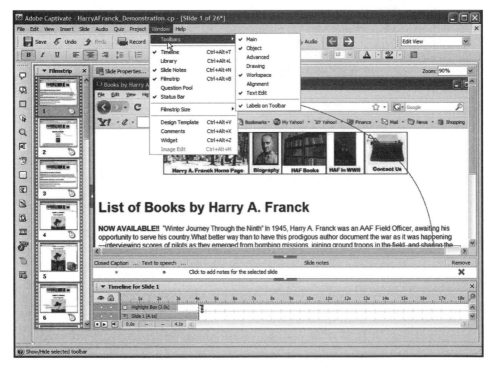

FIGURE 6-2 Use the Window menu to change the Edit view display.

2.   Display any of the listed elements or toolbars by clicking on the toolbar name to check it, or hide a toolbar or element by clicking on the name to remove the check mark. In the example in Figure 6-2, the Timeline, Slide Notes, Filmstrip, and Status Bar elements are displayed; all others are turned off. Under toolbars, you can see that the Advanced, Drawing, and Alignment toolbars have been turned off; the other toolbars are displayed.

Note: When you click a toolbar name, the Window menu changes to reflect the choice you made, then closes immediately. You'll know if the display changed by looking for the toolbar. Simply open the Window menu again to continue modifying your display.

3.   To change the location for any element (including toolbars), first display the element as described in Step 2. Move your cursor to the dotted line on one side of the toolbar until the cursor changes to an icon with four arrows. Hold down the mouse button and drag the toolbar to a new location. You can place the toolbars on any side of the Captivate window, or move them to the center of the Captivate window where they'll be opened in their own "floating" windows. You can move these windows around as needed, even move them off the Captivate window altogether (such as to a second monitor). You can also close any element by clicking the red "x" in the upper-right corner of the element.

FIGURE 6-3   **The Objects and Alignment toolbars are displayed in separate windows.**

Modifying the Filmstrip Display

Like the toolbars, the filmstrip can be on or off, and you can change the position of the filmstrip on the screen. You can also change the size of each slide icon (called thumbnails). For example, you may want to make the icons smaller (so you can see more slides at once) and display the filmstrip across the bottom of the screen. Follow these steps to do so:

1. There are two ways to turn on the filmstrip display:
   - From the Edit view screen, click **View** to display the viewing options, then click **Show Thumbnails**.
   - Hold down the **Ctrl** and **Alt** keys on your keyboard, and then press the letter **B**.

2. There are three ways to turn off the filmstrip display:
   - From the Edit view screen, click **View** to display the viewing options, then click **Show Thumbnails** to deselect it.
   - Hold down the **Ctrl** and **Alt** keys on your keyboard, and then press the letter **B**.
   - Click the **x** icon in the upper-left corner of the displayed filmstrip.

3. To change the location for the filmstrip, move your cursor to the dotted line on one side of the toolbar until the cursor changes to an icon with four arrows. Hold down the mouse button and drag the filmstrip to a new location. You can place the filmstrip on any side of the Captivate window, or move it to the center of the Captivate window where it will be opened in its own "floating" window. You can move these windows around as needed, even move them off the Captivate window altogether (such as to a second monitor).

4. To change the size of the slide icons, click the **Window** menu, choose **Filmstrip Size** to display the size options, then click the size option you want (Small, Medium, or Large). Alternatively, right-click on any thumbnail and select the desired size from the Thumbnail Size option on the context menu.

FIGURE 6-4   Display the filmstrip with small icons on the bottom of the screen.

Naming a Slide

You can assign a name to each slide by entering a slide label. The label will appear underneath the slide in Storyboard view and in the filmstrip portion of the Edit view. This can be useful if you have a lot of similar slides or if you're viewing the slides as small thumbnail icons. It can also be very helpful if you plan to construct a lot of branching for your movie (especially if you do not have a detailed storyboard or script).

> **TIP**
>
> You don't have to name all the slides, but it is useful to label at least the first slide for each task in your movie.

To name a slide:

1.   Open the slide that you want to name in Edit view.
2.   Double-click the slide, click the **Slide Properties** button, or choose **Properties** from the Slide menu to open the Slide Properties window.
3.   In the Slide Properties window, click the **Slide** tab.

FIGURE 6-5   **Add a slide label in the Slide Properties window.**

4.   In the Label box, type a short description of the slide. You can use spaces or punctuation as needed. For example, you might enter "List of Books" on the slide that begins that portion of the movie. Keep the labels short, since they may be truncated in your display, depending on your monitor settings and thumbnail size. For example, a large thumbnail may show the first 20 characters, while a medium thumbnail may only show the first six characters.

> **TIP**
>
> Even if the label under the slide is truncated, you can still view the full label by moving the cursor over the slide thumbnail.

5. Click **OK** to close the Slide Properties window and display the new label.

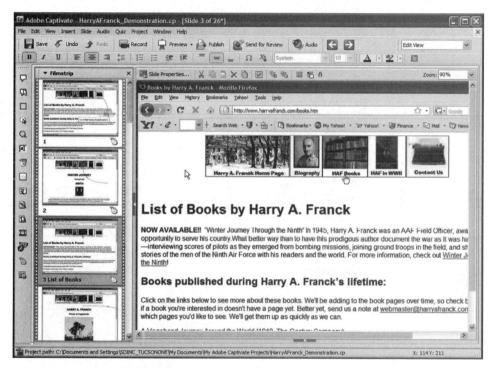

FIGURE 6-6   View the slide label in the filmstrip.

ADDING A SLIDE

You can add or delete slides from either the Edit view or the Storyboard view. The steps for adding a slide vary depending on the type of slide. There are seven main slide types.

TABLE 6-1 Types of slides.

Slide Type	Description
Blank	This is a slide with absolutely nothing on it. You can import elements later or use it a spacer.
Recording	Allows you to record additional slides and specify where the new slides will be placed within the movie.
Question	A question slide includes questions that the movie viewer is to answer. This type of slide turns your movie into an e-learning lesson (see Chapter 9 for more detail).
Random Question	Captivate allows you to create a set of questions in a "question pool." This type of slide will randomly display one of the questions from the specified pool.
Image	This type of slide contains an image. Image slides are useful for the first slide in a movie or to delineate between sections of your movie. You can use a logo, photo, or any other graphic you want. When you add this type of slide, you'll point to the image file you want to use. Make sure the image exists before you begin adding it. Images can be in JPG, JPEG, GIF, PNG, BMP, ICO, EMF, or WMF format.
PowerPoint	This lets you import Microsoft® PowerPoint® slides directly into your Captivate movie.
Animation	This type of slide contains an animation, like a movie within your movie. As you add this type of slide, you'll point to the file you want to use. Make sure the animation file exists before you add this type of slide. Animations can be in SWF, GIF, or AVI format. Your animation slide can even be another Captivate movie that you want to embed into the current project.

Once you've added the new slides to your movie, you can add more elements to it as described in later sections of this chapter. For example, you can add animations to an image slide or put questions into a slide that started as part of a PowerPoint presentation.

The rest of the sections in this chapter describe the blank, recording, image, PowerPoint, and animation slides. For question and random question slides, see Chapter 10.

Adding a Blank Slide

You can insert blank slides anywhere in your movie. You can use them as placeholders for information you want to add later, or you can create the slide and add elements to it right away. Once you've created the slide, you can add elements such as images, text, and animation. You can even turn it into a question slide or add interactivity as described in later chapters.

To add a blank slide, follow these steps:

1. Open the movie to which you want to add a blank slide.
2. Choose the location for the new slide within your movie by selecting the slide immediately before the one you want to add. For example, if you have the first slide open, the new slide will be inserted as slide number 2. You can move slides around later if needed.
3. From the **Insert** menu, choose **Blank Slide**. The new blank slide appears in your movie.

Adding a Recording Slide

A recording slide is simply a way to record and insert slides in the midst of an existing movie.

To add a recording slide, follow these steps:

1. Open the movie to which you want to add a recording slide.
2. From the **Insert** menu, choose **Recording Slide**.

FIGURE 6-7   **Specify location and application to record new slides.**

3.   To insert the new slides at the end of the movie, select **Record slides at the end of this project**. To insert the new slide in the middle of the current Captivate project, choose **Record slides and insert after the slide selected below**, then select the slide immediately before the location where you want the new slides. Click **OK** to display the Insert Slides window.

4.   From the **Insert** menu, choose **Blank Slide**. The new blank slide appears in your movie.

Adding an Image Slide

An image slide is simply a slide with an image on it. When you're recording new actions, you're actually creating image slides where the image is a screen capture (the movements and other elements are added separately). You can add an image slide anywhere in your movie. The image can be any stored file, such as a corporate logo or product photo. This is particularly useful as an opening, when you're introducing a new section of the movie, or for ending the movie.

Before you begin, check the image file you're going to use. It should meet these conditions:

- The image must be in one of the valid Captivate image formats (JPG, JPEG, GIF, PNG, BMP, ICO, EMF, WMF or PowerPoint template format POT).
- The image should be approximately the same size as your movie. If the image is too big, Captivate can either resize or truncate the image, but you may not get the exact results you expect.
- The image should be oriented the same way as the movie. For example, if you insert a vertical picture into a horizontally oriented movie, the slide will have white stripes on either side.

For example, to introduce a section of the movie about Harry Franck's family, we may want to start with an image slide with a photo from his wedding in 1919. Figure 6-8 shows the image scaled using Fit to Stage, and Figure 6-9 shows the image using the crop option.

> **TIP**
>
> An image slide stores the image as the background of the slide. You may want to consider creating a blank slide and importing a graphic onto it. You'll get more image options that way.

To create an image slide, follow these steps:

1. Open the movie to which you want to add an image slide.
2. Choose the location for the new slide within your movie by selecting the slide immediately before the one you want to add. For example, if you've got the first slide open, the new image will be inserted as slide number 2. You can move slides around later if you need to.
3. From the **Insert** menu, choose **Other Slide(s)** and then **Image Slide** to open a browser window that defaults to the last picture folder you used.
4. Browse to the correct folder, then select the image you want to insert and click **Open**. If the image is the same size as the movie (or smaller) you'll

see the image as a slide (and you're done!). If the image is larger than the
movie size, the Resize/Crop Image window displays.

FIGURE 6-8   **Crop or resize the image.**

5. Choose whether you want to crop the image or resize it to make it fit by
   selecting the appropriate option.

   ■ *Fit to Stage:* Resizes the image until the largest dimension
     fits within the designated space. This may mean that you'll
     end up with blank white spaces on either side of the image.
     You'll lose some resolution because tiny elements get more
     difficult to see. If you choose this option, you may also set
     the zoom. You may let the system choose the best fit, or you
     may specify a zoom factor by moving the Zoom slider or by
     choosing from the drop-down list.

   ■ *Crop:* Displays the image with an overlay that indicates
     the movie size. Move the red outline to the portion of
     the image that you want included in your movie. You can
     also resize the red outline if needed. Click the **Constrain**

proportions option to ensure that the cropped image has the same proportions as the finished movie.

FIGURE 6-9 **Crop or resize the image.**

6.   Click **OK** to import the image onto a new slide.

Adding a PowerPoint Slide

Captivate can use existing PowerPoint slides as the basis for a movie. When you add PowerPoint slides, some elements will be automatically converted to the Captivate format:

- Each PowerPoint slide will become one slide in the Captivate movie.
- Any content on the PowerPoint Notes page will be copied to the Captivate Notes function.
- Audio and interactivity will be carried over to the Captivate slide.

- The PowerPoint slide title will be stored as the Captivate slide label.

Each slide will be assigned a default time by the Captivate software—you can go back and edit the timing and other properties as needed.

To add one or more PowerPoint slides to your Captivate movie, follow these steps:

1. Open the movie to which you want to add one or more PowerPoint slides.
2. From the **Insert** menu, choose **Other Slide(s)** and then **PowerPoint Slide** to open a browser window that defaults to the last folder you used.
3. Browse to the correct folder, and then select the presentation that contains the slide or slides you want to insert. The PowerPoint slide options window displays the slides in the current movie.

FIGURE 6-10   **Select the PowerPoint slide options.**

4. To insert the new slide or slides at the end of the movie, select **Import slides at the end of this project**. To insert the new slide in the middle

of the current Captivate project, choose **Import slides and insert after the slide selected below**, then select the slide immediately before the location where you want the new slides. Click **OK** to display the Convert PowerPoint Presentations window.

FIGURE 6-11   **Choose the PowerPoint slides you want to add.**

5. Click the slides you want to add until the screen displays a green check mark below each slide. Note that you can easily select all slides or clear all the check marks using the buttons at the bottom of the selection window.

6. Specify whether you want slides to advance on a mouse click or automatically by choosing from the drop-down menu. If you choose to advance slides by mouse click, Captivate will automatically insert a click box over each of the slides. If you choose to advance slides automatically, Captivate will use the PowerPoint timings to determine how long each slide is displayed.

7. Click **Linked** if you want to maintain the link between the Captivate project and the original PowerPoint file. If selected, this option allows you to edit the original PowerPoint file from within the Captivate project. This is handy if you need to maintain both files, but can sometimes slow down the Captivate editing process.

8. Click **OK** when you're done to add the selected PowerPoint slides to your movie as Captivate slides.

TIP

The linking feature will not work with older versions of PowerPoint; the slides must be at least PowerPoint 2007 to link to the Captivate project.

Adding an Animation Slide

An animation slide is simply a blank slide that contains an animation file. Captivate can import .swf, .avi, or animated .gif files into any movie. When you add an animation slide, Captivate will create a blank slide and then place the animation file that you specify on that slide. Just like when you add an animation file to an existing slide, you can change the properties of the animation.

TIP

This process is useful when adding larger animations. To add smaller animated elements (such as an animated GIF or flashing arrow) to an existing slide, see the section in Chapter 7 titled "Importing Animations."

Before you begin, check the animation file you're going to use. It should meet these conditions:

- The animation must be in one of the valid Captivate animation formats (SWF, AVI, or GIF).
- If the animation is going to fill your whole slide, it should be approximately the same size as your movie. You will be able to resize your animation if necessary as described in Chapter 7.
- The animation frame rate should be appropriate for the movie you're creating. Captivate will play all imported animations at the setting specified in the Captivate movie preference settings (usually 30 Flash frames per second).

1. Open the movie to which you want to add an animation slide.
2. Choose the location for the new slide within your movie by selecting the slide immediately before the one you want to add. For example, if you've

got the first slide open, the new animation slide will be inserted as slide number 2. You can move slides around later if needed.

3. From the **Insert** menu, choose **Other Slide(s)** and then **Animation Slide** to open a browser window that defaults to the last folder you used.

4. Browse to the correct folder, and then select the animation you want to insert. The icon for the animation appears on a new slide in your movie.

Duplicating an Existing Slide

If you've got a slide just the way you want it, with borders or timing or transitions or other elements you've added, you can use that slide as a starting point for other slides. The only difference between the slides will be in the label on the new slide—it will be prefaced with "Copy of" and then the original slide title. There are two ways to duplicate slides. The duplicate function copies the selected slide and inserts the copy into the movie immediately after the original slide. The copy and paste function allows you to specify where you want the copy inserted.

To duplicate a slide, follow these steps:

1. Display the slide you want to duplicate, either by clicking on the slide in the filmstrip in Edit view or by highlighting the slide in Storyboard view.

TIP

You can select more than one slide by clicking the first slide, then holding down the Ctrl key before clicking each of the other slides you want to select. You can also select a series of sequential slides by clicking the first slide, holding down the Shift key, and then clicking the last slide in the series you want to select.

---

2. From the **Edit** menu, choose **Duplicate Slide** (or right-click on a slide and select **Duplicate Slide**) to insert a copy of the selected slide or slides into your movie immediately following the original slides.

To copy a slide and paste it somewhere else in the movie, follow these steps:

1. Display the slide you want to copy, either by clicking on the slide in the filmstrip in Edit view or by highlighting the slide in Storyboard view.

2.   From the **Edit** menu, choose **Copy Slide** to copy the selected slide or slides.

3.   Specify the location for the new slide by selecting the slide immediately before the location of the new slides.

4.   From the **Edit** menu, choose **Paste Slide**. The slides will be inserted into your movie immediately following the slide you selected in Step 3.

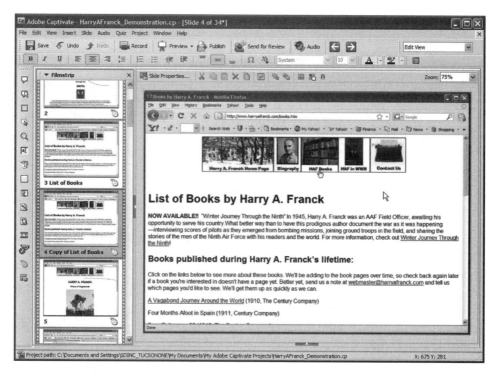

FIGURE 6-12   **The new slide is an exact copy of the old slide (except for the slide label).**

DELETING A SLIDE

As you work on a Captivate project, there may be times when you want to remove a slide or series of slides from a movie. For example, if you made a mistake while recording a task, it is sometimes simpler to remove the incorrect slides and record a few new ones rather than start recording the movie all over again. When you delete a slide from the movie, it is permanently removed from the movie, from the project, and from your computer.

To delete a slide from a movie, follow these steps:

1. There are a variety of ways to begin the deletion process. Do any one of the following:

    -   From Storyboard view, click the slide to select it, then click **Delete Slide** in the Slide Tasks pane.
    -   From Storyboard or Edit view, right-click on the slide to display the context menu, then choose **Delete Slide**.
    -   From Storyboard or Edit view, select the slide, then press the **Delete** key on your keyboard.
    -   From Storyboard or Edit view (with the slide for deletion selected or displayed), choose **Delete Slide** from the **Edit** menu.

Whichever method you use, a confirmation dialog appears.

2. Confirm that you want to delete the slide by clicking **Yes**, or cancel by clicking **No**.

HIDING A SLIDE

There may be times when you don't want the viewers to see a slide, but you don't want to delete the slide either. Captivate has a hide function that allows you to leave the slide in your project but prevent the slide from appearing in the finished movie. For example, you may want to hide slides if they aren't yet finished, if you are using them as placeholders for some future component, or if you are creating one movie that will be delivered to multiple audiences and you want to keep some slides hidden from some of the audiences.

Hidden slides will remain in the project, and you'll be able to see them in both Storyboard and Edit mode. Hidden slides are indicated by a diagonal line through the slide number and will not be exported when you publish the Flash movie.

FIGURE 6-13   Slides 6, 7, and 8 are hidden and won't be in the published movie.

To hide a slide, do any one of the following:

- From Storyboard view, click the slide to select it, then click **Hide Slide** in the Slide Tasks pane.
- From either view, right-click on the slide to display the context menu, then choose **Hide Slide**.
- From either view, choose **Hide Slide** from the **Slide** menu.
- From either view, select the slide, then hold down the **Shift** and **Ctrl** keys on your keyboard, and press the letter **H** on your keyboard.

> **TIP**
>
> Before distributing a movie with hidden slides, be sure to preview it carefully. It is very easy to hide one slide too many, and it can be very disconcerting for the viewers if you've hidden a slide that contains information they need.

To change a hidden slide back to normal viewing, do one of the following:

- From Storyboard view, click the slide to select it, then click **Show Slide** in the Slide Tasks pane.
- From either view, right-click on the slide to display the context menu, then choose **Show Slide**.
- From either view, choose **Show Slide** from the **Slide** menu.
- From either view, select the slide, then hold down the **Shift** and **Ctrl** keys on your keyboard, and press the letter **H** on your keyboard.

SUMMARY

This chapter described the various ways you can add, hide, and delete slides from your movie. It also explained the various views and the different types of slides. The following chapter describes how to add elements to and delete elements from a slide.

EDITING A SINGLE SLIDE

Chapter **7**

After you've created a movie full of slides, you'll usually need to go in and do a little bit of editing to get exactly the look or effect you want in your finished movie. No matter what type of slide you're working with, they all have the same basic components:

- Background, usually a screen capture or other image
- Visual elements such as text, captions, check boxes, mouse movement, etc.
- Transition information
- Audio (described in Chapter 8)

Most of the time, you'll be working in Edit view when you're editing a single slide.

WORKING WITH THE SLIDE BACKGROUND

When you look at an Adobe® Captivate® movie, most of what you see is the background of the slide. It is the surface on which the actions (such as mouse movement or the appearance of text captions) take place. The background of a slide will vary depending on the type of slide (and how you created it).

TABLE 7-1 Different types of slide backgrounds.

This type of slide:	Uses this for a background:
Recorded slide	The image of the screen when you captured it.
Image slide	The image you specified when you created the slide.
Blank	The background of the slide is a solid color as specified in the background preferences for the movie.
PowerPoint slide	The original Microsoft® PowerPoint® slide becomes the background. Note that once you've imported a PowerPoint slide into Captivate, you can no longer edit the text on the slides. However, you can add new text boxes to a slide with a PowerPoint background.
Question slide	The background of the slide is a solid color as specified in the background preferences for the movie.
Animation slide	The background of the slide is a solid color as specified in the background preferences for the movie.

You can't edit the contents of the background image within the Captivate software, but you can change the background of a slide to a new image. It's fairly simple to reimport the background into any slide, so if you need to make edits and have an external graphics program, you can make background changes. For example, if you've got a logo for a background, and your company logo changes, you can simply replace the old background logo with the new one. Any transitions or other elements on that slide remain in place.

In another example, sometimes when you're documenting a software product, a menu item might change. You could rerecord the slides that show that menu item, then edit the elements such as text captions or timings as necessary. Or you could copy the background image to your graphics package, change the one menu item, then replace the background of the slides with the new edited image. All of the other elements (captions, questions, click boxes, rollovers, buttons, etc.) will be retained.

Setting the Background Color

If you're working with slides that allow the background color of the movie to show through (such as question slides, blank slides, or animation slides with an animation smaller than the movie size), you can specify the default background color for the entire movie. By default, the background starts out white.

To set a new background color, follow these steps:

1. Open the Captivate movie.
2. From the **Edit** menu, choose **Preferences** to display the Preferences window.
3. Under the Global category in the list on the left of the window, choose **Defaults** to display the project settings.

FIGURE 7-1   **Set the background color in the Preferences window.**

4. Note that the current background color is displayed in a small rectangular box under Slide defaults. To change the color, click in the Background color box to open the Color window.

FIGURE 7-2   **Select a color for the movie background.**

5.   From this window, you can enter a color in any of the following ways:

   ■   Click one of the displayed colors.
   ■   Enter the hexadecimal value for the color (such as #000000
      for black and #FFFFFF for white).
   ■   Click the eyedropper icon, then click any area on the
      screen to copy the color of that area.
   ■   Click **More Colors. . .** to display the standard color
      selection tool. Use this option if you need to enter RGB
      values or Hue, Saturation, and Luminance values.

   Once you've chosen a color, the Color window closes and the selected color
   appears in the Background color box.

> **TIP**
> If your company has an official corporate color, you should be able to get the RGB
> values from your corporate art, marketing, or public relations department.

6.   Click **OK** to close the Preferences window and update all the slides in your
     movie with the new background color.

Copying a Slide Background

If you need to make a change to the background of a slide, you can easily copy the slide to your system clipboard and then paste the slide into a graphics package for editing. Select the slide that has the background you want to copy, then use any of the following methods:

- Click the right mouse button to display the context menu and choose **Copy Background**.
- From the **Edit** menu, choose **Copy Background**.
- Hold down the **Shift** and **Ctrl** keys on your keyboard, then press the **Y** key (**Shift+Ctrl+Y**).

The background of the slide is stored as an image onto the clipboard. You can then paste it into any graphics package for editing as necessary or paste from the clipboard to the background of any other slide.

Inserting a New Background Image

You can insert any image file as a new background into any slide. This can be the image that you copied from the slide (and edited), or it can be an entirely new image. You also have a choice of selecting an image from the Captivate library or from any other location.

Using a Background Image from the Library

You can import any image from the Captivate library to use as a slide background. The image will be referenced from the slide rather than copied into it. This allows you to make changes, if necessary, to the image file in the library, and to have those changes automatically display in the slides that use that image.

1. Select the slide by clicking on it. You can be in Storyboard, Edit, or Branching view.
2. From the **Slide** menu, choose **Properties** (or double-click anywhere on the slide background) to display the Slide Properties window.
3. From the Slide Properties window, click the **Change background image** button. A list of the current backgrounds and images in the movie displays.

FIGURE 7-3   **Change the background image by selecting a new background image.**

4. Use either of the following methods to select an image for the background of the slide:

    ■ Choose the background or image you want to use by clicking once on the filename to display a preview of the image in the left side of the window, and then click **OK** to select that image and close the image selection window.

    ■ If the image you want to use is not yet in the Captivate library, click the Import button to browse to the image location, click **OK** to select the file, copy it to the slide background and into the Captivate library, and then close the image selection window.

Using a Background Image that Isn't in the Library

You don't have to use the Captivate library to insert a new background; you can just cut and paste from any other application.

1. From a graphics or other display software, copy the image to your clipboard. This is usually done by pressing the **Ctrl** and **C** keys (**Ctrl+C**) or by using the software's copy function.
2. Open the Captivate movie that contains the slide or slides where you want to place the new background.
3. Select the slide by clicking on it. You can be in either Storyboard or Edit view.

> **TIP**
>
> You can update the background of multiple slides at once by selecting multiple slides. To select multiple slides, select the first slide, then hold down the **Ctrl** key as you click additional slides you want to select.

4. Paste the image from the clipboard into the slide using one of the following methods:

   - Click the right mouse button to display the context menu and choose **Paste as Background**.
   - From the **Edit** menu, choose **Paste as Background**.
   - Hold down the **Shift** and **Ctrl** keys on your keyboard, then press the **V** key (**Shift+Ctrl+V**).

5. Click **Yes** to confirm that you want to replace the background of the selected slide. The new image will be placed on the slide, and all the original objects such as mouse movements, captions, or highlight boxes will remain where they were.

ADDING AND EDITING VISUAL ELEMENTS

The real power of Captivate is not in the slide backgrounds or the screen capture images, but rather in the variety of elements that you can place on top of the background of the slides. Each element has a variety of options that you can set to fully customize the look and feel of your movie. The major elements are these:

- *Text captions:* Text captions contain words that describe the actions going on in each slide. These can be automatically generated by Captivate, or you can manually add them.
- *Highlight boxes:* Highlight boxes surround specific portions of the screen that you want the viewer to notice. These can be automatically generated by Captivate, or you can manually add them.
- *Rollover elements:* This category includes rollover captions, slidelets, rollover images, and zoom boxes. These elements are

displayed in the finished movie when the viewer rolls the cursor over specified areas of the slide. See Chapter 9 for more detail on this type of element.

- *Text entry boxes:* Text entry boxes allow the viewer to enter information, such as quizzing or other interactive applications. See Chapter 9 for more detail on this type of element.

- *Click boxes:* A click box is an area that the viewer must click before the next slide will be shown. See Chapter 9 for more detail on this type of element.

- *Buttons:* Buttons can be used to give the movie viewer a choice of what to do next while viewing your movie. See Chapter 9 for more detail on this type of element.

- *Drawing Objects:* This category includes lines, rectangles, ovals, and polygons.

- *Widgets:* A widget is a small piece of code that can be entered on a slide to perform a wide variety of functions. For example, one widget creates a course completion certificate that automatically pulls in the viewer's name. Another lets you create a unique type of question where the answer is displayed as a jumbled word and the viewer has to unscramble the letters. See Chapter 9 for more detail on this type of element.

- *Text Animations:* The letters you specify move around on the screen in different ways, such as flying in or spinning, or having fish float by.

- *Images:* In addition to using images as the background of your movie, you can add images to any slide. This gives you more control over the display of your image than just using the image as a background.

- *Animations:* You can import an existing animation file into a Captivate slide. Valid formats include SWF, AVI, and animated GIF. Captivate comes with a variety of predefined animations, such as arrows and spinning boxes, as well as a collection of animation schemes you can add to your text.

- *Flash Video:* You can import existing video files into your Captivate project.

Working with Text Captions

When you record your tasks, Captivate can automatically add some text captions to point out the specific tasks. For example, if you click on a link called "home page," Captivate will add a text caption that says "Click Here!" You can edit these captions, delete them, or create your own custom captions. For example, you may prefer to have the caption read "Click here to return to the home page."

You can also define the exact look of a caption, including the font, color, and size.

Adding Text Captions

Even if you use the automatic text captions, you may want to add a few captions of your own. For example, you could add a caption to point to a specific area of the screen or to insert a comment or special instruction. To add a text caption, follow these steps:

1. In Edit view, select the slide you want to edit.
2. From the **Insert** menu, select **Standard Objects**, and then **Text Caption**, or click the **Text Caption** icon to display the New Text Caption window.

FIGURE 7-4   **Add a new caption with the New Text Caption window.**

3. Type the text you want to display in the text caption.

TIP

Although the amount of caption text is unlimited, remember that it will be sitting on top of your slide background (which is often already very busy), and the more text you include, the smaller it will have to be to fit on the screen. The best captions are succinct and to the point. Use short, declarative phrases ("This is the main menu") or brief commands ("Click here to go to the next page").

---

4. If necessary, change the look of the caption by editing the following properties:

TABLE 7-2 Text caption properties.

To change this:	Do this:
Caption type	Choose a caption type from the list. The caption type defines the shape and color of the outline that will be placed around the text, as well as the default text color (although you can change this).
Font	Choose a font for the text from the list. The list of fonts will be determined by the fonts available on your system.
Size	Choose a size for the text from the list.
Color	Click the down arrow next to the letter A to choose a color for the text.
Highlight	Click the down arrow next to the highlight icon (a pen with ab next to it) to choose a color that will appear behind the text. Note that this is a color for the text background, and does not necessarily fill the caption outline.
Caption outline style	Many of the caption types include outlines that point in different directions. In the example in Figure 7-4, the "adobe blue" type has options that point in four different directions as well as an option with no direction. Click any one of the outline icons to select it for the current text caption.
Text style	If you want, set additional display options such as bold, italic, or underlined text, and text justification.

5. The changes you make to the caption properties will be applied to all subsequent text captions. If you want to apply these changes to all captions that are already in the movie, click **Apply to all** to apply the current settings as defined in the properties window. To view or change the properties settings, click the **Settings** button.

> **TIP**
>
> Note that if you change only part of a caption (such as making a single word bold or italicizing a phrase), these changes will not be applied to other captions.

FIGURE 7-5   Apply settings to previously created captions.

6. You can click the Options tab to set timing and transitions as described later in this chapter, click the Size and Position tab to set the default size and position, or click the Audio tab to set audio properties as described in Chapter 8.
7. Click **OK** to display the new caption in the center of the slide, as shown in Figure 7-6.
8. Using your mouse, click and drag the text caption to the desired location on the slide. You can also resize the caption box if necessary by clicking and dragging the corners of the outline.

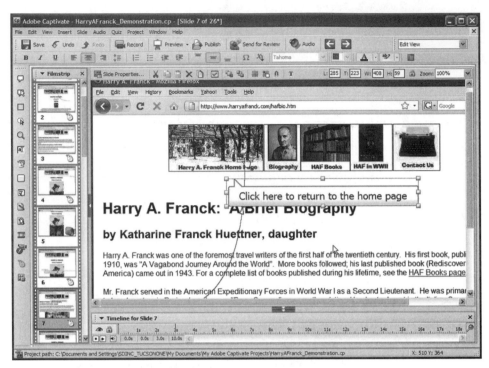

FIGURE 7-6 **The new caption appears on the slide.**

Editing Text Captions

Once you've created a text caption, you can move it around or resize it just like any other element on the slide. You can go back and edit the text as needed or change the look of the caption. You can also set the length of time the caption displays, as well as define the way the caption enters and leaves the screen during the movie (the transition).

1. In Edit view, select the slide you want to edit.
2. Double-click on the caption to open the Text Caption window (see Figure 7-7).
3. Make changes as necessary to the text caption properties. These are described in more detail in Table 7-2.
4. You can click the Options tab to set timing and transitions as described later in this chapter, click the Size and Position tab to set the default size

and position, or click the Audio tab to set audio properties as described in Chapter 8.

5.   Click **OK** to display the edited caption on the slide.

FIGURE 7-7   **Edit the text caption.**

Specifying Caption Language

Captivate automatically inserts captions as you record a Software Simulation. You can set the default language for these captions in the recording window that displays when you begin the recording process.

To change the caption language, follow these steps:

1.   Start the Captivate software. The first screen you'll see will be the Captivate main menu.

2.   Under **Create project**, choose **Software Simulation** to open the recording window.

3.   In the recording window, click the **Automatic Recording** icon (second one from the top) to display the recording options.

4.   Click the small, dark arrow next to the label **Advanced** to display the language options. The default will display the last language you used.

FIGURE 7-8   **Specify caption language.**

5. Choose a language for the captions from the drop-down list labeled **Captions In**. Available options as of this printing are Chinese-simplified, Chinese-traditional, Dutch, English, French, German, Italian, Japanese, Korean, Norwegian, Portuguese-Brazilian, Portuguese, Spanish, and Swedish. Note that only the captions will be translated into the selected language. The screen elements, such as buttons or menu items, remain in the original source language.

6. Click **Record** and continue to create the movie as normal. The finished movie will use the specified language for captions.

FIGURE 7-9   **A text caption and a failure caption in four languages.**

Working with Highlight Boxes

A highlight box is a rectangular, shaded area that is intended to draw the viewer's attention to a particular area on the slide. Depending on your recording settings, Captivate can automatically add highlight boxes whenever you click the mouse while recording. The highlight box will be placed around the link you clicked, whether it is a button or a text link. Whether you use the automatic function or add highlight boxes manually, you can always edit the highlight box shape, color, size, and placement.

For example, Figure 7-10 has two highlight boxes. One is around the button that goes back to the home page. The other is around the title of a book, *Winter Journey Through the Ninth.* Both highlight boxes are set to 50% transparency so that they show up clearly in this book; however, you may want to use a higher transparency so that viewers can see the button or text behind them. The words "highlight box" that appear in the center of the box will not appear in the finished movie.

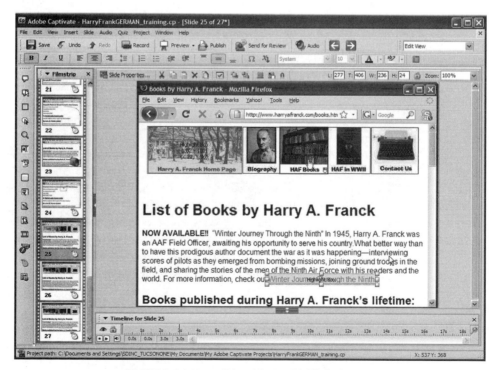

FIGURE 7-10   A slide with two highlight boxes.

Adding or Editing a Highlight Box

To add or edit a highlight box, follow these steps:

1. In Edit view, select the slide you want to edit.
2. To add a highlight box, from the **Insert** menu, select **Standard Objects** and then **Highlight Box**, or click the **Highlight Box** icon to display the New Highlight Box window. To edit an existing highlight box, double-click on the **highlight** box to display the Highlight Box properties window.
3. If necessary, change the look of the caption by editing the following properties. As you make changes, the preview in the center of the window changes to reflect each new selection.

TABLE 7-3 Highlight box properties.

To change this:	Do this:
Frame color	Click the colored box next to Frame color to display the Color window, and then choose a color for the border around the outside edge of the highlight box. This is usually a darker shade than the inside of the box.
Frame width	Specify the width, in pixels, for the border or frame of the highlight box. Set the width to 0 to remove the frame.
Fill color	Click the colored box next to Fill color to display the Color window, and then choose a color for the highlighting. This is usually a lighter shade than the frame of the box.
Fill transparency	Enter the percentage of transparency for the inside of the box. 0% would be completely solid; 100% would be completely transparent. Most of the time, you want something between these two values so that the highlight box is noticeable and yet the text behind the box still shows through.
Fill outer area	This option allows you to leave the designated highlight box area clear and shade the entire rest of the screen. Note that you can only see this form of highlighting in the preview or published slide (not in Edit mode).

FIGURE 7-11   **Set the new highlight box properties.**

4. The changes you make to the highlight box properties will be applied to all subsequent highlight boxes. If you want to apply these changes to all highlight boxes that are already in the movie, click **Apply to all** to apply the current settings as defined in the properties Settings window. To view or change the properties settings, click the **Settings** button.

FIGURE 7-12   **Apply settings to previously created highlight boxes.**

5. You can click the Options tab to set timing and transitions as described later in this chapter, click the Size and Position tab to set the default size and position, or click the Audio tab to set audio properties as described in Chapter 8.

6. Click **OK** to display the new highlight box in the center of the slide with the default size of 100x100 pixels.
7. Using your mouse, click and drag the highlight box to the desired location on the slide. You can also resize the highlight box if necessary by clicking and dragging the corners of the outline.

Working with Drawing Objects

Though not specifically a drawing package, Captivate does come with the ability to use basic objects (line, rectangle, oval, and polygon) to draw custom elements on your slides. Like other vector graphic programs, Captivate drawing tools allow you to specify a shape by indicating the line position, width, and style, and a fill color and transparency. Once defined, you can easily edit, move, or resize drawing objects just as you would other Captivate slide elements.

There are two ways to access the drawing tools:

- From the **Window** menu, select **Toolbars** and then **Drawing** to display the Drawing toolbar. This method gives you the most options and the most control over your drawing objects.
- From the **Insert** menu, select **Drawing Objects** and then click on the object you want to draw. This method is quick and easy, particularly if you've already set the drawing object defaults to the appearance of each object that you use most often.

Drawing objects in Captivate is similar to other vector-based graphic programs. As you create each object, the system uses the most recent settings for color and line width and a variety of other parameters. You can then go back in and change any of these settings for the exact look that you want.

Drawing an Object

To draw objects in Captivate, follow these steps:

1. In Edit mode, display the slide on which you want to create a new shape.
2. From the **Window** menu, select **Toolbars** and then **Drawing** to display the Drawing toolbar.

FIGURE 7-13 **Display the Drawing toolbar.**

3. Click on an icon in the toolbar to specify which type of object you want to draw (see Table 7-4).

TIP

You can also specify the shape you want to draw from the Insert menu by selecting **Drawing objects** and then the shape name.

4. Draw a shape as follows:

TABLE 7-4 Drawing objects.

Click this icon:	Then do this:
▲	Return to selection mode if you're in the middle of drawing a shape. Captivate automatically returns to selection mode after you've completed each shape. From here, you can select any object you want to edit.
╲	Draw a line by clicking once at the beginning and again at the end point of your line.
⬡	Draw a multisided, enclosed shape by clicking once at each corner of the shape. You can enter as many points as you want, but the shape will not be complete until you click on the starting point to enclose the polygon. You can also double-click on the last point to automatically connect it to the starting point.
▢	Draw a rectangle (or square) by clicking at the position of any corner, then holding down the left mouse button and dragging to the opposite corner of the desired rectangle before releasing the button. If you want to draw a square, hold down the **Shift** key while dragging to ensure that all four sides will be the same length.
◯	Circles and ovals are defined in the system as the largest oval that fits into a bounding box. Draw a circle by clicking on any corner of this box, then holding down the left mouse button and dragging the cursor to the opposite corner before releasing the button. Note that the two points you define do not actually touch the oval's perimeter; they define the corners of the bounding box. If you want to draw a perfect circle, hold down the **Shift** key while dragging.

5.   When you are done drawing a shape, Captivate automatically returns to Select mode. You can then draw additional shapes by repeating steps 3 and 4.

TIP

If you want to draw several shapes of the same type (such as a series of circles or a bunch of arrows), hold down the **Ctrl** key before you choose the shape. You'll still have to draw each shape individually, but you won't have to reselect the shape type each time. To stop drawing mode and return to selection mode, click the **Select** icon.

Editing Objects

Like other Captivate elements, you can select one or more drawing objects, move them around on the slide, resize as needed, and set a variety of properties. Though the drawing object properties vary slightly from type to type, the basic properties of line color, width, and style, and fill color and transparency are the same for all shapes.

Note: Captivate defaults to the last settings you used for each property, regardless of which shape you are modifying. If the last object you drew was a circle, and you set the fill color to red, then all subsequent polygons and squares will default to red fill.

To edit drawing properties, follow these steps:

1.   Select the shape you want to edit and choose **Properties** from the **Edit** menu (or simply double-click the shape) to display the properties for that shape.

FIGURE 7-14   **Set the drawing object properties.**

2. The properties window displays a preview of each shape based on the properties you set. Set any or all of the following properties listed in Table 7-5.

TABLE 7-5 Drawing object properties.

To set this property:	Enter this information:
Color of the shape outline	Choose a color from the drop-down box next to Stroke color. **Note**: For Line objects only, this is called the Line Color. Note that you can also set this property from the Drawing toolbar with the Stroke Color icon ( ).
Thickness of the shape outline	Enter a number (in pixels) in the Stroke width box. You can type in a number or use the up or down arrow keys.

TABLE 7-5 Drawing object properties (continued).

To set this property:	Enter this information:
Color of the shading inside the shape	Choose a color from the drop-down box next to Fill color. Note that you can also set this property with the Drawing toolbar Fill Color icon ( ).
Line beginning and ending shapes	(Object type Line only) Specify arrow, circle, diamond, or square for the first point on your line by choosing from the Start drop-down box. Specify arrow, circle, diamond, or square for the last point on your line by choosing from the End drop-down box.
Dotted or dashed lines	Choose the line appearance from the Stroke style drop-down box. You can choose solid or various types of dashed lines.
Fill color	Choose a color from the drop-down box next to Fill color. The Line object does not have a fill option.
Transparency of the fill color	Enter a number for the transparency in the Fill transparency box. Remember that the higher the number, the more transparent the color will be. 100 would be totally transparent (invisible), and 0 is completely solid. The Line object does not have a fill option.
Rounded corners on rectangular objects	(Object type Rectangle only) Enter a number in the Corner Radius box for the amount of curvature you want on the corners of a rectangular object. The highest number (50) indicates an oval or circular shape. Lower numbers will give slight rounding effects.

3. You can click the Options tab to set timing and transitions as described later in this chapter, click the Size and Position tab to set the default size and position, or click the Audio tab to set audio properties as described in Chapter 8.

4. Click **OK** to close the properties window and display the edited shape or shapes.

5. To quickly change the colors of all selected objects to black lines with white fill, click the **Black/white** icon ( ) on the Drawing toolbar.

6. To quickly reverse line and fill colors, click the **Reverse colors** icon ( ) on the Drawing toolbar.

Working with Images

For most movies, you'll use an image or series of images as the background of each slide. In many cases, this will be a screen capture, logo, or photograph (see the section called "Working with the Slide Background" earlier in this chapter). When you create an image slide, you're importing an image as the background. Background images cannot be edited or changed within Captivate.

You can also import an image as an element on top of a slide background. Like other visual elements, the image can have unique timing and transition settings. You can resize the image or move it around on the slide. You can also specify a transparency setting for the image.

Valid image formats include JPG, JPEG, GIF, PNG, BMP, ICO, EMF, and WMF.

TIP

Although you can add images of any size, this process works best with smaller images, such as an arrow or a small icon or button that you will make interactive. If you need to import an image that will take up the entire slide area, see the section titled "Adding an Image Slide" in Chapter 6.

TIP

Captivate comes with a gallery of images for buttons that you can import into your movies. By default, they're stored in the Adobe Captivate 4\Gallery\Buttons folder.

Adding or Editing an Image

Once you've imported an image, you can move it around or resize it just like any other element on the slide. You can also set the length of time it displays, as well as define the way the image enters and leaves the screen during the movie (the transition). You cannot, however, actually edit the image (such as change colors or erase parts of the image). For that type of task, you'll need to use an external graphics package.

To add or edit an image, follow these steps:

1. In Edit view, select the slide you want to edit.
2. To add a new image, from the **Insert** menu, select **Image**, or click the Image icon to display the images available in the last folder you used. Browse to the location of the image you want to import, highlight the image name, and click **Open**. To edit an existing image, double-click on the image in the slide.

FIGURE 7-15   **Import an image as an element on the slide.**

3. The image you selected appears in the center of the window. Enter the percentage of transparency for the image. 0% would be completely solid; 100% would be completely transparent.

4. You can specify that Captivate import the image but make the background color of the image transparent. For example, if you are adding a logo that is a custom shape, such as a shield, you might not want the rectangular outline of the image file to show.

TIP

Be careful to check your images after you import them, particularly if you use a transparent background. Captivate will make all areas the color of the background transparent. For example, if you have an image of a black circle with white lettering and a white background, and you make the white background transparent, then Captivate will make all white portions of the image transparent (including the letters). If this isn't the look you wanted, use a graphics program to make the background or the letters slightly different shades of white.

---

5. The changes you make to the image properties will be applied to all subsequent images. If you want to apply these changes to all images that are already in the movie, click **Apply to all** to apply the current settings as defined in the properties Settings window. To view or change the properties settings, click the **Settings** button.

FIGURE 7-16   **Apply settings to previously created images.**

6. You can click the Options tab to set timing and transitions as described later in this chapter, click the Size and Position tab to set the default size and position, or click the Audio tab to set audio properties as described in Chapter 8.

7. Click **OK** to display the new image in the center of the slide.

8. Using your mouse, click and drag the image to the desired location on the slide. You can also resize the image if necessary by clicking and dragging the corners of the outline.

Working with Animations

There are three types of animations within Captivate. The primary difference between the animation types is the way the files are created.

- Full Motion Recordings are actually AVI animations that are created by Captivate and stored as Flash files displayed on a single slide. These Full Motion Recordings take up the full area of the slide and thus cannot be moved. The icon for the animation appears in the center of the slide. Full Motion Recording is described in Chapter 4.
- Imported animations are files that were created outside of Captivate. Valid animation formats for importing are AVI, SWF, and animated GIF.
- Text animations are predefined animations that come with Captivate. Use these to make any text you enter move in various ways.

For all three animation types you can modify parameters such as transparency, timing, and transitions.

> **TIP**
>
> With Captivate Release 4.0, you can also import SWF widgets. Unlike standard SWF animations, a widget allows for customization at run-time. See Chapter 9 for more information about widgets and interactivity.

Importing Animations

You can import .avi, .swf, or animated .gif files into your Captivate movie. Like Full Motion Recordings, these mini-movies will be stored on a single slide. You'll be able to modify the placement of the animation, as well as the other standard element properties.

> **TIP**
>
> Captivate comes with a gallery of animated arrows and boxes that you can import into your movies. By default, they're stored in the Adobe Captivate 4\Gallery\ SWF Animation folder.

To import an animation, follow these steps:

1. In Edit view, open the slide on which you want the animation.
2. From the **Insert** menu, select **Animation** or click the **Animation** icon to open the last-viewed folder.
3. Browse to the appropriate folder and choose the animation you want to import. For this example, we'll import an animation from the Captivate Gallery that shows a blue arrow moving diagonally downward (Adobe Captivate 4\Gallery\SWF Animation\Arrows\Blue Fade\downleft.swf).
4. Click **OK** to open the selected animation in the New Animation window. A preview of the animation is displayed on the left side of the window; statistics for the animation are displayed on the right side of the window.

FIGURE 7-17   **Insert an animation and set transparency.**

5. If after viewing the preview you decide that it isn't the right animation, click the **Import** button to choose a new file.

6. Make changes as necessary to the Transparency setting. Remember, the lower the transparency setting, the less transparent (or more solid) the animation will appear.

7. The changes you make to the transparency will be applied to all subsequent animations. If you want to apply these changes to all animations that are already in the movie, click **Apply to all** to apply the current settings as defined in the properties Settings window. To view or change the properties settings, click the **Settings** button.

FIGURE 7-18 Apply settings to previously created images.

8. You can click the Options tab to set timing and transitions as described later in this chapter, click the Size and Position tab to set the default size and position, or click the Audio tab to set audio properties as described in Chapter 8.

9. Click **OK** to display the animation on the slide. Note that the animation won't be playing—you'll just see an icon that represents the animation.

10. If necessary, use your mouse to click in the center of the image and drag it to a different area of the screen. For example, we might drag this animation icon so that the bottom corner (where the arrow is pointing) is close to the link for Harry A. Franck's books. When played, the arrow will move from the upper-right corner of the animation box to the lower-left corner, fading in as it moves.

11. If necessary, use your mouse to click on the square handles on the sides or corners of the animation, and then drag them outward or inward to create the size and shape you need.

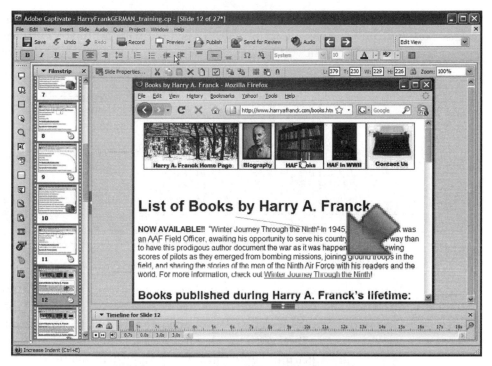

FIGURE 7-19   **Move or resize the animation as needed.**

TIP

Use the handles on the corners of the animation rather than the sides to maintain the aspect ratio (the relative height and width). This will prevent distorting the shapes.

Adding Text Animations

Captivate comes with a selection of animations specifically designed to add motion to the text that you enter. Some of the animations cause the text to enter or exit the slide in colorful or spectacular ways, while others make the letters in your text move about for the duration of the animation.

For example, you could have text shuffle in (like cards), spin like a top, pop in when bulbs break, or scroll onto the screen with a filmstrip effect. There are many others, but you'll have to view the list that comes with Captivate to see them all.

FIGURE 7-20   **A few of the Captivate text effects.**

To add text animation to a slide, follow these steps:

1. In Edit view, open the slide to which you want to add the text animation.
2. From the **Insert** menu, select **Text Animation** or click the **Text Animation** icon to display the new Text Animation window. The window displays the words "Sample Text" with the first animation from the list. In the sample below, the "Aquarium" effect has blue-striped fish swimming about and nibbling at the letters in the text.

FIGURE 7-21   **Type your text and choose a text animation effect from the list.**

3. Type the text you want to animate in the Text box. Note that you can enter multiple lines of text and use any punctuation or special symbols.

> **TIP**
>
> There is no limit to the amount of text you can animate, but it works best if you animate smaller phrases rather than long strings of text. You can press the **Enter** key to create multiple lines of text in one animation, or you can create several one-line animations for the same slide.

4. Choose the animation effect you want from the Effect list. As you select from the list of animations, a preview of the selected animation will display on the left side of the window, using the words you've entered in the text box. For example, for a slide introducing Harry A. Franck books, we may want to create a title slide that makes it appear that a pen is writing out the letters on the slide. This is the animation called "Feather."

5. If you want to change the font, size, or color of your text, click the **Change font** button to display the Font window, and then choose the font, style, size, and color you want. For example, we may want to use a font that looks more like handwriting.

FIGURE 7-22   **Specify font, size, and color for your text.**

6. Click **OK** to close the Font window and display the changes in the new Text Animation window.

7. Make changes as necessary to the Transparency setting. Remember, the lower the transparency setting, the less transparent (or more solid) the animation will appear.
8. Specify the time delay between frames of the animation.

Note: This is in frames, not in seconds. A frame delay of 1 makes for a very fast, smooth movie. A higher delay between frames will cause the letters to come in (or fly out, or whatever the animation does) very slowly. Regardless of the frame delay, the animation will not run longer than the timing setting on the Options tab.

9. The changes you make to the animation properties will be applied to all subsequent animations. If you want to apply these changes to all animations that are already in the movie, click **Apply to all** to apply the current settings as defined in the properties Settings window. To view or change the properties settings, click the **Settings** button.

FIGURE 7-23   **Apply settings to previously created animations.**

10. You can click the Options tab to set timing and transitions as described later in this chapter, click the Size and Position tab to set the default size and position, or click the Audio tab to set audio properties as described in Chapter 8.
11. Click **OK** to display the new animation in the center of the slide.
12. Using your mouse, click and drag the animation to the desired location on the slide. You can also resize the animation if necessary by clicking and dragging the corners of the outline.

Merging Visual Elements into the Background

As we've seen throughout this chapter, you can add elements on top of the background of any slide. These elements usually remain separate from the background so that you can modify them, move them around, and control their individual timing. However, there may be some instances where you want to merge an element into the background. For example, to make a type of watermark background, you could import an image of your logo as an object. This would allow you to edit the size, placement, and transparency of the logo to make it almost transparent. Then, merge the image into the background and use that background for other slides.

> **Note:** Once you merge an object into the slide background, you can no longer edit that object.

To merge any object into the background of the slide, follow these steps:

1. In Edit view, add the object to a slide and make whatever changes you want. Remember, you won't be able to change the object after it is merged with the background.
2. Click once on the object to select it.
3. From the **Edit** menu, select **Merge into Background** (or right-click on the object and select **Merge into Background**) to display the confirmation dialog.

FIGURE 7-24   **Merging an object and background cannot be undone.**

4. Click **Yes** to complete the merge. Any objects you had selected are now part of the background of the slide.

> **TIP**
>
> If you merge animations into the background, the animations are converted to a single image. The result will display only the last frame of the animation.

REARRANGING ELEMENTS ON A SLIDE

Once you've inserted the various elements (such as images, animations, or captions) onto a slide, you can move them, resize them, align them with each other, or even delete them. The functions described in this section apply to all of the elements that you add on top of slides, but not to the background of the slides. If, for example, you've created an animation slide or an image slide, that animation or image is part of the slide background and not a separate object.

> **TIP**
>
> You can tell the difference between background and editable elements because the background elements do not have "handles" for resizing. Also, double-clicking a background will only display the slide property window (not the window for the element type).

Selecting Elements

In order to perform actions like moving or resizing elements on a slide, you must first specify which elements you want to work with. You can do this in the following way:

- Click once on an element to select it, either in the edit window or from the timeline. The outline of a selected element displays small square boxes (called "handles") in each corner and on each side of the outline.

> **TIP**
>
> If you accidentally double-click on an element, the properties window for that element appears. Simply click **Cancel** to close the window. The element will remain selected.

To select multiple elements at once, do any one of the following:

- Click on one element to select it, then hold down the **Shift** key while you click on one or more subsequent elements.
- Click on one element to select it, and then from the **Edit** menu, choose **Select All**. Note that this option only becomes available after you've selected one object.
- Using the mouse, click anywhere on the slide, then hold down the left mouse button while you drag the mouse across the screen. This will draw a dotted line box, and any object within the box will be selected when you release the mouse button.

There are two elements in Figure 7-25: one text caption and one highlight box. The text caption is selected (you can see the square handles); the highlight box has not been selected.

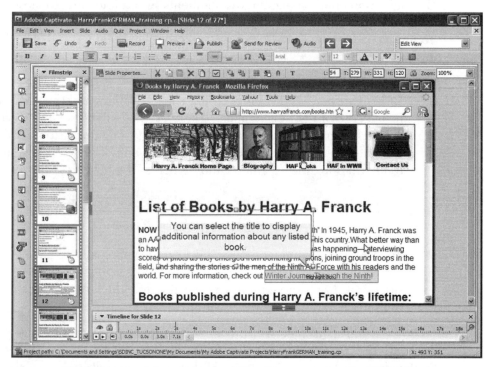

FIGURE 7-25 Selected elements, like this text caption, have "handles."

To remove the elements from selection, simply click once anywhere on the slide background.

Moving Elements

Once an element or set of elements has been selected, simply click anywhere within the selected element outline, hold down the mouse button, and drag the element to a new location.

For more exact placement of the element, use the up, down, left, or right arrow keys to move the element one pixel at a time in the direction of the arrow. This is sometimes referred to as "nudging."

If you're moving several elements at once, they will move as a group, retaining their positions relative to each other.

Aligning Elements

Though you could manually move elements into a line with each other, it is easier and more accurate to use the alignment function when you want elements to line up perfectly. There's even a toolbar of alignment icons that makes this task very easy.

To turn on the Alignment toolbar, follow these steps:

1.   In Edit view, from the **View** menu, click **Toolbars** and then **Alignment** to select it, or right-click on any displayed toolbar and select **Alignment**. A check mark appears on the menu, and the Alignment toolbar displays in the location you last placed it. If you haven't displayed the Alignment toolbar before, the default location is across the bottom of the screen.

FIGURE 7-26   **The Alignment toolbar.**

2.   To move the Alignment toolbar, click on the vertical dotted line on the far left (or top) of the toolbar, then drag the toolbar to a new location on any side of the Captivate screen. You can also drag the toolbar to the center of the screen to display it in a "floating" window.

When you align objects, Captivate will move all the elements you select in a line with the first one selected (the "anchor" element). You can easily see which is the anchor element because it will have white handles, and subsequently selected objects will have black handles.

To align objects, follow these steps:

1. Select two or more objects.
2. Click the icon representing the type of alignment you want.

TABLE 7-6 Alignment options.

Click this icon:	To align the elements like this:
	Align the left side of each element along the left side of the anchor.
	Align the horizontal center of each element along the horizontal center of the anchor.
	Align the right side of each element along the right side of the anchor.
	Align the top of each element along the top of the anchor.
	Align the vertical center of each element along the vertical center of the anchor.
	Align the bottom of each element along the bottom of the anchor.
	Space the elements so that there is an equal distance between the horizontal centers of each one.
	Space the elements so that there is an equal distance between the vertical centers of each one.
	Align the horizontal center of all elements, then center them horizontally on the slide.
	Align the vertical center of all elements, then center them vertically on the slide.
	Resize all elements so that they are the same height as the anchor.
	Resize all elements so that they are the same width as the anchor.
	Resize all elements so that they are the same height and width as the anchor.

TIP

If you change your mind about anything you do within Captivate, you can use the undo function to step back through actions you've performed since you opened the project. Choose **Undo** from the **Edit** menu or press **Ctrl+Z** to undo the previous action.

Placing Elements with the Grid

For more precise placement of elements on a slide, you can display a grid in Edit view and specify the distance between both horizontal and vertical grid points. You can then either manually place elements on the grid or have Captivate automatically place the elements along the lines formed by the grid points.

Note: The grid is a tool for placement of elements like captions, animations, and images. It will not display in the finished movie.

To use the grid for placing elements, follow these steps:

1. In Edit view, from the **View** menu, choose **Show Grid**. A grid composed of dots displays on the slide.
2. Click **Snap to grid** if you want Captivate to automatically place elements so that they are touching the nearest grid lines or click the checked box to turn off Snap to grid.
3. For finer control over placement, you can set the dots to be closer together. From the **Edit** menu, choose **Preferences** to display the Captivate Preferences window.
4. Under **Global** in the left-side Category panel, click **General Settings** to display the global options.

FIGURE 7-27   Set the grid size in the Global area of the Captivate Preferences window.

5.   The default grid size is 16 pixels between each dot, both horizontally and vertically. Set this to the number that works for your project. Larger numbers allow more space between the grid dots; smaller numbers allow for more precise placement.

6.   Click **OK** to close the Captivate Preferences window and return to the gridded slide.

7.   If you selected Snap to grid, any element you move will automatically be placed along the grid. If you don't have Snap to grid turned on, you can still use the grid as a guideline for alignment.

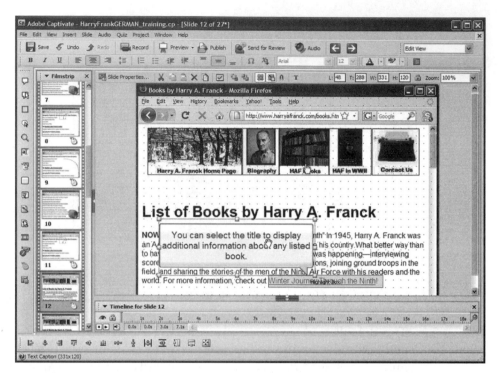

FIGURE 7-28   **Text captions and other elements snap into alignment on the grid.**

8.   When you're finished moving things around, from the **View** menu, choose
     Show Grid again to remove the check mark and turn off the grid.

Resizing Elements

Each element you add to a slide starts out with a default size. Captivate creates
text captions so that they're just big enough to fit the text you enter. It imports
animations and images at their original size, and bases the size of text animations
on the font size and type of animation. You can change the size of any element
using the handles on the corners and sides of the selected objects.

There are three ways to change the size of Captivate elements:

■   Dragging the handles works just like it does in other
    applications. This is the quickest way to change a single element.

- Enter the size and placement in the shortcut menu at the top of the Edit view. This is quick and easy, like dragging, but allows for more accurate placement.
- Specify the size and placement on the Size and Position tab in the element's properties window. This option gives you more control, and is particularly useful when resizing several elements at once. It can store your changes for all subsequent elements of the same type, or can be set to change all elements of the same type in the movie.

To use the drag method, follow these steps:

1. Select the element or elements.
2. Click on one of the handles, hold the mouse down, and drag the handle away from the element to make it bigger or toward the center of the element to make it smaller. Hold down the **Shift** key, and drag the handles in the corners of the element to maintain the aspect ratio and to keep the same general shape of each element. Use the handles on the sides or top or bottom of the element to stretch in one direction only.
3. Release the mouse button when the element or elements are the size you want them to be.

To use the shortcuts at the top of the Edit view, follow these steps:

1. Select the element or elements.
2. When you select an element, the current position and dimensions of the selected element display at the top of the Edit view. If you select several elements, the position and dimension boxes appear, but are empty. To specify a position and/or dimension, enter a number for any of the displayed boxes.

TABLE 7-7 Size and Position options.

The number in this box:	Does this:
L	Align the left side of each element the specified number of pixels from the left side of the screen.
T	Align the top of each element the specified number of pixels from the top of the screen.
W	Resize all elements to the specified number of pixels in width.
H	Resize all elements to the specified number of pixels in height.

FIGURE 7-29   Set the exact size and position of an element or group of elements.

To use the Size and Position tab in the element's properties window, follow these steps:

1. Double-click the element to display the properties window.
2. Click the **Size and Position** tab.

FIGURE 7-30   The Size and Position tab in the properties window adjusts element location.

3. Specify the position of the element by entering the number of pixels the left edge of the element should be from the left of the slide, and the number of pixels the element should be from the top of the slide. For example, the very top leftmost position would show 0 in both the left and top boxes.

4. Specify the size of the element by entering the width and height in pixels. If you want to ensure that the proportion of width to height remains the same as you change the numbers, click either the **Constrain proportions** box to check it or the lock symbol to display a closed lock. This is similar to "Maintain aspect ratio" in other programs.

5. The changes you make to the element's properties will be applied to all subsequent elements of that type. If you want to apply these changes to all similar elements that are already in the movie, click **Apply to all** to apply the current settings as defined in the properties Settings window. To view or change the properties settings, click the **Settings** button.

6. Click **OK** to save your changes and close the properties window.

Deleting Elements

When you delete an element from a slide, you're deleting it permanently. Make sure this is what you want to do before you start to delete!

TIP

If you change your mind about anything you do within Captivate, you can use the undo function to step back through actions you've performed since you opened the project. Choose **Undo** from the **Edit** menu or press **Ctrl+Z** to undo the previous action.

To delete an element, follow these steps:

1. Select the slide that contains the element you want to delete and open it in Edit view.

2. Select the element you want to delete.

3. Do any one of the following:

    - From the **Edit** menu, choose **Delete**.
    - Right-click on the element to display the context menu, then choose **Delete**.
    - Press the **Delete** key on your keyboard.

Whichever method you use, a confirmation dialog appears.

FIGURE 7-31   **Confirm that you want to delete the element.**

4.   Confirm that you want to delete the element by clicking **Yes**, or cancel by clicking **No**.

TIP

Although you can click the **Don't ask me this again** check box in the delete confirmation window to save a mouse click whenever you're deleting, it is a good idea to leave this unchecked. Once deleted, you cannot retrieve elements, and an extra confirmation step may one day save your project from accidental disaster.

CHANGING CURSOR MOVEMENT

When you record actions on the screen, Captivate automatically stores the movements of your cursor as you move it around on the screen using the mouse or other pointing device. Rather than store the exact path, Captivate stores only the beginning and ending locations of the cursor on each slide. When the movie is played, Captivate fills in the cursor movement using the mouse settings you've entered for properties such as cursor icon, speed, path, and mouse click. One exception to this is if you record your movie in Full Motion Recording mode. Full Motion Recording captures the exact motions of your cursor.

Within Captivate, the cursor movement is also called the mouse movement, since it is typically created by recording your use of the mouse, although you can use other pointing devices such as a pen on a tablet. Sometimes the cursor is also called the pointer, even when it is a nonpointing icon such **as a timer** or cross-hatch.

Unlike other elements on a slide, you cannot delete cursor movement. You can, however, set the mouse movement so that it doesn't show. The beginning and ending points are still stored, and you can show them again later if you need to, but the mouse will not display on the slide in the finished movie.

Displaying Cursor Movement

The cursor movements are recorded along with your screenshots whenever you record a movie. As you work with movie files, you can turn the display of these movements on or off. There are three ways to do this:

- Set the default recording options for cursor movement display (on or off) before you record the movie. You can always override the cursor display for each slide later.
- Turn the cursor display on or off for a single slide through the Mouse menu.
- Set the cursor defaults with the Mouse Properties window. This window allows you to specify whether you want the new settings to apply to a single slide or become the new default for all slides.

To change the default cursor display, follow these steps:

1. From the **Edit** menu, choose **Preferences**.
2. From the displayed Preferences window, click the **Mode(s)** option in the Recording area of the Category panel on the left side of the window.

FIGURE 7-32   **Set the Recording options.**

3. Specify the recording mode for which you want to change the default cursor display (Demonstration, Assessment Simulation, Training Simulation, or Custom). Remember that these are the options that you'll choose when you begin the recording process.

4. Click **Show mouse location and movement** to select it and display the cursor on your slides. Deselect this option to hide the cursor movement.

5. Click **OK** to close the Preferences window. All subsequent recordings, whether new movies or new slides in an existing movie, will use the new settings. The next time you record a movie, the cursor movement will display by default.

You can turn the cursor movement on or off for specific slides using the mouse menus.

Note: Turning the display off does not remove the cursor movement from the file. It is just hidden until you turn it on again. Hiding the cursor movement on one slide does not change the cursor start positioning for the next slide, so you may appear to have a cursor pop out of nowhere if you hide cursor movement on a slide that actually had some movement. When you hide a slide, Captivate adjusts the start position of the cursor on the subsequent slide to match the previous slide.

Access the Mouse menu in any of the following ways:

- In the Storyboard view Slide Tasks pane, click **Mouse**.
- In Edit view, right-click anywhere on the background of the slide to display a context menu, then choose **Mouse**.
- From the **Slide** menu, click **Mouse**.

FIGURE 7-33   **Display the Mouse menu.**

From the Mouse menu, select (or deselect) the **Show Mouse** option to turn the cursor movement display on or off.

Changing the Cursor Icon

For each slide, you can designate a different icon to be used as the cursor. You can choose from the variety of cursor icons that come with your Windows system, or you can use your own icon (as long as it is in valid Windows cursor format). For example, on some slides you may want to leave the standard image of a hand pointing to various objects; on other slides you may want to use a timer or cross-hatch.

To change the cursor icon, follow these steps:

1. Display the slide that contains the icon you want to change.
2. Display the Mouse menu by doing any one of the following:
    -   In the Storyboard view Slide Tasks pane, click **Mouse**.
    -   In Edit view, right-click anywhere on the background of the slide to display a context menu, then choose **Mouse**.
    -   Double-click on the cursor on the slide.
    -   Double-click on the **mouse** element in the timeline.
    -   From the **Slide** menu, click **Mouse**.
3. Choose either **Project Pointers** (for a display of all icons in the cursor folder on your system) or **Current Theme Pointers** (for a display of the icons that match your current Windows theme).
4. Click the cursor icon you want to use for the current slide or select **Browse** to navigate to the file containing the icon you want to use.

FIGURE 7-34   Choose a new icon for the cursor from either the project pointers or current theme pointers.

5. If you want to use the currently selected cursor for all the slides in the current movie, display the Mouse menu again (as in Step 2) and choose **Use current mouse pointer for all slides**.

Changing the Cursor Path

Captivate stores the beginning and ending points of your cursor movements, then displays the path as a line between those two points. When you play the movie, the selected cursor icon moves along a path that represents the movement you made when recording the slides. Note that this isn't necessarily the same path you actually took—if you moved the mouse in a squiggly pattern or in circles, Captivate will still represent this as a direct line between the beginning and end points. In general, beginning and end points are set for each slide when you click the mouse button.

You can display the line either straight or curved, or you can move the end point of the movement to a new location. When you move the end point of a cursor path, Captivate automatically adjusts the start point of the path on the next slide to match, giving you a smooth transition when the movie is played. You can also move the starting point by selecting the cursor and dragging the red anchor to a new location.

To change the way the cursor moves across the screen, follow these steps:

1. In Edit view, select the slide with the cursor movement you want to change. Note that the path displays an arrow indicating the direction of movement. The arrow points toward the end point of the path, which displays the selected icon.

2. To change the path from curved to straight (or from straight to curved), open the Mouse menu in any of the following ways:

   - In the Storyboard view Slide Tasks pane, click **Mouse**.
   - In Edit view, right-click anywhere on the background of the slide to display a context menu, then choose **Mouse**.
   - From the **Slide** menu, click **Mouse**.

   Then click **Straight Pointer Path** to select it (for a straight path) or click again to deselect it (for a curved path).

3. Change the end point of the path in any one of the following ways:

   - Click the icon at the end of the path, and drag it to a new location.
   - From the Mouse menu, choose **Align to Previous Slide** to move the end point of the current slide to match the end point of the previous slide. This will place the two points

exactly on top of each other, making the cursor remain still for the duration of the current slide.

- From the Mouse menu, choose **Align to Next Slide** to move the end point of the current slide to match the end point of the next slide. Because the end of the current slide is always the same as the beginning point of the next slide, this places the two points (beginning and ending) on the next slide on top of each other, making the cursor remain still for the duration of THAT slide.

As you move the end point on the current slide, the beginning point of the path on the next slide will also be changed.

TIP

If you change your mind about anything you do within Captivate, you can use the undo function to step back through actions you've performed since you opened the project. Choose **Undo** from the **Edit** menu or press **Ctrl+Z** to undo the previous action.

Changing the Cursor Speed

Captivate automatically moves the cursor icon along the specified path. You can define how long this takes by setting the mouse properties. The faster the cursor moves, the less time the slide will take to play, but the more difficult it may be for the viewer to follow the cursor.

To set the cursor speed, follow these steps:

1. In Edit view, open the slide that contains the movement you want to edit.
2. Open the Mouse menu in any of the following ways:
   - In the Storyboard view Slide Tasks pane, click **Mouse**.
   - In Edit view, right-click anywhere on the background of the slide to display a context menu, then choose **Mouse**.
   - From the **Slide** menu, click **Mouse**.

3. Choose **Properties** from the Mouse menu to display the Mouse Properties window.

FIGURE 7-35 Set the cursor speed in the Mouse Properties window.

4. Click **Reduce speed before click** to slow the cursor down just before the end of the path. This allows relatively high-speed movement, but lets the viewer see where the clicks occur.

5. Click the **Timing** tab to display the timing options for the cursor movement.

FIGURE 7-36   Set the length of time for the cursor movement.

6. Set the total length of time, in seconds, that you want the cursor to take to move between the beginning and end points by entering a number in the Display time box. You can enter time in increments of one-tenth of a second.

7. Set the total length of time, in seconds, that you want the slide to appear BEFORE the cursor movement starts by entering a number in the Appear after box. You can enter time in increments of one-tenth of a second.

8. The changes you make to the cursor properties will be applied to all subsequently created slides. If you want to apply these changes to all slides that are already in the movie, click **Apply to all** to apply the current settings as defined in the properties Settings window. To view or change the properties settings, click the **Settings** button.

9. Click **OK** to close the Mouse Properties window and display the slide.

Note: You can also set cursor speed using the timeline as described later in this chapter.

Adding Special Mouse Click Effects

There are two options that let you define the way the cursor movement mimics the movement of your mouse. Unlike the other elements, the cursor movement does not have a separate audio component, and although the mouse click effects are noises based on audio files, Captivate does not treat them like other audio components. They are linked to and part of the movement element and cannot be treated separately.

To set the special mouse click effects, follow these steps:

1. In Edit view, open the slide that contains the movement you want to edit.
2. Open the Mouse menu in any of the following ways:
   - In the Storyboard view Slide Tasks pane, click **Mouse**.
   - In Edit view, right-click anywhere on the background of the slide to display a context menu, then choose **Mouse**.
   - From the **Slide** menu, click **Mouse**.
3. Choose **Properties** from the Mouse menu to display the Mouse Properties window, as shown in Figure 7-35.
4. Select **Show mouse click** to cause a small animation to display when the cursor reaches its end position on the path. This graphic represents the clicking of a mouse. By default, a small blue dot appears when the cursor reaches the end of the movement path.
5. If you've chosen to show the default mouse click graphic, select **Default**. You can change the color of the graphic by clicking in the color box (shown in Figure 7-35 as a dark box next to the word Default).
6. If you've chosen to show a graphic to represent the mouse click but don't want to use the default graphic, select **Custom** and then choose a graphic from the drop-down list. The box next to the list displays a preview of what each graphic looks like.
7. To play a sound when the cursor reaches the end of its movement path, select the **Mouse click sound** check box, then choose one of the available sounds (click, double-click, or browse to choose a sound file of your own). Sound files must be in either WAV or MP3 format.
8. The changes you make to the cursor properties will be applied to all subsequently created slides. If you want to apply these changes to all slides that are already in the movie, click **Apply to all** to apply the current

settings as defined in the properties Settings window. To view or change the properties settings, click the **Settings** button.

9.   Click **OK** to close the Mouse Properties window and display the slide.

CHANGING THE TIMING OF ELEMENTS ON A SLIDE

When Captivate creates the Flash movie from your slides, each slide is displayed for a set length of time. The elements on each slide display in turn, also for a set length of time. You can create a wide variety of effects for your movie by modifying the length of time that each element displays and specifying when the element should appear on the slide.

There are two main functions that determine the length of time that a slide and the elements on it are displayed.

■   Transitions set the way that an element appears on the slide and how the element is removed from the slide when the set element timing expires.

■   Timing determines the length of time that each element is displayed and the delay, if any, between the display of the background slide and the start of the individual element displays. Timing can be set either through the element properties or with a unique Captivate tool called the timeline. This is a visual representation of the elements on a slide, placed along a graph that represents the total length of time the slide is displayed. It is very similar to the Flash Timeline, with most (though not all) of the same features.

Changing Element Transitions

The transitions for each element define the way the element enters and leaves the screen during the movie. You can set transitions for any elements except mouse movement, zoom areas, click boxes, and buttons. To set transitions for any element that allows transitions, follow these steps:

1. In Edit view, select the slide that contains the element you want to edit.
2. Double-click on the element to open the properties window for that type of element.
3. Click the **Options** tab to display transition parameters. For this example, we're looking at the Highlight Box window, but the other elements use similar windows.

FIGURE 7-37   Set transitions in the properties window.

4. Choose a transition effect for the object.
    - *Fade in:* The element will appear very dim at first and will gradually become more solid until it reaches the defined transparency setting.
    - *Fade out:* The element will gradually become more transparent until it is gone from the slide display completely.
    - *Fade in and out:* The element will appear dim, then gradually get more solid. Then it will gradually become

more transparent until it is gone from the display completely.

■ *No transition:* The element simply displays and then is removed after the specified timing.

5. For fading effects, you'll also need to specify how long or how gradual the effect should be. The default is 0.5 seconds.

TIP

It is usually best to show some restraint in adding effects to your movie. If you already have a lot going on, multiple animations and transition effects can be more distracting than entertaining.

---

6. The changes you make to the transition properties will be applied to all subsequently created elements of this type. If you want to apply these changes to all similar elements that are already in the movie, click **Apply to all** to apply the current settings as defined in the properties Settings window. To view or change the properties settings, click the Settings button.

7. Click **OK** to close the properties window.

Changing Element Timing Properties

1. In Edit view, select the slide that contains the element you want to edit.

2. Double-click on the element to open the properties window for that type of element.

3. Click the **Options** tab to display timing properties. For this example, we're looking at the new animation window, but the other elements use similar windows.

FIGURE 7-38 Set the timing parameters.

4. Set the length of time the element will display by choosing one of the following from the list of Display for options:

-   *Specific time:* Enter the number of seconds you want the element to display. If you enter a time longer than the current length the slide is displayed, the slide timing will be adjusted to the new length of time. For example, if your slide is currently set to display for 3 seconds, and you enter 5 seconds in the animation timing area, the slide timing will be extended to display for 5 seconds. You can enter times in increments of one-tenth of a second.

-   *Rest of slide:* Displays the element for as long as the slide is displayed.

-   *Rest of movie:* Displays the element for the entire rest of the movie.

-   *Duration of Animation* (Animation and Text Animation elements only): Displays the element for the length of time needed to display the entire animation.

> **TIP**
>
> If you use the Rest of movie setting, make sure you test the whole movie. This setting makes it easy to accidentally cover up important information on a later slide without realizing it.

5. You can specify that the element displays a certain length of time after the slide first appears by typing a number of seconds in the box labeled **Appear after**. Leave this number set to 0.0 if you want the caption to display as soon as the slide displays. You can enter times in increments of one-tenth of a second.

> **Note:** If you've specified a duration for the text caption, the slide will display for at least as long as the total of the Appear after and the Display for times. For example, a Display for setting of 5 seconds and an Appear after setting of 3 seconds would display the slide a total of 8 seconds.

6. The new Animation options window has a unique check box that the other options windows don't have. The **Synchronize with project** option lets you control the length of time that the animation plays using the timeline (see the next section).
7. The changes you make to the timing properties will be applied to all subsequently created elements of this type. If you want to apply these changes to all similar elements that are already in the movie, click **Apply to all** to apply the current settings as defined in the properties Settings window. To view or change the properties settings, click the **Settings** button.
8. Click **OK** to close the properties window.

Using the Captivate Timeline

While working in Edit mode, you can display the Captivate timeline for a quick view of the elements on the slide and when each will display. Instead of opening the properties of each element, then adjusting the timing, you can simply drag the elements on the timeline to specify when each will display and for how long.

Understanding the Timeline Basics

The timeline itself is a horizontal representation of the duration of a slide, with a ruler across the top that marks out the slide display in seconds. Each element is represented by a rectangular box in the timeline. By default, most elements are displayed as soon as the slide is displayed. Many will remain on display for the full time that the slide is displayed.

To display the timeline, you must be in Edit view. Then go to the **View** menu and select **Show Timeline**.

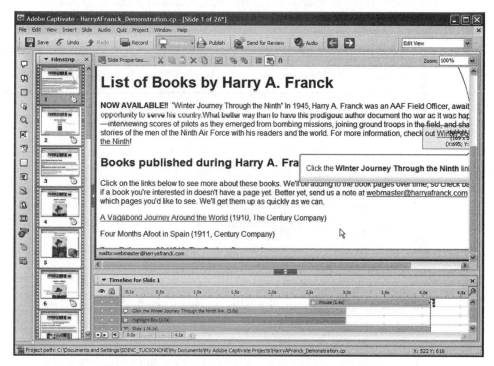

FIGURE 7-39   **View the slide elements on the timeline.**

In Figure 7-39, the timeline displays a "stack" of three elements plus the slide itself (on the bottom of the stack). This particular slide will be displayed for 4.1 seconds. The slide displays the background, highlight box, and text as soon as the slide is opened. After the slide has been displayed for 2.5 seconds, the mouse element (representing the cursor movement) is displayed and begins to move along the designated cursor path. One-half second later (at 3.0 seconds into the display of this slide), the text box and highlight box disappear. The mouse, however, continues its path until the end of the slide.

The timeline controls are displayed at the bottom of the timeline. The first two allow you to preview elements on the slide, just as they will appear within the movie. The first, a square icon, stops the preview, and the second, a triangular icon, starts the preview. As you preview the slide, a red line moves across the timeline, indicating the time on the slide. This red line is the playhead, and you can use it to view exactly what the slide looks like at any given point; you also can drag the playhead to see how objects (including audio) will play back.

TIP

This feature can delay a little when you have more complex animations and audio. Proper levels of available system memory help tremendously in using this handy feature.

There is also a scroll bar that is part of the timeline in case the slide lasts longer than the displayed amount of time (in this case, 4.5 seconds or so).

To use the timeline, click on an element in the timeline and drag it to the desired position on the timeline. You can change either the length of time the element displays (the duration) or the amount of time before or after the element displays.

- Click in the center of the element on the timeline, then drag the entire element. The duration of the element remains the same, but the amount of time before and/or after the element will change.
- Move the cursor to the right side of the element in the timeline until the cursor becomes a set of vertical lines. This indicates that you're on the edge of the element. Click and drag the edge outward or inward to change the duration of the element.
- Drag the right side of a timeline object to a different position on the timeline to lengthen or shorten the time the element is displayed.

- Drag the center line in a timeline object to change the pause location.

For example, if you want the slide to display for a second and a half before the text box displays, you would click on the left side of the text element and drag it until it lines up with the 1.5-second mark. Similarly, click in the center of the mouse movement element on the timeline and drag it until the left edge of the element is at the 2-second line on the timeline.

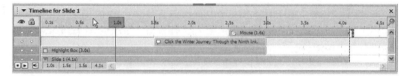

FIGURE 7-40   **Make changes to element timing on the timeline.**

Note: If you stretch or drag an element on the timeline past the duration for the whole slide, the slide duration (as represented by the bottom of the stack) will automatically be extended.

Previewing a Slide

There are several ways to preview the way a slide will look when it is played.

- Click the **Preview** icon, then choose **Play this slide**.
- Press **F3** to display from the playhead to the end of the slide.
- Press the **Spacebar** to display from the playhead to the end of the slide.
- On the lower portion of the timeline, click the **Play** icon.
- Drag the playhead across the timeline.

Note: Previewing a single slide does not let you preview interactive elements. You must preview multiple slides to access interactive features.

In any preview, the playhead, represented by a vertical red line, moves across the timeline as the slide plays. If you use the playhead method to preview your slide, you can stop and examine the way the slide will look at any given point in the display.

To manually move the playhead, click on the rectangle at the top of the red playhead line and drag the playhead across the timeline. This is called "scrubbing" the playhead. It's a common tool in movie editing software and it can be done in reverse as well as forward to check animation, movement, etc., and is powerful for quickly checking and adjusting timing.

In Figure 7-40, the playhead is at 1.0 seconds into the slide display. At this point in the preview, the highlight box has appeared, but the cursor and text box have not yet displayed.

TIP

As you move the playhead, the slide elements will display according to the timing settings. When you release the mouse button and the playhead stops moving, all elements will display, regardless of the location of the playhead. To see just the elements at that particular moment, click the top of the playhead and hold the mouse button down as if you were dragging the playhead.

Setting Element Timing Using the Timeline

In addition to the ability to move elements individually, the timeline includes some functions that let you set the timing for elements by moving the elements on the timeline using shortcuts. You can use any of these shortcuts for a single element, or you can select several elements in the timeline and move them all at once.

To select multiple elements, click on any element to select it, then hold down the **Ctrl** key and click on additional elements.

Once you've selected the element or elements for which you want to set a timing option, do any of the following:

TABLE 7-8 Using the timeline to set timing options.

To set this timing:	Do this:	Or use these keys:
Start the element as soon as the slide displays.	Click and drag the element or elements to the left side of the timeline.	
Start the element at the time indicated by the current position of the playhead.	Right-click to display a context menu, then select **Sync with Playhead**.	Ctrl+L
Extend the timing of the element so that it remains visible for the whole time the slide is displayed.	Right-click to display a context menu, then select **Show for rest of slide**.	Ctrl+E
Shorten the whole slide duration.	Click the end of the slide element and drag it toward the beginning of the slide. Each element will move as needed to fit in the allotted time. {Note that you can't make the slide duration shorter than the timing for the longest element.)	

Changing the Timeline Display

Like the other Captivate toolbars, you can turn the timeline display on and off as needed. In addition, you can change the size of the displayed timeline and the amount of time that is displayed.

To change the way the timeline displays, follow these steps:

1. If it isn't already displayed, display the timeline. In Edit view, from the **Window** menu, choose **Timeline**.
2. To change the position of the timeline, click on the four dots in the top-left corner of the timeline to display a four-headed arrow, then hold down the left mouse button and drag the timeline to a new location. Note that the timeline will be displayed in a new window but will remain horizontally oriented.

Note: If you move the timeline to the top or the bottom of the slide display, it will "dock" or become part of the slide window.

3.   You can change the size of the increments in the ruler that represent seconds in the timeline. For example, if you currently are showing 19 or 20 seconds on the timeline, but only need 5 or 6, you could make the increments larger. Valid ruler display options are tiny, small, normal, medium, and large. The actual number of seconds that will display for each option varies by the type of monitor you have and your system display settings. To change the seconds on the timeline ruler, do one of the following:

- Click the magnifying glass icon in the upper-right corner of the timeline to display a list of size options, and then click the one you want.
- Click anywhere on the timeline ruler, then use your mouse wheel to scroll through the available ruler sizes.

PREVENTING CHANGES TO A SLIDE

After you've made all these edits to a slide to make it exactly what you want, you can lock the slide so that the objects on it cannot be moved, deleted, or changed. Locking a slide prevents changes to the elements on the slide, but it does not prevent changes to the slide as a whole. In other words, although no one but you will be able to delete the captions from a locked slide, anyone would be able to move the whole slide to another part of the movie or change the slide transitions.

> **TIP**
>
> Anyone with access to these Captivate project source files can lock (or unlock) any slide or element on a slide. Though this feature is very useful to prevent accidental or unintended changes, it does not prevent others from unlocking the file and making changes.

Another method of preventing accidental changes is to temporarily hide elements on a slide. Like the lock elements feature, the hide feature can easily be undone by anyone.

Locking a Slide

To lock a slide, do any of the following:

- From the **Slide** menu, choose **Lock Slide**.
- Right-click on the slide to display the context menu, then choose **Lock Slide**.
- Click the **Properties** icon or double-click the slide to display the properties window, then click the **Lock Slide** check box.
- Press **Ctrl+K** on your keyboard.

Locking or Hiding Individual Elements on a Slide

You can also prevent changes to individual elements on a slide by locking just those elements. Or you can hide individual elements from the slide (though they'll still appear on the timeline). On the far left side of the timeline, there is a matrix of radio buttons with an eye symbol and a lock symbol in the top row.

FIGURE 7-41   **Locking individual elements on a slide prevents changes.**

To lock an object on the slide, click in the column under the lock icon and in the row for the selected element. To unlock the element, click in that same radio button to deselect it. To lock all elements in the slide, click the **lock** icon itself.

To hide an element on the slide, click in the column under the eye icon and in the row for the selected element. To view the element, click in that same radio button to deselect it. To hide all elements on the slide, click the **eye** icon itself.

In Figure 7-41, the highlight box and text caption are locked, and the mouse is hidden.

SUMMARY

This chapter described how to work within a single slide. It covered the slide background, adding and editing various types of elements, and adjusting the timing and transitions for a slide. The next chapter will discuss how to record and add audio to your movie.

Chapter 8

DEFINING WHAT THE USER HEARS—ADDING AUDIO

Adobe® Captivate® software allows you to add sound to your movies, either by recording sounds as you record the visual elements or by adding separate audio files later. You can add sounds to a single element on a slide, for the duration of a slide, or even for the whole movie. For example, you may want to include special sounds for certain actions (like getting a question right—or wrong) or to narrate your actions on the screen. You can also include sound files as needed for accessibility purposes, or you can simply add some background music that plays throughout the movie.

Like other elements (see Chapter 7), you can move audio files around on the timeline, or copy, paste, and delete them as needed. You can also adjust the sound level so that your audio volume is consistent from slide to slide.

RECORDING NEW AUDIO FILES

There are several ways to record audio in Captivate. You can record a voice narration while you're recording a movie; you can record audio for an existing movie; you can record individual audio files for each slide; or you can record audio for each individual element (such as a click box or a caption). Before recording any audio, you must first set up the appropriate audio equipment and calibrate it for use with Captivate.

Setting Up Audio Equipment

In order to record audio files for use with Captivate, you must have the following minimum configuration:

- Computer with sound card to record the audio.
- Microphone with stand. The better your microphone, the more professional your audio will sound. You'll need the stand to avoid unnecessary noises from microphone movement.
- Speakers so that you can hear the recorded audio.

In addition, you may want to consider some of the following equipment to ensure a clean audio file:

- Microphone preamplifier to boost the signal of the microphone.
- Headphones to use while recording to avoid distracting feedback.
- Recording software that lets you edit audio files or create sound effects. Choose whichever software works for you, but it must be able to create MP3 or WAV formatted files.

Once you've got everything set up, you'll need to calibrate the audio input to make sure that Captivate can recognize your microphone and your voice. Each time you begin to record an audio session, Captivate displays a message asking you if you want to check your recording levels. You can calibrate each time you record, or you can do it whenever you begin a session or change hardware, even if you aren't recording anything at the time.

To have Captivate calibrate your recording levels without recording anything, follow these steps:

1. Make sure your microphone is plugged in and turned on.
2. Open an existing Captivate project.
3. From the **Audio** menu, choose **Settings**.

FIGURE 8-1   Display the Audio settings window.

4. Choose one of the available sources for audio input:

    ▪   CD Player
    ▪   Microphone
    ▪   Line In
    ▪   Wave Out Mix

5. Click the **Calibrate input** button to display the Calibrate audio input window. Depending on the input method, the window may vary slightly. For microphone input, you'll need to speak a sample sentence. For other input types, the calibration is automatic.

FIGURE 8-2   Speak into the microphone to set the audio levels.

6.   For microphone input, as soon as the Calibrate microphone window displays, start speaking into the microphone with a normal voice. Read the sentence on the window, or say anything else you like. As you speak, the meter level indicator on the right of the calibration window will move, and as soon as the system has a good audio level setting, the text message will turn green and switch from Checking input level to Input level OK.

7.   Once the level is set, click **OK** to close the Calibrate microphone window.

FIGURE 8-3   **Captivate indicates if an acceptable recording level exists.**

8.   Click **OK** to close the Audio settings window.

Setting Audio File Size

When you record Captivate audio files, the system records your voice in WAV format and then converts it to MP3 format for storage with each slide. During this conversion process, you have the option of also compressing the audio to reduce file size. However, this will also lower the quality of the audio sound. You'll need to set the audio options based on the needs of your audience. For example, if many of your viewers will be downloading your movie over a slower, dial-up connection, you may be more concerned with keeping the file size small. On the other hand, if you're delivering on a CD, you may decide to set the audio to a higher quality even though it increases the file size.

To set the audio recording quality, follow these steps:

1.   Make sure your microphone is plugged in and turned on.

2.   Open an existing Captivate project.

3.   From the **Audio** menu, choose **Settings**.

FIGURE 8-4   Set audio quality.

4.   Choose one of the available sources for audio input:

- CD Player
- Microphone
- Line In
- Wave Out Mix

5.   Choose one of the encoding frequencies. This is the number of times per second the original sound wave is translated into digital form. A higher frequency results in a more accurate digital representation of the sound.

- 44,100 KHz: The most frequent sampling gives the highest quality (near CD quality).
- 22,050 KHz: Comparable to FM radio.
- 11,025 KHz: Fewer samples per second, lower quality sound; this frequency is generally considered equivalent to telephone quality, but it's actually a little higher.

6.   Choose one of the encoding bitrates. This specifies the amount of audio information (in kbps) that will be stored per second of a recording.

- CD Bitrate (128 kbps) gives you the highest quality and largest file size.

- Near CD Bitrate (96 kbps) is close to CD quality, but results in a smaller file size.
- FM Radio Bitrate (64 kbps) creates the smallest file size.
- Custom Bitrate: You must specify the rate in kilobytes per second at which you want to record the audio.

7. Set the speed at which you want to encode the audio for output. A lower number creates a higher-quality audio file.

8. Click **OK** when you are done to close the Audio settings window.

Recording Audio While Recording a Movie

One way to get all of your audio files recorded quickly is to record them as you record the actions for each slide. This sort of narration is easy to do—you just talk aloud as you move the mouse or click through your application. Captivate will record your voice and store it as a series of audio clips, one for each slide that you create.

Note: For more details on the nonaudio options available while recording, see Chapter 4.

To record audio while you're creating a new Captivate movie, follow these steps:

1. Start the program you want to record, and then start the Captivate software. The first screen you'll see is the Captivate main menu.

2. From the **Edit** menu, choose **Preferences** to display the Preferences window.

3. Click the **Settings** option under **Recording** to display the recording settings.

FIGURE 8-5   Set narration in the recording options window.

4.   Select the **Narration** check box to turn on the audio recording whenever you record a movie. Captivate will use the defaults you've set in the Audio settings window (see prior section).

Note: If you have Record narration selected, you won't have the option to turn on camera sounds. The camera sounds are tools that help you record—even when turned on, they don't play in the finished movie.

5.   The first time you record audio in a session, a message is displayed. If you've recorded audio already, skip to Step 8.

FIGURE 8-6   **Determine whether or not you want to calibrate your microphone.**

6. Click **Yes** to begin calibration.

TIP

Even though you don't have to calibrate for each recording session (you can click **No** or even turn off the message by selecting **Don't ask me this again**), it is a good idea to test the audio levels each time you record. This will help identify the myriad little things that can go wrong between recording sessions, such as a shift of cables that loosens a connection or something being placed on a table that blocks the microphone enough to impact audio levels.

---

7. When the calibration is complete, click **OK** to close the Calibrate audio input window.
8. A series of three countdown windows displays to let you know exactly when to begin speaking. Perform the actions you want to record, and speak into the microphone to create the audio.

TIP

For easier editing later, do not speak while you are doing actions, but instead speak and then click the mouse or choose a menu item. Remember, each slide gets a separate audio file, and each time you click usually creates a new slide. You don't want to end up with half a word on one audio file and half on the next. Although they should play seamlessly when you publish the movie, splits like this could make adding or deleting slides more difficult.

---

9. When you finish, press the **End** key to stop recording, generate the slides and audio files, and display the new movie in Storyboard view.

Recording Audio for Individual Elements

In some cases, you may want to record an audio file that will play when a specific element displays, such as a click box or caption. Captivate lets you record audio or import existing audio files for each element. If you're importing audio, you can choose from the library of sounds that comes with Captivate, or you can import a sound file of your own.

To record an audio file for a specific element on a slide, follow these steps:

1. Open the slide that contains the element to which you want to add audio.
2. Double-click the element to display the properties for that element.
3. Click the **Audio** tab to display the audio properties. Figure 8-7 shows the audio settings for a text caption, but all elements have similar audio properties.

FIGURE 8-7 View, record, or edit audio files.

4. Click the **Record** icon (round red circle) to display the Record Audio window. If this is the first time you're recording audio this session, a message is displayed. If you've recorded audio already, skip to step 7.
5. Click **Yes** to begin calibration.

> **TIP**
>
> Even though you don't have to calibrate for each recording session (you can click **No** or even turn off the message by selecting **Don't ask me this again**), it is a good idea to test the audio levels each time you record. This will help identify the myriad little things that can go wrong between recording sessions, such as a shift of cables that loosens a connection or something being placed on a table that blocks the microphone enough to impact audio levels.

6. When the calibration is complete, click **OK** to close the Calibrate audio input window and display the Record Audio window.

7. Click the **Record** icon (round red circle) to begin recording audio for this element.

8. Begin speaking into the microphone. The Record Audio window displays a status bar that shows the audio level and a timer. Try to keep your voice in an even tone so that you don't cause the level to go into the red zone. The following example shows a recording at about two seconds.

FIGURE 8-8 **The Record Audio window displays the audio level as you record.**

9. When you are finished recording, click **OK** to stop recording, close this window, and display the audio in the audio properties window with information about the new audio recording. In Figure 8-9, the audio file is a little over 8 seconds long, with the default name of Recording4.

> **TIP**
>
> If, as you're recording, you notice a mistake in your audio, it may be easier to simply repeat (and correct!) the misspoken portion as part of the current audio file. It is simple to delete the incorrect audio later.

FIGURE 8-9 **The audio properties window displays information about the recorded audio.**

10. Click **OK** to close the audio properties window.

Recording Audio for an Existing Slide

You can record new audio files for each individual slide, rather than for a single element or for the entire movie. When you record slide narration, you have the option to preview the action on the slide as you record, as well as to see the captions and any notes you may have stored with the slide. You can then read this text while recording, much as an actor would read a script. The resulting audio file is associated with the slide; by default, it begins when the slide is first displayed. You can change the timing of the audio for each slide, or you can do other audio editing as necessary. This is particularly useful if you've already recorded audio for an entire movie and you just need to change one or two slides.

To record new audio for an existing slide, follow these steps:

1. Open the slide to which you want to add audio.

2.   There are two ways to begin recording for a slide:

- Double-click the background of the slide (not on any elements) or click the **Properties** icon to display the properties for that slide. Then click the **Audio** tab to display the audio properties, and click the **Record** icon. OR

- Click the **Audio** icon at the top of the Captivate screen (in any view) to immediately display the audio recording window.

FIGURE 8-10   **The recording window displays captions and slide notes.**

3.   If this is the first time you're recording audio this session, a message is displayed. If you've recorded audio already, skip to step 6.

4.   Click **Yes** to begin calibration.

TIP

Even though you don't have to calibrate for each recording session (you can click **No** or even turn off the message by selecting **Don't ask me this again**), it is a good idea to test the audio levels each time you record. This will help identify the myriad little things that can go wrong between recording sessions, such as a shift of cables that loosens a connection or something being placed on a table that blocks the microphone enough to impact audio levels.

---

5.   When the calibration is complete, click **OK** to close the Calibrate audio input window and display the Record Audio window.

6.   The recording window has three areas:

- The top area displays information about the associated audio file (if any).

- The middle area displays a preview of the slide or slides for which you're creating audio. The preview includes a timer that shows how much time is left for the slide as the various elements display. For example, animations will run, captions will display or dissolve, and the cursor will move across the screen (if you've defined them to do so).

- The bottom area displays the captions (if any) and the slide notes (if any). Captions come directly from the text captions created while recording or that were added manually. These elements display on the slide while the movie is running (see Chapter 7). Slide notes are for your own use while recording or editing, and (effective with Captivate 4.0) can also be used as the script for the Captivate Text-to-Speech function.

When you're ready, click the **Record** icon to begin recording audio for this slide.

FIGURE 8-11   **The elements move on the slide preview as you record.**

7. Begin speaking into the microphone. You won't get the countdown display as when recording audio with screens, but you will see a progress bar with a timer that lets you know that the voice is being captured.

8. When you are finished recording, click **OK** to stop recording and return to the Record Audio window.

9. Click **OK** to close the Record Audio window.

FIGURE 8-12   **The audio information is displayed in the audio properties window.**

10.   If you began recording from the properties window, click **OK** to close the audio properties window.

Recording Background Audio for a Movie

You can record audio files that will run in the background throughout the entire movie. When other audio elements play (such as for a caption or for a slide), Captivate can automatically lower the volume of the background audio. If the background audio file is shorter than the movie length, Captivate can repeat the background audio in a loop until the end of the movie.

To record background audio, follow these steps:

1.   From the **Audio** menu, choose **Background Audio**.

FIGURE 8-13   **Record background audio.**

2. Click the **Record** icon to display the Record Audio window. If this is the first time you're recording audio this session, a message is displayed. If you've recorded audio already, skip to step 6.

3. Click **Yes** to begin calibration.

> **TIP**
>
> Even though you don't have to calibrate for each recording session (you can click **No** or even turn off the message by selecting **Don't ask me this again**), it is a good idea to test the audio levels each time you record. This will help identify the myriad little things that can go wrong between recording sessions, such as a shift of cables that loosens a connection or something being placed on a table that blocks the microphone enough to impact audio levels.

4. When the calibration is complete, click **OK** to close the Calibrate audio input window and display the Record Audio window.

5. Click **Record** to begin recording background audio for this movie.

6. Begin recording your background audio. You won't get the countdown display as when recording audio with screens, but you will see a progress bar with a timer that lets you know that the audio is being captured.

7. When you are finished recording, click **OK** to stop recording and close the recording window.

FIGURE 8-14   **The audio information displays in the Audio for Background window.**

8.   Click the check box to lower the volume of the background audio on slides that have other audio elements on them. If the check box is not selected, the background audio will play at the same volume even when other audio is playing.

9.   Click the **Loop audio** check box to repeat the background audio so that it will last as long as the movie lasts. If the check box is not selected, the audio file will play through just once.

10.   Click the **Stop audio at end of project** button if you want the audio to end when the project ends. If this check box is not selected, the audio will play until the end of the audio file, even if the project is finished.

11.   Click **OK** to close the Audio for Background window.

Importing Existing Audio Files

If you already have audio files that you want to add to your Captivate movie, you can do so in any of the following ways:

- Add existing audio to an element on a slide.
- Add existing audio to an entire slide or series of slides.
- Add existing audio to the background of a movie.

The existing audio must be in either WAV or MP3 format. If you use WAV format, Captivate will automatically convert the files to MP3 format for inclusion in your movie.

> **TIP**
>
> Captivate comes with a gallery of existing audio elements. By default, these are stored in Adobe Captivate 4\Gallery\Sound. The import audio function defaults to this location.

ADDING AUDIO TO INDIVIDUAL ELEMENTS

You can add audio to any of the elements on a slide, such as buttons, click boxes, and success/failure captions. You can add voice files if you have them or sound effects such as a ringing bell or buzzer. When you associate audio with an element, the audio will not begin to play until the element appears on the slide. To add existing audio to an element, you can choose from an audio file that exists within your project already, or you can browse to import a file from elsewhere on your system.

To add an audio file to a specific element on a slide, follow these steps:

1. Open the slide that contains the element to which you want to add audio.
2. Double-click the element to display the properties for that element.
3. Click the **Audio** tab to display the audio properties.

FIGURE 8-15   View, record, or edit audio files.

4. Click **Import** to display the most recently used folder of sound files, or click **Library** to display the list of sound files in the current movie.

Note: Unless you've imported an external library, the audio library will display only those individual audio files you've already imported or recorded in the current movie. If you don't have any audio in the current movie yet, the Library button will not be available.

5. Click the name of the audio file you want to play when the element appears, then click either **OK** (for the Audio library) or **Open** (to import files).

FIGURE 8-16   **You can import from the folder of sounds on your system.**

FIGURE 8-17   **You can choose from the library of sounds already in the movie.**

> **TIP**
>
> If you're choosing from the audio library, you can click the Play icon (a dark triangle above the sound wave image) to hear what each audio file sounds like before you select it.

6. You can specify a fade-in time to start the sound file gradually or a fade-out time to make the sound file gradually get softer as it ends. Enter a time in seconds in the Fade in or Fade out boxes. You can specify fade times with an accuracy of a tenth of a second. For example, to fade out for half a second, enter 0.5.

7. Once you've added an audio file, you can click the **Play** icon to hear how it will sound or preview the audio in the slide timeline (see Chapter 7).

> **TIP**
>
> Though the Play icon lets you know how the audio will sound, this audio preview may not incorporate all of the options that are part of the overall slide. For example, if you have defined a fade-in time delay, you'll need to preview the slide (or the whole project) in order to see this delay.

8. Click **OK** to close the audio properties window.

Adding Audio to a Slide

You can add audio to an entire slide. This type of audio begins playing as soon as the slide displays. Unlike audio attached to elements, you can modify the audio to begin or end whenever you like within the slide timeline. To add existing audio to a slide, you can choose from an audio file that exists within your project already, or you can browse to import a file from elsewhere on your system.

To add an audio file to a slide, follow these steps:

1. Open the slide to which you want to add audio.
2. Double-click anywhere on the background of the slide (not on an element) to display the properties for that slide.
3. Click the **Audio** tab to display the slide audio properties.

FIGURE 8-18   Import audio files.

4. Click **Import** to display the most recently used folder of sound files, or click **Library** to display the list of sound files in the current movie.

TIP

You can also import audio from the Captivate sound library by selecting the slide, then choosing **Import to slide** from the **Audio** menu. This option does not let you choose from files already in the movie.

Note: Unless you've imported an external library, the audio library will display only those individual audio files you've already imported or recorded in the current movie. If you don't have any audio in the current movie yet, the Audio library button will not be available.

5. Click the name of the audio file you want to play for this slide, and then click either **OK** (for the audio library) or **Open** (to import files).

> ┌─ **TIP** ──
> If you're choosing from the audio library, you can click the Play icon (a dark triangle above the sound wave image) to hear what each audio file sounds like before you select it.

6. You can specify a fade-in time to start the sound file gradually or a fade-out time to make the sound file gradually get softer as it ends. Enter a time in seconds in the Fade in or Fade out boxes. You can specify fade times with an accuracy of a tenth of a second. For example, to fade out for half a second, enter 0.5.

7. Once you've added an audio file, you can click the **Play** icon to hear how it will sound or preview the audio in the slide timeline (see Chapter 7).

8. Click **OK** to close the audio properties window.

Adding Background Audio for a Movie

Background audio plays for the entire movie, regardless of which slide is displayed or how long a slide is on the screen. When other audio elements play, you can lower the volume of the background audio. If the background audio file is shorter than the movie length, you can repeat the background audio in a loop until the end of the movie.

To add background audio to a movie, follow these steps:

1. From the **Audio** menu, choose **Background Audio**.

FIGURE 8-19 Import background audio.

2.   Click **Import** to display the most recently used folder of sound files, or click **Library** to display the list of sound files in the current movie.

> **Note:** Unless you've imported an external library, the audio library will display only those individual audio files you've already imported or recorded in the current movie. If you don't have any audio in the current movie yet, the Audio library button will not be available.

3.   Click the name of the audio file you want to play for this slide, then click either **OK** (for the audio library) or **Open** (to import files).

> ⌐ TIP ┐
>
> If you're choosing from the audio library, you can click the **Play** icon (a dark triangle above the sound wave image) to hear what each audio file sounds like before you select it.

4.   You can specify a fade-in time to start the sound file gradually or a fade-out time to make the sound file gradually get softer as it ends. Enter a time in seconds in the Fade in or Fade out boxes. You can specify fade times with an accuracy of a tenth of a second. For example, to fade out for half a second, enter 0.5.
5.   Click the check box to lower the volume of the current audio file when audio for specific slides or elements is available.
6.   Click the **Loop audio** check box to repeat the current audio file as many times as necessary to fill the background of the entire movie.
7.   Click the **Stop audio at end of project** check box to stop playing the audio when the movie ends, no matter where in the audio file that ending hits.
8.   Click **OK** to close the Audio for Background window.

VIEWING AND REMOVING AUDIO FILES

Once you've got audio in your movie, you can easily check to see the status of all the audio files in a single place. You don't have to open each individual element's audio properties window. You can play the files, or you can remove them from your movie. You can also export the .mp3 audio files you've created in Captivate for use with other programs.

Note: You cannot change the audio properties from this view. To make changes to the audio, such as replacing a file or adjusting timing, go to the audio file properties as described in the section called "Editing Audio Files."

To view the audio for your entire movie, follow these steps:

1. From the **Audio** menu, select **Audio Management** to display the Advanced Audio Management window.

FIGURE 8-20   **Display the sound files for the entire movie.**

The Advanced Audio Management window displays a row of information for each slide in the movie, and also includes a row for the background audio, if any.

TIP

You may need to resize the window to display all of the information, or use the scroll bars across the bottom and on the side of the window.

TABLE 8-1 Audio file properties.

This column:	Displays this information:
Slide Object	The slide number or slide label if there is one.
Sound	Yes indicates that there is an audio file associated with the slide. No indicates that there isn't. Note that this does not include audio for individual elements unless you check the Show object level audio option. Therefore, a slide may contain objects with audio but still show up on this window with a No.
Duration (s)	The length of the sound file in seconds.
Fade in (s)	The number of seconds it will take for the audio file to increase to full volume. 0.0 means that it will stay at the same volume the whole time.
Fade out (s)	The number of seconds it will take for the audio file to decrease in volume. 0.0 means that it will stay at the same volume the whole time.
Size (MB)	The size of the sound file in megabytes.
Original filename	The name of the sound file. Note that Captivate automatically names the files as you record them.
Display name	The name of the file as it displays within Captivate. This is particularly useful for audio files that are split across multiple slides.
Audio sample rate (KHz)	An indicator of the sound quality set during recording. A higher sample rate gives a more realistic sound but requires a larger file size. The sample rate for CD-quality audio is 44,100 samples per second, expressed in kilohertz.
Bit rate (kbps)	The number of bits the audio file uses per second, expressed as kilobits per second (kbps). A higher bit rate gives a more realistic sound but requires a larger file size.
CC	Indicates whether or not there is a text version of the audio for use with closed captioning.

2.   Click **Show object level audio** to display the sound files associated with the individual elements in the movie.

TIP

It is a good idea to click this check box to see if there are audio files for slides that don't have slide-level audio. For example, in Figure 8-20, you can see that slides 1 and 3 have no sound, but the elements on those slides have associated audio files.

---

3.   To play a file, click anywhere on the row for that file to select it, and then click the **Play** icon (the triangle at the bottom of the screen). You can click the **Stop** icon (the square at the bottom of the screen) to stop the file, or simply let it play until it is done.

4.   To copy an audio file from within your Captivate movie to a different location on your system, select the file and then click **Export** to display a window that lets you browse to an appropriate folder. Click **OK** in the folder window to export both the MP3 and WAV versions of the audio file to the selected destination folder.

5.   To remove a file from the movie, click anywhere on the row for that file to select it, and then do either of the following:

■   Right-click to display a menu, and then choose **Remove**.

■   Press the **Delete** key.

TIP

Once you remove a file that was created within Captivate, it will be removed entirely from your movie and from your system. If you think you might want to use the audio file again, in this or other movies, export the file as described in Step 4.

Click **OK** in the confirmation dialog that displays to complete the file removal.

6.   When you finish, click **OK**.

EDITING AUDIO FILES

Captivate includes a basic audio editing tool that lets you adjust the audio files to fit your needs. You can add silence (described in Table 8-3), delete parts of the audio, or adjust volume for an audio file. For example, you may want to remove a single word rather than rerecord the whole audio clip. Or you may want to remove some of the extra silence that is often recorded at the beginning and ending of an audio file.

| TIP |

Don't remove all of the silence—you need a little bit of space at the beginning and end of each file so that if the audio plays near another piece of audio it will sound more natural. You may also want to use a small sample of silence in other places within your movie to maintain ambient room noise and create a seamless effect.

To edit an audio file, follow these steps:

1. Open the audio properties window for the specific type of element.

TABLE 8-2 Audio properties windows.

For this type of element:	Do this:
Element (such as a click box or caption)	In Edit view, double-click the element on the slide, and then click the **Audio** tab.
Slide	Double-click the background of the slide to display the properties, and then click the **Audio** tab.
Background Audio	Choose **Background Audio** from the **Audio** menu.

2. From the audio properties window, click the **Edit** button.

FIGURE 8-21   **Open the audio file to edit it.**

3.   Set the display of the audio file to one that is appropriate for your needs by clicking the magnifying glass icons with the plus or minus signs. For example, Figure 8-21 shows an audio file that lasts 8 seconds. Click the **"plus" magnifying glass** icon to zoom in on the file so that you can see the audio components more clearly or the **"minus"** to zoom out and see more of the audio file.

FIGURE 8-22   **Zoom to display the audio file in an appropriate size.**

4. You can export the displayed audio file to either a .wav or .mp3 file by clicking the **Export to podcast** button.

5. Click the **Play** icon (the blue triangle) to play the audio file. As the file plays, a vertical line called the playhead moves across the window to indicate exactly which part of the displayed file is playing at any moment. In Figure 8-22, for example, the playhead indicates that 2.9 seconds of the audio has played. In this example, that's just about between the first two words. Notice that as the audio is playing, the Play icon changes to two vertical lines to become a Pause icon. You can hit the **Pause** icon or the **Stop** icon (the square) at any time. You can also select a portion of the audio and press the spacebar to preview the selected portion only.

6. Make any of the edits described in Table 8-3 to your audio file.

TABLE 8-3 Edit options for audio files.

To make this change:	Do this:
Select a specific piece of audio	Click on the audio graphic and drag the cursor to highlight a specific area.
Delete a part of the audio	Select the part you want to delete, then right-click and choose **Delete** (or press the **Delete** key) to remove the audio from the file.
Copy a part of the audio	Select the part you want to copy, then right-click and choose **Copy** (or press **Ctrl+C**) to copy the audio to the clipboard.
Cut a part of the audio	Select the part you want to cut, then right-click and choose **Cut** (or press **Ctrl+X**) to cut the audio from the audio file.
Paste in a new piece of audio	Copy the part you want to paste, then click on the audio graphic so that the playhead displays in the location where you want to add the new piece of audio. Right-click to display a menu, and then choose **Paste** (or press **Ctrl+V**). Note that you can only cut and paste audio within a single file.

TABLE 8-3 Edit options for audio files (continued).

To make this change:	Do this:
Add silence	Click on the audio graphic so that the playhead displays in the location where you want to begin a period of silence, and then click the **Insert silence** button. A window displays that allows you to specify the length of the silence and lets you choose a location for the silence (at the playhead location, the beginning, or the ending of the audio file). Enter a number in seconds, and then click **OK**.
Add a new piece of recording	You can add to an existing audio file by clicking the **Record** button (the circle on the bottom left of the window). The new audio will be inserted starting at the point where the playhead is displayed. **Tip:** This can be tricky. It works best if your audio setup is exactly as it was when the original audio was recorded.
Undo a change	Click the **Undo** icon in the menu across the top of the window.

> **TIP**
>
> Use discretion when editing audio files. It is all too easy to make audio edits that cause your file to sound stilted or awkward or to create something that doesn't make sense. Often, it is easier and quicker to rerecord the entire audio file.

7. If necessary, you can adjust the volume of the entire audio file or simply a portion of it. For example, if the person speaking turned slightly while recording, a word or two may be quieter than you like. You can select these words in the audio graphic and make them a little bit louder. To display the Adjust Volume window, click the **Adjust volume** button.

FIGURE 8-23   Adjust volume as needed.

8.   Move the **Volume** slider up (to make the audio louder) or down (to make the audio quieter) to change the volume of the selected portion of the audio file.

9.   You can also adjust the audio by selecting either (or both) of the following processing options:

■   *Normalize:* Adjusts the sound volume automatically. This will keep the sound level consistent across the selection or entire audio clip.

■   *Dynamics:* Automatically increases the volume for the quietest portions of the audio file. You can set a maximum ratio to specify the factor by which the quietest audio should be increased. You can also set a noise threshold, which specifies the relative volume of the quietest audio that you want to amplify. For example, you may have an audio file where most of the sound is at an acceptable level, but some portions are too quiet. A Ratio of 2 would double the volume of the quietest portions of the audio. A Threshold setting of 10% would specify that portions of the audio that are 10% or less of the audio level of the rest of the file should NOT be amplified by that ratio (they are likely to be background noise).

10. Click **OK** to close the Adjust Volume window.
11. When you finish editing the audio file, click **OK** to close the Edit Audio window.

CONVERTING TEXT TO SPEECH

If you've entered notes for a slide (see Chapter 12), you can choose to have an automated voice read the slide notes while the movie is playing. To make use of the Text-to-Speech feature, follow these steps:

1. From View menu, select the **Slide Notes** to display the notes area.
2. Click the **Notes** tab to display the notes area.

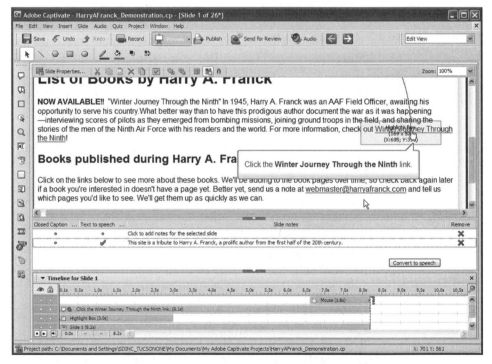

FIGURE 8-24   **Display the Speech Management window.**

3. Type the notes that apply to the displayed slide.

4. Click the **Convert to speech** button to display the Speech Setting window.

FIGURE 8-25   **Display the Speech Setting window.**

5. Choose the voice you want for the speech, then click **OK**. Captivate will create a .wav file using the automated voice to read the text in the notes. This file will be stored as the audio file for the slide, and can be viewed or edited like any other audio file.

SUMMARY

This chapter described the audio functions available with Captivate. You saw how to record new audio; add existing audio to elements, slides, and the entire movie; and how to use the audio editing functions. The following chapter describes how to add interactivity to your movie by inserting interactive elements and a variety of captions.

Chapter 9

Defining What the User Does—Adding Interactivity

When you recorded your actions on the screen, the recording options determined whether the resulting movie would be a demonstration that the viewers would simply watch (and learn from) or a more interactive project where the movie pauses while the viewer clicks or types to move from one slide to another. Another type of interactivity allows the viewers to get more information using a rollover function. When the viewer moves the cursor over a certain spot, you can have either a text caption or an image display on the screen. This is particularly useful for functions similar to tool tips in other packages.

A very powerful feature of Adobe® Captivate® software allows you to add multiple interactive elements to a single slide and specify different actions based on which element the viewer clicks. For example, you could replicate your main menu within the movie by putting a click box over each icon and then displaying different slides based on which box the viewer clicks. Or you could add buttons that skip over certain parts of the movie or that allow the viewer to repeat various sections. Giving the viewer this type of flexibility and control over the way the movie plays is often called "branching" or "contingency branching" in e-learning applications. Captivate lets you display these options for presentation of slides in a Branching view (see Chapter 11 for more information on branching).

You can manually add these interactivity features to any slide in any movie, or you can have Captivate automatically add some interactive elements, such as click boxes, while you're recording the movie. See Chapter 4 for more information on recording movies.

ADDING INTERACTIVITY WITH BOXES AND BUTTONS

There are three main types of interactive elements in this category:

- Click boxes specify an area where the viewer should click.
- Text entry boxes specify an area where the viewer will type and the text will display on the slide.
- Buttons specify an area where the viewer will click, usually to go to another slide.

These interactive elements can be added automatically when you're recording a movie, or you can enter them manually for more exact control of how the viewer will interact with your movie.

For each type of element, you'll need to specify a variety of properties:

- Instructions on what happens in the movie when the viewer successfully clicks in the specified area (such as go to the next slide or display a URL).
- Instructions on what happens in the movie when the viewer clicks outside of the designated area (or types an invalid text string).
- Optional captions that are displayed upon success or failure, or when the viewer moves the mouse over the specified interactive area.
- Timing, such as whether or not the movie should pause while awaiting viewer input.
- Audio, if necessary, as described in Chapter 8.
- Instructions on how you want Captivate to store information about the viewer's success or failure actions. This reporting information can then be imported into other e-learning applications.

When you add the basic interactive elements, you'll do so in the following major steps:

Step 1: Specify the type of interactive element and indicate how to proceed when the viewer interacts with the movie.

Step 2: For buttons only, define how you want the button to look.

Step 3: Set interactive element options, such as captions, timing, or audio.

Step 4: Adjust the interactive elements and associated components to place them exactly where you want on the slide and to display the text you want.

Step 1: Specify an Interactive Element

When you're adding interactivity, you'll need to decide which type of element you want to use.

- *Click boxes:* Click boxes allow you to specify an area where the viewer should click. For example, you might use this if you want the movie to pause until the viewer clicks a specific link or clicks on a menu option.
- *Text entry boxes:* Text entry boxes are rectangular areas where you want the viewer to type specific text. The text will display on the slide as it is typed; it must match any one of the correct answers that you provide before the movie will continue. You can display the outline of the box or not. Each text entry box defaults to having a submission button, but you can turn this off if desired.

Note: The text entry box button is not the same as the regular interactive buttons and has only a subset of the interactive button functionality.

- *Buttons:* Buttons are visual elements that you want the viewer to click. You can control the appearance of the button using either a text label or an image. To the end viewer, a button will appear to be very similar to a click box.

TIP

The main difference between a click box and a button is that the click box defines an area but doesn't have a visual component—the viewer can't see where a click box is without additional elements such as a highlight box.

To add an interactive element, follow these steps:

1. In Edit view, open the slide to which you want to add interactivity.
2. From the **Insert** menu, choose **Standard Objects**, then select the type of element you want to add (**Text entry box**, **Click box**, or **Button**). The properties window that displays will vary slightly depending on the element you choose, but most property options are the same for all interactive elements. Figure 9-1 shows the properties window for a text entry box.

FIGURE 9-1   **Set the interactive element properties.**

3. *For text entry box elements only,* enter the text that you want to display when the viewer first sees the text box. This might be something like "type your name here." You can select the **Retain Text** check box if you want the text that the viewer enters to display on subsequent viewings of the text box (for the current instance of the movie only).
4. *For text entry box elements only,* enter the text that you want the viewer to type in the Correct entries box. Click on a row in the box, then type an answer exactly as you want the viewer to type it. You can enter as many

correct answers as you like. Click the **Delete** button to the right of the Correct entries box to remove an entry, or click the **Font** button to set the way you want the text to look as the viewer types it.

5. For all interactive elements, choose from the **On success** drop-down list to specify what you want the movie to display when the viewer clicks within the click box. Valid options are listed in Table 9-1.

TABLE 9-1 Destination options based on viewer success (or failure) to perform certain actions.

Choose this option:	For this effect:	Also enter this information:
Continue	Continue playing the rest of the current slide and the rest of the movie.	None necessary
Go to previous slide	Display the previous slide, and then continue the movie from that point, even if all the actions for the current slide have not yet been performed.	None necessary
Go to next slide	Continue on to the next slide in the movie, even if all the actions for the current slide have not yet been performed.	None necessary
Go to last visited slide	Display the slide that was viewed immediately before the current one.	None necessary
Jump to slide	Display the specified slide and continue the movie from there.	Choose from the drop-down list of slides. Note that slide labels, if any, appear in the list instead of slide numbers. This makes it easy to find the slide you're looking for!

TABLE 9-1 Destination options based on viewer success (or failure) to perform certain actions (continued).

Choose this option:	For this effect:	Also enter this information:
Open URL or file Open other movie	Display the specified URL or file in the viewer's default browser, or play another Flash movie. The viewer must have an active Internet connection to view URLs, and the specified file or movie must exist on the viewer's system. Note that the URL will not be visible on the finished movie.	Enter the URL or filename, or browse to the location of the file by clicking the button with three dots (. . .). For movies, you can also choose from a drop-down list. Click the black triangle button to choose the type of window in which the URL or file will display. Valid options are Current, New, Top, or Parent.
Send e-mail to	Create an e-mail message to a specified address in the viewer's default e-mail program. The viewer will still have to fill in the message and subject and click Send.	Enter the e-mail address to which you want the e-mail sent. Click the check box to indicate whether or not the current movie should continue playing.
Execute JavaScript	Run JavaScript commands.	Enter the JavaScript code you want to run.
Execute advanced action	Run a custom ActionScript that you've created through the Advanced Action feature.	Choose the name of the action.
Show	Display an element that had previously been hidden	Choose the element on this slide that you want to display if the viewer successfully performs the required task. Similar to a success caption, this can be any element type. For example, you may want to show an additional button or display a different graphic.
Hide	Remove a displayed element from sight.	Choose the element on this slide that you want to hide if the viewer successfully performs the required task. This is particularly powerful when used in conjunction with the Show option (and Multiple Actions) to change the buttons available based on user interaction.

TABLE 9-1 Destination options based on viewer success (or failure) to perform certain actions (continued).

Choose this option:	For this effect:	Also enter this information:
Enable	Activate a previously disabled element.	Specify the element you want to activate.
Disable	Cause an active element to become inactive. The element will still display, but none of the assigned interactivity will work.	Specify the element you want to inactivate.
Assign	Enter a value into a variable.	Choose from the list of variable names, and specify a value to assign to that variable.
Increment	Increase the value of a numeric variable.	Choose the variable from the drop-down list, then enter the number you want to add to the variable.
Decrement	Decrease the value of a numeric variable.	Choose the variable from the drop-down list, then enter the number you want to subtract from the variable.
Multiple Actions	Choose this option to display a window that allows you to set more than one action for the current element. The available actions are the same as in the properties drop-down box.	Click the **More** button (. . .) to display the Set Multiple Actions window. Choose the actions you want and specify additional information as necessary, then click **OK** to return to the properties window.
No Action	Take no action, not even continue the movie.	None necessary

6. By default, Captivate allows the viewer an unlimited (infinite) number of tries to get the correct action (click in the click box or on the button, or type the correct text in the text entry box). If you want to limit the number of attempts, click the **Infinite attempts** check box to deselect it, then specify the number of attempts you want to give the viewer. If you leave Infinite attempts selected, the movie will pause until the viewer gets it right or performs some action that causes the movie to move on to another

slide. If you specified a number of attempts, choose an option from the **After last attempt** drop-down list to specify what you want the movie to display after the last unsuccessful attempt. Valid options are the same as for successful actions and are listed in Table 9-1.

7. *For button elements only,* choose the way you want the button to look by choosing from the drop-down menu (see "Step 2: Set Button Properties").

8. *For text entry box elements only,* click the **Options** tab and choose the way you want the entry box to display on the screen by selecting one of the following transition parameters:

   ■ *Fade in:* The box will appear very dim at first and will gradually become more solid until it reaches the defined transparency setting.

   ■ *Fade out:* The box will gradually become more transparent until it is eliminated from the slide display completely.

   ■ *Fade in and out:* The box will appear dim, then gradually get more solid. Then it will gradually become more transparent until it is eliminated from the display completely.

   ■ *No transition:* The box simply displays and then is removed after the specified timing.

   For fading effects, you'll also need to specify how long or how gradual the effect should be. The default is 0.5 seconds.

TIP

It is usually best to show some restraint in adding effects to your movie. If you already have a lot going on, multiple animations and transition effects can be more distracting than entertaining.

---

9. If you want to automatically apply the current settings to all elements of this type in the movie, click the **Apply to all** check box. Depending on the type of element, this check box may be on the main tabs, on the Options tab, or unavailable at all.

10. Each interactive element has a default shortcut key that sends the action to the controls of the Flash movie. For example, the action for a click box

defaults to a mouse click. The action for a text entry box defaults to the Enter key. You can change the shortcut key for each element by clicking **Select keys** to display the Shortcut key window.

FIGURE 9-2   **Set a shortcut key combination.**

Select **Allow mouse clicks** to let the viewer use the mouse to click in the element. Select **Attach a shortcut** to activate the shortcut options, then choose a new key combination. You can choose any combination of keys, but don't choose so many that it is difficult for the viewer to enter them.

TIP

Try to avoid key combinations that are likely to conflict with other software. For example, F1 is often designated as a Help button, and Ctrl+C is often for copy functions.

---

11.   Click **OK** when you are done to close the Shortcut key window and return to the display of the properties window.

12. You may choose to enter the options as described in the following sections of this chapter or set audio properties (see Chapter 8). You can also set properties that relate to e-learning and quizzes, which are described in Chapter 10.

13. Click **OK** when you are done to close the element properties window and view the new interactive element on your slide. The element will appear in the center of your slide, along with associated components, if any. For example, a text entry box will display with a button, and success or failure captions will display if you have them turned on (as described in the following section).

FIGURE 9-3   **Buttons and text entry boxes often have several associated elements.**

Step 2: Set Button Properties (for Buttons Only)

If you're adding a button, you have a lot of control over the appearance of the button. You can set the color and transparency, and either enter text for the button or choose an image.

There are three types of buttons:

- *Text button:* A rectangular button with text on it. You can have the button itself be transparent, making it look like a text link. Or you can define the color, size, and style of the text. This button type is quick and easy to add but does not let you modify the color or shape of the button.

- *Transparent button:* This type of button functions like a combination click box and highlight box, allowing the viewer to see the borders of the button and making full use of the interactive properties. By placing a transparent button on top of other elements on the background of a slide, such as a menu item, icon, or background button, you can make it look like the menu item or icon is actually working.

- *Image button:* A set of images that display one at a time, depending on the state of the button:
  - Up state is before the button is clicked.
  - Down state is after the button has been clicked.
  - Over state is when the mouse is over the button but it hasn't been clicked yet.

To define the unique button properties, follow these steps:

1. From the Edit view, either create a new element as described in "Step 1: Specify an Interactive Element" or double-click on an existing element to open the element properties window.

2. Set the success and failure options just as you would for any other element, as described in the previous section.

3. Choose the button type from the drop-down list. Depending on the option you choose, the bottom portion of the properties window will change to reflect the different options available.

4. If you chose **Text button**, type the button text in the Button text box. You can click the **Font** button to change or hide the background and borders of the button (only the text displays in the movie).

FIGURE 9-4   Set the Text button properties.

5. If you chose **Transparent button**, choose the colors for the button by clicking on the color box and clicking on a color from the palette. You can also set the width of the frame around the button, along with the transparency percentage. The default, 0%, is a solid button (not transparent at all). Set this to a higher number (50% or 60%) to let the viewer see through the button to the background of the slide.

FIGURE 9-5   **Set the Transparent button properties.**

6.   If you chose **Image button**, you'll be presented with three options. Captivate will display a different image for each of the three possible states of the button:

■   Up image (the first in the row of buttons) is displayed before the button is clicked.

■   Down image (the middle image) is displayed after the button has been clicked.

■   Over image (the third image in the row of buttons) is displayed when the mouse is over the button but hasn't been clicked yet.

The default is to use three gray rectangles with varying border colors to indicate the three possible image states.

FIGURE 9-6   **Set the Image button properties.**

Click the selection button to browse the folders on your system and choose an image for each of the three button states. You can also set the buttons to have a transparent color by selecting the **Transparent buttons** check box. When this is selected, Captivate will make whatever color is in the upper left-corner of the button image be transparent throughout the button image. For most buttons, this allows the slide to show through the body of the button.

> **TIP**
>
> Captivate comes with a variety of buttons that you can use anywhere within your movie. They're usually stored in the default folder at Adobe Captivate 4\Gallery\ Buttons. You can create your own buttons by following the naming conventions for the three button states and placing the corresponding graphics in this folder.

FIGURE 9-7   **Samples of the gallery buttons in the Button property window.**

7. You may choose to enter options for the button as described in the following sections of this chapter or set audio properties (see Chapter 8). You can also set properties that relate to e-learning and quizzes, which are described in Chapter 10.

8. Click **OK** when you are done to close the element properties window and view the new button on your slide, along with the success or failure captions if you have them turned on (as described in the following section).

Step 3: Set Interactive Element Options

Each interactive element has a variety of additional options that you can set to control exactly how the element will behave when the movie is playing. To set the interactive properties, follow these steps:

1. From the Edit view, either create a new element as described in "Step 1: Specify an Interactive Element" or double-click on an existing element to open the element's properties window.
2. Click the **Options** tab to view the options for the element. For example, if you are creating or editing a click box element, the options look like Figure 9-8.
3. Set the length of time the element will display by choosing one of the following from the list of **Display for** options:

   ▪ *Specific time:* Enter the number of seconds you want the element to display. If you enter a time longer than the current length the slide is displayed, the slide timing will be adjusted to the new length of time. For example, if your slide is currently set to display for 3 seconds, and you enter 5 seconds in the Display for area, the slide timing will be extended to display for 5 seconds. You can enter times in increments of one-tenth of a second.

   ▪ *Rest of slide:* Displays the element for as long as the slide is displayed.

FIGURE 9-8 **Set properties for a click box.**

4. You can specify that the element displays a certain length of time after the slide first appears by typing a number of seconds in the box labeled **Appear after**. Leave this number set to 0.0 if you want the element to display as soon as the slide displays. You can enter times in increments of one-tenth of a second.

> **Note:** If you've specified a duration for the element, the slide will display for at least as long as the total of the Appear after and the Display for times. For example, a Display for setting of 5 seconds and Appear after setting of 3 seconds would display the slide a total of 8 seconds.

5. *For text entry boxes and buttons only,* specify the length of time after the element displays that you want to pause the movie and wait for the viewer input. For example, you may have other animation or mouse movement going on for 2 or 3 seconds after a text entry box first displays. Set the **Pause after** setting for 3 seconds so that the action on the slide can complete before you pause the movie.

6. Click any of the following options to select it, or click on a selected item to deselect it.

TABLE 9-2 Options for interactive elements.

Select this:	To cause this:
Success caption	Include a special text caption that displays when the viewer clicks in the box, presses the button, or types correct text.
Failure caption	Include a special text caption that displays when the viewer does not successfully click in the box, press the button, or type correct text.
Hint caption	Include a special text caption that displays when the viewer moves the mouse over the click box.
Show hand cursor over "hit" area	*For click boxes and buttons only,* change the cursor to a pointing hand icon when the viewer moves the mouse over the click box.
Pause project until user clicks	*For click boxes only,* stops the movie until the viewer clicks in the box.
Double mouse click	*For click boxes only,* allows viewers to double-click the click box.
Right mouse click	*For click boxes only,* allows viewers to click the right mouse button to choose the click box.

TABLE 9-2 Options for interactive elements (continued).

Select this:	To cause this:
Pause for success/ failure captions	Stops the movie until all success and failure captions have displayed.
Show button	*For text entry boxes only,* displays a button that the viewer clicks to indicate the text entry is complete (like a Submit or Enter button). Note that this button is not the same as a fully interactive button; it is a component of the text entry box element.
Show text box frame	*For text entry boxes only,* displays a border around the text box.
Password	*For text entry boxes only,* causes the text that the viewer enters to be displayed on the screen as asterisks, just as many passwords display.
Case-sensitive	*For text entry boxes only,* requires that the viewer enter the text exactly as it is entered in the properties box, with all upper- and lowercase letters typed correctly.

7. You may choose to enter audio properties (see Chapter 8). You can also set properties that relate to e-learning and quizzes, described in Chapter 10.

8. Click **OK** when you are done to close the element properties window and view the new element on your slide, along with the success or failure captions and any other components you have turned on.

Step 4: Adjust Interactive Elements and Components

If you used the automatic functions to create interactive elements while recording, the elements are likely to be placed at the appropriate points in the slide (such as click boxes over links that you click and success or failure captions right next to the elements the viewer is supposed to click, such as a menu icon). When you create new interactive elements on your slide, Captivate defaults to placing them in the center of the slide at a default size. You'll need to move and resize these elements as appropriate, exactly as you would move or resize or align any other element, by clicking and dragging the whole element to a new location or by dragging the handles of the element to resize it (see Chapter 7). You can also move the associated components, such as success captions or hints.

In addition, you'll probably want to change the text that appears on the additional components of interactive elements. If you're adding new elements, the default text just says things like "Enter success text here." Even if you're using the automatically generated text, you may want to change the wording. You can also change the color schemes and other properties of the success, failure, and hint captions.

To change the appearance of interactive captions, follow these steps:

1. From Edit view, double-click on a success caption, failure caption, or hint caption to display the properties window, as shown in Figure 9-9.
2. Type the text you want to display in the caption. As of Captivate 4, you can also type in a variable that will be filled in when the movie plays. Click the variable icon ("X" with an arrow) to choose from a list of User or System icons, or type the variable name surrounded by double dollar signs. For example, type $$cpInfoCurrentYear$$ to display the four-digit year in the text caption.

TIP

While there is no limit to the amount of text you can include in a caption, remember that this caption will be sitting on top of your slide background (which is often already very busy), and the more text you include, the smaller it will have to be to fit on the screen. The best captions are succinct and to the point.

FIGURE 9-9   Enter new text in the Success Caption properties window.

3.   If necessary, change the look of the caption by editing the properties shown in Table 9-3.

TABLE 9-3 Interactive element caption properties.

To change this:	Do this:
Caption type	Choose a caption type from the list. The caption type defines the shape and color of the outline that will be placed around the text, as well as the default text color (though you can change this). The icons below this field display the look of each caption type.
Font	Choose a font for the text from the list. The list of fonts will be determined by the fonts available on your system.
Size	Choose a size for the text from the list.
Color	Click the down arrow next to color icon (large letter A) to choose a new color for the text. The text color does not change the color of the caption type outline.
Caption style	Many of the caption types include outlines that point in different directions. In Figure 9-9, the "adobe green" type has options that point in four different directions as well as an option with no direction. Click any one of the type icons to select it for the current text caption.
Text style	If desired, set additional display options such as bold, italic, or underlined text, and text justification.

4.   The changes you make to the caption properties will be applied to all subsequent text captions. If you want to apply these changes to all captions that are already in the movie, click **Apply to all** to apply the current settings as defined in the properties window. To view or change the properties settings, click the **Settings** button.

Note: Selecting this check box applies the caption style, font type, font size, font color, and transition properties to all success or failure or hint captions in the movie. It does not change the wording of the text, nor does it change the text style (such as bold, italic, or justification).

5.   You can click the **Options** tab to set timing and transitions as described in Chapter 7, or click the **Audio** tab to set audio properties as described in Chapter 8.

6.   Click **OK** to close the properties window and display the new text.

CREATING USER-DEFINED VARIABLES

Throughout Captivate, you can make use of any of the system variables such as system date or quiz score. The system variables as of this printing are typically available in drop-down lists where appropriate. In addition, you can create your own variables for additional flexibility and customization.

To create a user-defined variable, follow these steps:

1. From the **Project** menu, select **Actions** to display the Actions Dialog window and then click the **Variables** tab.
2. Select **User** from the Type drop-down list.
3. Click the **Add New** button, and enter a name for the new variable. At this point, the **Add New** button will change to the **Save** button.

FIGURE 9-10   **Create a new user-defined variable.**

4. Enter an optional default value for the variable. This might be useful, for example, if you have a variable that specifies a software version number. Insert the variable instead of the number, and you can change the version

number wherever it appears throughout the whole movie by changing the default value.

5. Enter a description for the variable. Though this is optional, it's a good idea to describe the variable well enough so that if someone else needs to use that variable, they'll understand what the purpose is.

6. Click **Save** to store the new variable and display it in the list of user-defined variables in the lower portion of the Variables tab.

7. Click **Close** to close the Actions Dialog window.

8. Whenever you want to use the variable, you can type the variable name surrounded by double dollar signs ($$User_Name$$) or simply choose from the drop-down list in the caption or button properties windows.

ADDING INTERACTIVITY WITH ROLLOVERS

Rollover captions, rollover images, and rollover slidelets are a cross between the static elements (text captions and images) and their more interactive equivalents. The rollover elements are interactive in that they only appear if the viewer takes an action (like moving the cursor over the designated area). But they do not require this action. The movie will continue whether the rollover caption displays or not.

A rollover element consists of two components: the area that the viewer must "roll over" and the caption, image, or secondary slide that appears. Rollover captions are particularly useful when you're documenting complex screens with many options. In such situations, you can use the rollover caption to create a sort of interactive job aid describing the use and purpose of each option.

Adding a Rollover Caption

To add a rollover caption, follow these steps:

1. In Edit view, select the slide you want to edit.

2. From the **Insert** menu, select **Standard Objects** and then **Rollover Caption** or click the Rollover Caption icon to display the New Rollover Caption window, as shown in Figure 9-11.

3. Type the text you want to display when the viewer rolls the mouse over the designated area. As of Captivate 4, you can also type in a variable

that will be filled in when the movie plays. Click the variable icon ("X" with an arrow) to choose from a list of User or System icons, or type the variable name surrounded by double dollar signs. For example, type $$cpInfoCurrentYear$$ to display the four-digit year in the text caption.

TIP

While there is no limit to the amount of text you can include in a caption, remember that this caption will be sitting on top of your slide background (which is often already very busy), and the more text you include, the smaller it will have to be to fit on the screen. The best captions are succinct and to the point. Use short declarative phrases ("This is the main menu") or brief commands ("Click here to go to the next page").

FIGURE 9-11   Set the rollover caption parameters.

4.   If necessary, change the look of the caption by editing the properties shown in Table 9-4.

TABLE 9-4 Rollover caption properties.

To change this:	Do this:
Caption type	Choose a caption type from the list. The caption type defines the shape and color of the outline that will be placed around the text, as well as the default text color (though you can change this). The icons below this field display the look of each caption type.
Font	Choose a font for the text from the list. The list of fonts will be determined by the fonts available on your system.
Size	Choose a size for the text from the list.
Color	Click the down arrow next to the color icon (large letter A) to choose a new color for the text. The text color does not change the color of the caption type outline.
Caption style	Many of the caption types include outlines that point in different directions. In Figure 9-11, the "adobe blue" type has options that point in four different directions as well as an option with no direction. Click any one of the type icons to select it for the current text caption.
Text style	If desired, set additional display options such as bold, italic, or underlined text, and text justification.

5. The changes you make to the caption properties will be applied to all subsequent text captions. If you want to apply these changes to all captions that are already in the movie, click **Apply to all** to apply the current settings as defined in the properties window. To view or change the properties settings, click the Settings button.

> **Note:** Selecting this check box applies the caption style, font type, font size, font color, and transition properties to all rollover captions in the movie. It does not change the wording of the text, nor does it change the text style (such as bold, italic, or justification).

6. You can click the **Options** tab to set timing and transitions as described in Chapter 7, or click the **Audio** tab to set audio properties as described in Chapter 8.
7. Click **OK** to display the new rollover caption and the text that you entered in the center of the slide.

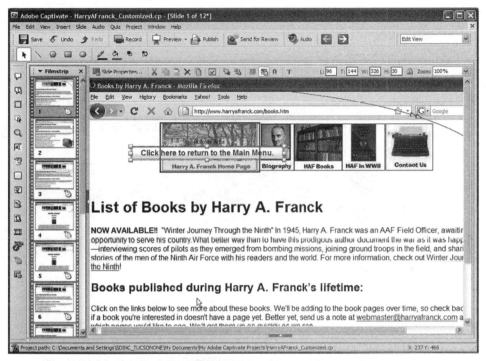

FIGURE 9-12   **The new rollover caption appears on the slide.**

8. Click and drag the text box that displays to the location where you want it to appear when the viewer rolls the mouse over the designated area.

9. Click and drag the rollover area box—it's difficult to see, particularly if the slide is very busy—from the center of the slide to the area where you want the viewer to click. In this example, we'll drag the outline that surrounds the words "rollover caption" to the top of the slide and resize it until it just matches the first icon in the menu.

> **Note:** Once the movie is running, the rollover captions will only display when the mouse is in the designated rollover area. If you have several rollover captions, don't worry if the text boxes pile up on each other. It may be difficult to see while you're editing, but they'll only appear one at a time during the movie. For example, if we continue adding rollover captions to the icons in the menu in Figure 9-12, the result in Edit view looks like Figure 8-13. It will get even more crowded when we add click boxes and/or success and failure captions.

> **TIP**
>
> You can't see the rollover captions when you use the Play this slide function (by pressing F3). To see what the captions will look like when the movie is played, use either Preview from this slide (F8) or Preview Next 5 slides (F10) from the Preview menu.

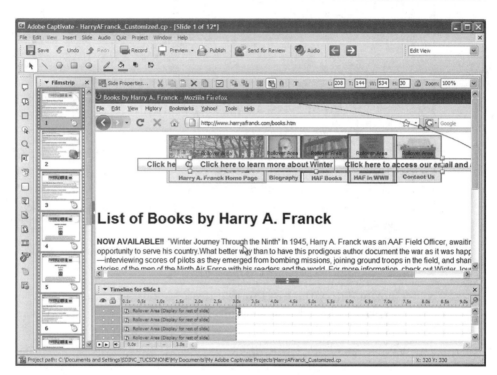

FIGURE 9-13   **Many rollover captions pile up in the Edit view but display one at a time when the movie is played.**

Adding a Rollover Image

To add a rollover image, follow these steps:

1. In Edit view, select the slide you want to edit.
2. From the **Insert** menu, select **Standard Objects** and then **Rollover Image** or click the Rollover Image icon to display the images available in the last folder you used.

3. Browse to the location of the image you want to display when the viewer moves the mouse over the designated area, and then highlight the image name.

TIP

Captivate comes with a gallery of buttons that you can import as images. By default, they're stored in the Adobe Captivate 4\Gallery\Buttons folder.

---

4. You can use rollover images for many things, such as close-ups of the background or showing categorization icons. Remember, though, that a rollover image does not require a click; the viewer only has to roll the mouse over the designated area. For this example, we'll add a series of close-ups of the background image. As the viewer moves the mouse around on a map, the various regions display in higher resolution as separate images. Browse to the image you want to use for the rollover, then click **OK** to select the image and display it on the current slide.

5. Double-click the image to display the Rollover Image window.

FIGURE 9-14   **Import an image as an element on the slide.**

6. The image you selected appears in the center of the window. Enter the percentage of transparency for the image. 0% would be completely solid; 100% would be completely transparent.

7. You can specify that Captivate import the image but make the background color of the image transparent. For example, if you are adding a logo that is a custom shape, such as a shield, you might not want the rectangular outline of the image file to show.

TIP

Be careful to check your images after you import them, particularly if you use a transparent background. Captivate will make all areas the color of the background transparent. For example, if you have an image of a black circle with white lettering and a white background, and you make the white background transparent, then Captivate will make all white portions of the image transparent (including the letters). If this isn't the look you wanted, use a graphics program to make the background or the letters slightly different shades of white.

---

8. You can click the **Crop** button to choose a portion of the displayed image.

9. The changes you make to the properties will be applied to all subsequent rollover images. If you want to apply these changes to all rollover images that are already in the movie, click **Apply to all** to apply the current settings as defined in the properties window. To view or change the properties settings, click the **Settings** button.

TIP

If you want the rollover area to be invisible, set the frame width to zero and the frame fill to 100% transparency.

---

10. You can click the **Options** tab to set transitions as described in Chapter 7, or click the **Audio** tab to set audio properties as described in Chapter 8.

11. Click **OK** to display the new rollover image in your slide. By default, the rollover area and image are in the center of the slide.

12. Click and drag the image to the location where you want it to appear when the viewer rolls the mouse over the designated area.

13. Click and drag the rollover image box—it's difficult to see, particularly if the slide is very busy—from the center of the slide to the area where you want the viewer to click. In this example, we'll drag the outline that surrounds the words "Rollover Image" to the area of the map that corresponds to the close-up image. When the viewer moves the mouse over the designated area (in Figure 9-15, it's the boxed area), the specified image displays.

TIP

You can't see the rollover images when you use the Play this slide function (by pressing F3). To see what the images will look like when the movie is played, use either Preview from this slide (F8) or Preview Next 5 slides (F10) from the Preview menu.

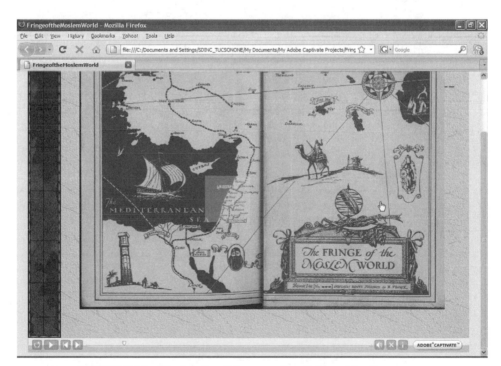

FIGURE 9-15 Preview the slide to see the designated rollover area.

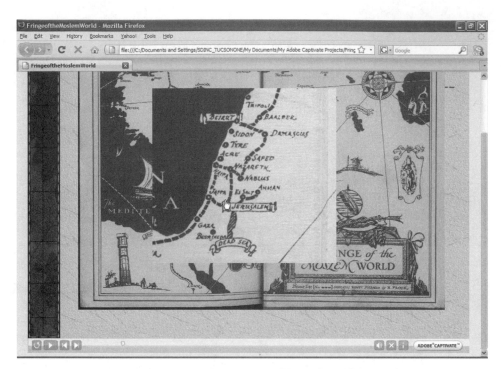

FIGURE 9-16   **Move the mouse to display the rollover image.**

Adding a Rollover Slidelet

A slidelet is a miniature slide that displays when the viewer rolls the mouse over a specified area. This gives you lots of options, since a slidelet can contain most of the elements that a full slide can contain.

> **TIP**
>
> Slidelets can be tricky to implement well. Remember that the slidelet displays on top of the current slide, which can make for a very busy screen. Also, it is easy to put too much into a slidelet, making each element very small (sometimes too small to read).

You'll need to define both the rollover area and the slidelet contents.

To add a rollover slidelet, follow these steps:

1. In Edit view, select the slide you want to edit.
2. From the **Insert** menu, select **Standard Objects** and then **Rollover Slidelet** to display the slidelet properties window, as shown in Figure 9-17.

FIGURE 9-17   Set the slidelet properties.

3. If necessary, change the look of the caption by editing the properties described in Table 9-5. As you make changes, the preview in the center of the window changes to reflect each new selection.

TABLE 9-5 Rollover slidelet properties available on creation.

To change this:	Do this:
Border color	Click the colored box next to Border color to display the Color window, and then choose a color for the border around the outside edge of the rollover box. This is usually a darker shade than the inside of the box.
Border width	Specify the width, in pixels, for the border or frame of the rollover box.
Fill color	Click the colored box next to Fill color to display the Color window, and then choose a color for the rollover box. This is usually a lighter shade than the frame of the box.
Fill transparency	Enter the percentage of transparency for the inside of the box. 0% would be completely solid; 100% would be completely transparent. Most of the time, you want something between these two values so that the highlight box is noticeable and yet the text behind the box still shows through.
Slidelet background	Click **Select image** and browse to the image you want as the slidelet background.

4. The changes you make to the properties will be applied to all subsequent rollover images. If you want to apply these changes to all rollover images that are already in the movie, click **Apply to all** to apply the current settings as defined in the properties window. To view or change the properties settings, click the **Settings** button.

5. You can click the **Options** tab to set transitions as described in Chapter 7, or click the **Audio** tab to set audio properties as described in Chapter 8.

6. Click **OK** to display the new rollover slidelet in your slide. By default, the rollover area (labeled "Rollover Slidelet") and the content box (unlabeled) are in the center of the slide.

7. Click and drag the rollover area box—it's difficult to see, particularly if the slide is very busy—from the center of the slide to the area where you want the mouse movement to trigger the rollover display.

8. To set the rollover properties, double-click on the rollover area box, or click the box and click **Properties** to display the properties window. This defaults to the appearance properties you set when creating the slidelet, but it also gives you a few extra options.

FIGURE 9-18 **Set rollover area properties.**

9. Most of the tabs are similar to those you've seen on other property windows (such as audio settings, size and position, and most of the options). The Options tab does include one extra option that you won't see for other elements. Click the **Options** tab and select the **Show Runtime Shadow** check box to display a shadow behind the slidelet when it displays. This can help to differentiate the slidelet content from the slide behind it.

10. Define the actions you want to occur if the user clicks inside the rollover area. Remember, most rollover areas don't have a clickable functionality, so many users will not expect to click in the area. Click **OK** when finished.

TABLE 9-6 Rollover slidelet properties available while editing.

Set this:	For this action:
Navigate	If the viewer clicks in the rollover area, take the action specified in the On Click drop-down box (such as Go To Next Slide or Continue).
Stick Slidelet	Leave the slidelet on the screen, even after the viewer moves the cursor out of the rollover area.
Shortcut Key	Specify a key (or combination of keys) to trigger the display of the rollover content.

11. Click and drag the content box to the location where you want it to appear when the viewer rolls the mouse over the designated rollover area.

12. Define the content for the rollover by inserting elements into the content box by highlighting the box and choosing elements from the Insert menu. See Chapter 7 for details on the available elements.

> **TIP**
>
> Though you can add many types of elements to the content box, remember that this is a rollover element, and is usually displayed temporarily. Also, the content will be displayed on top of whatever else is on the slide. Don't try to put too much information in a rollover slidelet.

WORKING WITH WIDGETS

A widget is a small piece of code that you can use to automate certain functions at movie run-time. If you're familiar with Adobe's ActionScript® scripting language, you can create and import your own widgets. Captivate comes with a few widgets to get you started. To incorporate a widget into your movie, follow these steps:

1. From the Edit view, open the slide on which you want to place the widget.

2. From the **Insert** menu, choose **Widgets** to display the available widget files. The widgets that come with Captivate are stored in the Adobe Captivate 4\Gallery\Widgets folder.

3. If necessary, browse to display the widget you want to use, then select the filename and click **OK** to display the widget properties.

FIGURE 9-19   A sample widget file property window.

Note: Because each widget is unique, the properties windows will vary. Figure 9-19 shows the Course completion certificate widget property window.

4.   You can set any of the options, audio, or size and position settings with the appropriate tabs. These are all optional.

5.   You must, however, click the **Widget Parameters** tab to specify the additional information needed by each particular widget.

FIGURE 9-20   **A sample Widget Parameters window.**

Note: The widget in Figure 9-20 requires that you enter the name of the course (this will go on the certificate). It also includes instructions about what the widget requires in terms of user variables. In this case, you'll need to use a text entry box (TEB) to collect a user name variable. The widget needs this variable to be called v_Name.

6.   Enter the information required by the selected widget. This will vary greatly by widget type. Click **OK** when you are done.

ADDING INTERACTIVE ELEMENTS WHILE RECORDING

When you record tasks for a movie, Captivate can automatically add various visual elements for certain actions. For example, if you're recording an assessment simulation type of movie, failure and hint captions will automatically be added whenever you click on a menu item or link. To specify whether or not Captivate should add interactive elements automatically for you, you have to edit the movie recording options. To do this, follow these steps:

Note: You do not have to have an open movie to change the recording options.

1. From the **Edit** menu, choose **Preferences**, then in the **Recording** category, choose **Mode(s)** to display the current settings.

FIGURE 9-21   **Specify recording settings in the Preferences window.**

2. Choose the recording mode from the Mode drop-down menu. There are four options:

    ■ Demonstration automatically adds captions and highlight boxes, and records mouse movement.

    ■ Assessment Simulation adds click boxes and failure boxes but does not insert captions or mouse movement.

- Training Simulation adds click boxes and hints but no mouse movements.
- Custom mode allows you to set the recording options manually but defaults to including text captions.

3. For each mode, specify the options that you want Captivate to automatically add by choosing the appropriate check boxes.

4. Click **OK** to close the Preferences window. The options you've set will be used for all subsequent recordings (both for new movies and recording additional slides in an existing movie).

PUTTING IT ALL TOGETHER: ONE EXAMPLE

With all the options, actions, variables, and element types, Captivate can create a wide variety of highly customized movies. With all the possibilities, however, it can sometimes be difficult to ensure that all components are in place. This section steps through just one simple example of an interactive implementation. For example, you may want to include the viewer's name in the success captions for click boxes. To do this, follow these steps:

1. Set up a variable for the user name by selecting **Actions** from the **Project** menu and clicking the **Variables** tab. For this example, let's call it First_ Name (see "Creating User-Defined Variables").

2. On an introductory slide in the movie, enter a text entry box where the viewer will enter a name. Associate the text box with the user name variable by clicking the **Advanced actions** tab and then choosing the variable name you created in Step 1. Be sure to set On success to **Continue** and **Turn Off Validation** in the Options tab (see "Adding Interactivity w/Boxes + Buttons"). You may also want to include default text such as "Enter your first name here" in the text entry box.

3. On the first slide where you want the user to click in a specific area (for example, on a button or icon or menu item), create a click box with captions (see "Adding and Editing Interactive Elements").

4. Double-click the click box to display the properties window. In the text area for the success caption for the new click box, enter "Good Job $$First_Name!" and save the caption properties.

5.   Save and publish the movie as usual (see Chapter 14).

When the movie runs, the first screen will display a text box. To proceed with the movie, the viewer must enter a first name (or any string) in the text box. Later, if the viewer clicks in the click box at the appropriate point in the movie, the success caption will use the entered name.

SUMMARY

This chapter covered the basics of adding interactive elements to your slides, such as for demonstrations and simulations. The following chapter takes this interactivity a step further into e-learning, where you can create quizzes in a variety of question formats, and you can store or export your viewer's quiz results.

Chapter 10 CREATING e-LEARNING CONTENT

In the previous chapter, you learned how to add interactive elements to a slide and how to display different captions or continue on to different slides based on whether or not the viewer performed certain tasks correctly. Taking this one step further, the Adobe® Captivate ® program can store the results of all those interactive tasks, making the entire movie into a quiz that you can automatically grade and score and even integrate into other learning management systems.

QUESTIONS AND QUIZZES

Captivate also offers a powerful, easy-to-use feature called a question slide that automatically creates interactive slides in a variety of question formats, such as multiple choice, true or false, or short answer. Like the other interactive elements, you can specify what displays when the viewer gets a question right or when the viewer gets a question wrong. And like the other interactive elements, questions can be included in quizzes.

The Captivate Quiz Manager helps you define the properties of a quiz that automatically apply to all of the interactive elements, such as scoring and output format. The Quiz Manager also defines the defaults for elements on the question slides (such as "try again" messages or the text for Next and Submit buttons). You can also export the pass/fail information to other learning systems or to Questionmark™ Perception™ or Macromedia® Authorware®. You can track the number of correct and incorrect answers, and you can provide students with feedback based on whether their responses are correct or incorrect.

Before you begin to create questions and quizzes, you'll need to make some basic decisions:

- Decide what you want the viewer to do and what format you want to use to request the viewer input. There are two ways to get and store input from the viewer:
  - Report on interactive elements, such as whether or not the viewer clicked in the right place or entered the correct text in a text entry box. This type of interaction takes place on normal slides during the course of the movie. You'll need to create the interactive element (such as a click box or button) as well as the instructions for it (usually with a text caption and an optional highlight box).
  - Have the viewer read and answer question slides. A question slide is a unique type of slide that sits between the other slides in your movie and displays a question in any of a variety of formats (such as multiple choice or short answer questions). The interactivity is already built in, and all you have to do is input the questions and answers. You can also make some questions that will be graded (pass or fail) and others that are not graded (survey questions).
- Decide what you want to have happen if the viewer enters the correct answer or clicks in the right spot, and what you want to have happen if the viewer doesn't do the right thing. For example, you can pause the movie until the viewer clicks the right location or answers the question correctly, or display a different slide depending on whether the input is right or wrong. The display of different slides lets you give the viewer choices in the way the movie displays. This is described more in Chapter 11, "Working with the Branching View."
- Decide whether or not to use the quizzing functions to store and display a summary that shows how the viewer did overall. This is in addition to the success or failure captions that display for each interactive element or question. You can even decide to track some interactive elements and not others within the movie.

- If you use a quiz, decide what a passing score should be, what should happen when the viewer gets a passing score, and what should happen when the viewer doesn't pass. For example, will there be an option to try again? Will you let the viewer keep watching the movie or go to another area? You could also run some JavaScript based on the viewer's score (pass or fail).
- If you use a quiz, decide what you will do with the data once it's collected. You can have the results e-mailed to you, or you can create output files that you can then integrate with other programs.

- Decide if you want to use the Question Pool functionality to let Captivate generate random questions at specified places throughout the movie.

As you can see, Captivate offers a lot of options and thus gives you a lot of control over the movies you create.

WORKING WITH QUESTION SLIDES

Captivate lets you insert six types of question slides into your movie. For each slide, you'll need to define one question and enter answers. You'll also need to set the question slide options, such as which slide to display when the viewer answers correctly and whether or not to display buttons that allow the viewer to skip a question.

You'll also need to specify whether or not you want to track the answers for each question with the reporting function.

Entering Questions and Answers

Each of the eight types of question slides has its own requirements for entering the question and answer (or in some cases, multiple answers).

TABLE 10-1 Types of question slides.

For this type of question:	Do this:
Multiple choice	Enter a list of possible answers, and indicate whether the viewer can choose one or more than one and which one or ones are correct.
True/False	Indicate which is correct.
Fill in the blank	Supply the correct answer or a list of answers from which the viewer must choose. If you give a list of answers, indicate which are correct.
Short answer	Enter the correct answer.
Matching	Supply two lists of items that the viewer must pair up (one from column a, one from column b) and the correct matches.
Hot Spot	Similar to a multiple choice question, the hot spot question is displayed in a number of areas on the slide (the hot spots) that the viewer must click. You can specify up to 10 hot spots, and you can specify one or more that are correct.
Sequence	Similar to a matching question, this type of question asks the viewer to put the possible answers in order or sequence This can be done by typing the letters of each answer (like a matching question) or by dragging the answers around on the slide to put them in the order you've specified as correct.
Rating Scale (Likert)	Give a list of statements that the viewer must rate on a scale that you define. This type of question is not graded—there is no "right" or "wrong."

Defining Multiple Choice Questions and Answers

Multiple choice question slides allow the viewer to choose from a list of answers that you provide. You can specify one correct answer, or several. If there are several correct answers in your list, the viewer would have to select all of them in order for the answer to be considered correct (no partial scores here!).

To add a multiple choice question slide, follow these steps:

1. In either Storyboard or Edit view, choose where you want the slide to be placed by selecting the slide just before the question. Captivate will insert the new slide immediately after the selected slide.
2. From the **Insert** menu, choose **Other Slide(s)** and then **Question Slide** to display the list of question types.

FIGURE 10-1   **Select from the list of question types.**

3. Click on the **Multiple choice** icon or text description to select it.
4. Specify whether this question will be graded (that is, part of a quiz) or
    not by choosing either **Graded Question** or **Survey Questions**. Survey
    question results will be tabulated, but they will not be used to determine
    a score for the viewer. Once you've clicked either of these buttons, the
    window closes and the appropriate Edit Question window is displayed.

FIGURE 10-2   **Enter a question and multiple answers.**

5.   Enter a title in the Name box. This text will be displayed across the top of the slide when the movie is played. It won't be stored or tracked anywhere else.

TIP

You can type unique titles for each question, or you can use the title to categorize your questions for the viewer. For example, you might have the first few questions (regardless of question type) titled Navigation Tasks, the next few titled Message Board, and the final ones titled Feedback (or whatever categories fit your movie).

---

6.   Type the question, exactly as you want it to display, in the Question box. You can include text, numbers, and special characters including punctuation, and you may include instructions if necessary.
7.   If you specified a graded question, you can enter a number in the Points box to indicate the value or weight of the question within the context of the quiz. If you specified a survey question, this box is not available.
8.   Type an answer into each of the rows in the Answers area. You must enter at least two answers, but you can enter as many as you need. The answers will appear in the question slide in the order in which they display here. You can delete answers by highlighting the answer and clicking the **Delete** button or the **Delete** key on your keyboard.

TIP

You can click in each row or you can use the up and down arrow keys to move from one answer to the next within the Answers area.

---

9.   From the Type box, choose whether you want to indicate just one correct answer or several by choosing an option from the drop-down menu.
10.   Back up in the Answers area, indicate which answers are correct by clicking the radio button next to the answer.
11.   Select the **Shuffle Answers** check box to display the available answers in a different order each time the slide is displayed. Captivate will keep track

of the correct answer or answers, regardless of the order in which they are displayed. If this box isn't selected, the slide will always display the answers in the same order (so, in Figure 10-3, answer "B" will always be correct).

12. From the Numbering box, choose an option from the drop-down menu to indicate whether you want the answers to be listed with uppercase letters, lowercase letters, or numbers. The choice you make will be reflected in the answers that are currently displayed in the Answers area.

FIGURE 10-3   **Specify the correct answer.**

13. You may set options for this question as described in a later section in this chapter, or you can leave the default settings so that all your questions will act the same way.

14. You may set reporting options for this question as described later in this chapter.

15. Click **OK** when you are done to display the new question slide. Note that the slide displays the correct answer or answers as selected.

FIGURE 10-4   **A multiple choice question slide.**

Defining True/False Questions and Answers

A true/false question slide only gives the viewer two possible answers. You can choose whether the two answers will be True and False or Yes and No.

To add a true/false question slide, follow these steps:

1.   In either Storyboard or Edit view, choose where you want the slide to be placed by selecting the slide just before the question. Captivate will insert the new slide immediately after the selected slide.

2.   From the **Insert** menu, choose **Other Slide(s)** and then **Question Slide** to display the list of question slide options.

FIGURE 10-5 **Select from the list of question types.**

3. Click anywhere on the **True/False** icon or text description to select it.

4. Specify whether this question will be graded (that is, part of a quiz) or not by choosing either **Graded Question** or **Survey Questions**. Survey question results will be tabulated, but they will not be used to determine a score for the viewer. Once you've clicked either of these buttons, the window closes and the appropriate Edit Question window is displayed.

FIGURE 10-6 **Enter a question and specify the correct answer.**

5. Enter a title in the Name box. This text will be displayed across the top of the slide when the movie is played. It won't be stored or tracked anywhere else.

> **TIP**
>
> You can type unique titles for each question, or you can use the title to categorize your questions for the viewer. For example, you might have the first few questions (regardless of question type) titled Navigation Tasks, the next few titled Message Board, and the final ones titled Feedback (or whatever categories fit your movie).

6. Type the question, exactly as you want it to be displayed, in the Question box. You can include text, numbers, and special characters, including punctuation, and you may include instructions if necessary.
7. If you specified a graded question, you can enter a number in the Points box to indicate the value or weight of the question within the context of the quiz. If you specified a survey question, this box is not available.
8. From the Type box, choose either **True/False** or **Yes/No** from the drop-down menu. If you want the answers to be anything else, you must edit them in the Answers section.
9. Back in the Answers area, indicate which answer is correct by clicking the radio button next to the answer.
10. From the Numbering box, choose an option from the drop-down menu to indicate whether you want the answers to be listed with uppercase letters, lowercase letters, or numbers. The choice you make will be reflected in the answers that are currently displayed in the Answers area.
11. You may set options for this question as described in a later section in this chapter, or you can leave the default settings so that all your questions will act the same way.
12. You may set reporting options for this question as described later in this chapter.
13. Click **OK** when you are done to display the new question slide.

FIGURE 10-7   **A true/false question slide.**

┌─ **TIP** ───┐

If the question you entered doesn't appear in full on the slide, you can make the
text box bigger (or move elements around as needed) as described in Chapter 7,
"Editing a Single Slide."

└──┘

Defining Fill-in-the-Blank Questions and Answers

A fill-in-the-blank question slide starts with a question that is really a sentence
with one or more blank spaces where words should be. You can let the viewer
type in the correct answer, or you can provide a list of possible answers from
which the viewer should choose.

To add a fill-in-the-blank question slide, follow these steps:

1. In either Storyboard or Edit view, choose where you want the slide to be placed by selecting the slide just before the question. Captivate will insert the new slide immediately after the selected slide.

2. From the **Insert** menu, choose **Other Slide(s)** and then **Question Slide** to display the list of question slide options.

FIGURE 10-8 **Select from the list of question types.**

3. Check on the **Fill-in-the-blank** icon or text description to select it.

4. Specify whether this question will be graded (that is, part of a quiz) or not by choosing either **Graded Question** or **Survey Questions**. Survey question results will be tabulated, but they will not be used to determine a score for the viewer. Once you've clicked either of these buttons, the window closes and the appropriate Edit Question window is displayed.

FIGURE 10-9   **Enter a question and multiple answers.**

5. Enter a title in the Name box. This text will be displayed across the top of the slide when the movie is played. It won't be stored or tracked anywhere else.

TIP

You can type unique titles for each question, or you can use the title to categorize your questions for the viewer. For example, you might have the first few questions (regardless of question type) titled Navigation Tasks, the next few titled Message Board, and the final ones titled Feedback (or whatever categories fit your movie).

---

6. Type a description in the Description box. This will appear on the slide beneath the title in slightly smaller text.
7. If you specified a graded question, you can enter a number in the Points box to indicate the value or weight of the question within the context of the quiz. If you specified a survey question, this box is not available.

8.   Select the **Shuffle List Answers** check box to display the available answers in a different order each time the slide is displayed. Captivate will keep track of the correct answer or answers, regardless of the order in which they are displayed. If this box isn't selected, the slide will always display the answers in the same order.

9.   Type the phrase, exactly as you want it to be displayed, in the Phrase box. Do not include the missing word! You can include text, numbers, and special characters, including punctuation.

10. When you get to where the missing word should be in your phrase, click the **Add Blank** button to display the Blank Answer window.

11. In the Blank Answer window, choose how you want the viewer to input the answer (either by typing or selecting from a list).

12. Specify the correct answer or answers. If you want the user to type in an answer, any item in the list will be considered correct. If you want the user to choose from a list in a drop-down box, you must specify which answer or answers are correct. You must select at least one correct answer.

FIGURE 10-10   Specify the correct answer or answers for fill-in-the-blank question slides.

13. To edit the correct answers, you can use the Add or Delete button, or you can simply use your arrow keys to move from one answer row to the next.

14. If the user has to type in an answer, select **The answer is case-sensitive** if you want the answer entered with the exact capitalization that you've specified. In other words, if you select this check box and have "Home" as a possible answer, the answer "home" would be considered incorrect. Ensure that this check box is not selected to allow both "Home" and "home" as correct answers.

15. Click **OK** to close the Blank Answer window and return to the New fill-in-the-blank question window. You can open this window again later if you need to by highlighting the answer and clicking on the **Edit Blank** button. Note that the question window displays only the correct answers.

FIGURE 10-11   Correct answers display in the Blanks box.

16. Repeat steps 11 through 15 for each blank you want to be included in this question.
17. You may set options for this question as described in a later section in this chapter, or you can leave the default settings so that all your questions will act the same way.
18. You may set reporting options for this question as described later in this chapter.
19. Click **OK** when you are done to display the new question slide.

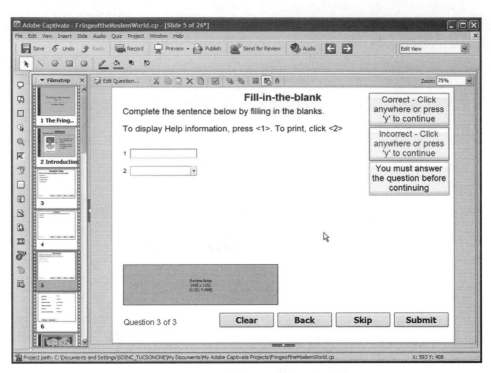

FIGURE 10-12   A fill-in-the-blank question slide.

Defining Short Answer Questions and Answers

A short answer question requires that the viewer type text into a text box. This text can be matched against a list of correct answers that you've provided, or you can simply store the entered text with the quiz results. For example, you could ask for comments or let the viewer submit suggestions with a short answer.

To add a short answer question slide, follow these steps:

1.   In either Storyboard or Edit view, choose where you want the slide to be placed by selecting the slide just before the question. Captivate will insert the new slide immediately after the selected slide.

2. From the **Insert** menu, choose **Other Slide(s)** and then **Question Slide** to display the list of question slide options.

FIGURE 10-13 Select from the list of question types.

3. Click on the **Short answer** icon or text description to select it.
4. Specify whether this question will be graded (that is, part of a quiz) or not by choosing either **Graded Question** or **Survey Questions**. Survey question results will be tabulated, but they will not be used to determine a score for the viewer. Once you've clicked either of these buttons, the window closes and the appropriate Edit Question window is displayed.

FIGURE 10-14   Enter a question and (optional) multiple answers.

5.   Enter a title in the Name box. This text will be displayed across the top of the slide when the movie is played. It won't be stored or tracked anywhere else.

TIP

You can type unique titles for each question, or you can use the title to categorize your questions for the viewer. For example, you might have the first few questions (regardless of question type) titled Navigation Tasks, the next few titled Message Board, and the final ones titled Feedback (or whatever categories fit your movie).

---

6.   Type the question, exactly as you want it to display, in the Question box. You can include text, numbers, and special characters, including punctuation, and you may include instructions if necessary.

7.   If you specified a graded question, you can enter a number in the Points box to indicate the value or weight of the question within the context of the quiz. If you specified a survey question, this box is not available.

8. If you chose a graded question, click **Add** and enter the correct answers in the box. The viewer will have to type the exact string in order for the answer to be considered correct. Each row represents a separate and equally "correct" answer. Note that you can type more than the displayed length—the characters will scroll within each row. If you initially chose a survey question, the viewer's text will not be marked correct or incorrect, but it will be stored as an answer and output in the same way as other questions in the quiz. You must have reporting functions (described later in this chapter) turned on in order to store any answer.

TIP

You can click in each row or you can use the up and down arrow keys on your keyboard to move from one answer to the next within the answer list area.

---

9. Choose whether you want to require the viewer to enter the exact short answer, including all capital and lowercase letters, by selecting or deselecting the check box labeled **The answer is case-sensitive**.
10. You may set options for this question as described in a later section in this chapter, or you can leave the default settings so that all your questions will act the same way.
11. You may set reporting options for this question as described later in this chapter.
12. Click **OK** when you are done to display the new question slide.

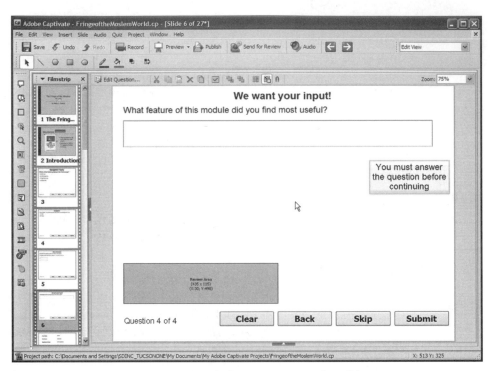

FIGURE 10-15   A short answer question slide.

Defining Matching Questions and Answers

A matching question slide has two lists on it. The viewers must match the items in the first list to the items in the second list. They do this by typing the letter or number of each entry from the second list into a box next to each entry in the first list. To set this up, you must enter the two lists and indicate which items match each other.

To add a matching question slide, follow these steps:

1. In either Storyboard or Edit view, choose where you want the slide to be placed by selecting the slide just before the question. Captivate will insert the new slide immediately after the selected slide.

2. From the **Insert** menu, choose **Other Slide(s)** and then **Question Slide** to display the list of question slide options.

FIGURE 10-16   **Select from the list of question types.**

3.   Click on the **Matching** icon or text description to select it.

4.   Specify whether this question will be graded (that is, part of a quiz) or not by choosing either **Graded Question** or **Survey Questions**. Survey question results will be tabulated, but they will not be used to determine a score for the viewer. Once you've clicked either of these buttons, the window closes and displays the appropriate Edit Question window.

FIGURE 10-17   **Enter two lists.**

5. Enter a title in the Name box. This text will be displayed across the top of the slide when the movie is played. It won't be stored or tracked anywhere else.

TIP

You can type unique titles for each question, or you can use the title to categorize your questions for the viewer. For example, you might have the first few questions (regardless of question type) titled Navigation Tasks, the next few titled Message Board, and the final ones titled Feedback (or whatever categories fit your movie).

---

6. Type the question, exactly as you want it to be displayed, in the Question box. You can include text, numbers, and special characters, including punctuation, and you may include instructions if necessary.

7. If you specified a graded question, you can enter a number in the Points box to indicate the value or weight of the question within the context of the quiz. If you specified a survey question, this box is not available.

8. Select the **Shuffle Answers** check box to display the available answers in a different order each time the slide is displayed. Captivate will keep track of the correct answers, regardless of the order in which they are displayed. If this box isn't selected, the slide will always display the answers in the same order.

9. In the Answers area, the default names for the two lists are Column 1 and Column 2. If you want to, you can click in either list title box to change these to more specific names for your two lists.

10. In each of the two columns, enter a list of answers. You can click **Add** to add a new entry with default text, or simply click in the row to enter text. You can use the up and down arrow keys at the bottom of each list to move the entries within each list, or click the **Delete** key as necessary to remove entries.

FIGURE 10-18   **Indicate which items are "matches."**

11. Specify the correct correlations between the two columns by clicking once on an answer in the first column, clicking once on the corresponding answer in the second column, and then clicking the Match button. You'll see a line connect the two "matched" entries. Repeat for each of the matches. Note that you can match any answer from the first column to any in the second column, even one that's already been matched.

TIP

You can also match entries by clicking on an entry in column 2 and dragging it to the matching answer in column 1.

---

12. Specify the way you want the viewer to make matches, either by dragging and dropping or by choosing from a drop-down list.
13. Specify the numbering for the questions, either capital letters (A, B, C), lowercase letters (a, b, c) or numbers (1, 2, 3).

14. You may set options for this question as described in a later section in this chapter, or you can leave the default settings so that all your questions will act the same way.

15. You may set reporting options for this question as described later in this chapter.

16. Click **OK** when you are done to display the new question slide.

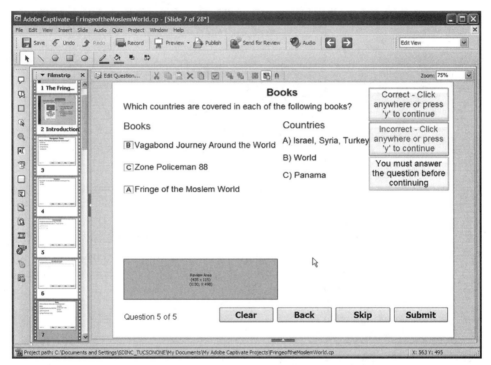

FIGURE 10-19   A matching question slide.

Defining Hot Spot Questions and Answers

A hot spot question lets you define areas on the slide (the hot spots) that the viewer must click. You can specify up to 10 hot spots, and you can specify one or more that are correct. For example, you might want the viewer to click on a set of icons or other images. Or you might make the hot spots over portions of the slide simulate clicking navigation areas. Like multiple choice questions, the viewer must select all of the correct hot spots (and none of the incorrect ones) in order to get this question correct. To add a hot spot question slide, follow these steps:

1. In either Storyboard or Edit view, choose where you want the slide to be placed by selecting the slide just before the question. Captivate will insert the new slide immediately after the selected slide.

2. From the **Insert** menu, choose **Other Slide(s)** and then **Question Slide** to display the list of question types.

FIGURE 10-20   **Select from the list of question types.**

3. Click on the **Hot Spot** icon or text description to select it.

4. Specify whether this question will be graded (that is, part of a quiz) or not by choosing either **Graded Question** or **Survey Questions**. Survey question results will be tabulated, but they will not be used to determine a score for the viewer. Once you've clicked either of these buttons, the window closes and the appropriate Edit Question window is displayed.

FIGURE 10-21 **Enter a question and specify the number of hot spots.**

5. Enter a title in the Name box. This text will be displayed across the top of the slide when the movie is played. It won't be stored or tracked anywhere else.

TIP

You can type unique titles for each question, or you can use the title to categorize your questions for the viewer. For example, you might have the first few questions (regardless of question type) titled Navigation Tasks, the next few titled Message Board, and the final ones titled Feedback (or whatever categories fit your movie).

---

6. Type the question, exactly as you want it to be displayed, in the Question box. You can include text, numbers, and special characters, including punctuation, and you may include instructions if necessary.

7. If you specified a graded question, you can enter a number in the Points box to indicate the value or weight of the question within the context of the quiz. If you specified a survey question, this box is not available.

8. Specify the number of hot spots you want to use for this question (from 1 to 10).

9. As the viewer clicks on each hot spot, Captivate displays a small animated icon that indicates the hot spot has been selected. You can change this animation by clicking the **Select** button next to the Choose box, then choosing from the list of available animations.

10. Select **Allow Clicks On Hot Spots Only** to force the viewer to select only areas you have defined as hot spots. If this option is not selected, the animated icon will display wherever they click, even if it isn't a defined hot spot.

11. You may set reporting options for this question as described later in this chapter, or you may set the branching option as described in Chapter 11.

12. Click **OK** to display the hot spots on your slide. In Figure 10-22, we've got four hot spots.

FIGURE 10-22   **The hot spots are displayed on the question slide.**

13. Next, you'll want to add the images (or background) that will be displayed on the finished slide by selecting the **Insert** menu, then **Image**, then selecting the image. You can edit, move, or resize the images or do any of the other tasks described in Chapter 7, "Editing a Single Slide."

14. Edit, move, or resize each hot spot box so that it is displayed over the images or slide area that you want the viewer to click. This is the same technique you might use to place a highlight box or click box.

15. Specify which hot spots are "correct" by editing the properties for each hot-spot element. Access the properties by selecting the hot spot, then clicking the **properties** icon, or by right-clicking on the hot spot and choosing **Properties**, or by double-clicking the hot spot element. The properties box looks much like the properties window for other elements, and it allows you to specify color and shading.

FIGURE 10-23   **Specify the correct hot spots.**

16. Select the **Correct Answer** check box for each correct hot spot, and ensure that this box is not selected for each incorrect hot spot. Click **OK** when finished, then repeat for each hot spot on the slide. When viewing the slide

within Captivate, the correct hot spots will be displayed with a green check mark; the check mark does not display on incorrect hot spots.

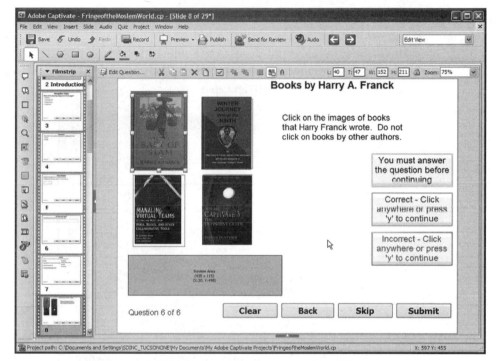

FIGURE 10-24   A hot spot question slide.

> **TIP**
>
> Note that in this example, the slide "Question" element has been moved and resized. You don't have to leave the question text centered at the top of each slide!

Defining Sequence Questions and Answers

A sequence question asks the viewer to put the possible answers in order or sequence. This can be done by typing the letters of each answer (like a matching question) or by dragging the answers around on the slide to put them in the order you've specified as correct.

To add a sequence question slide, follow these steps:

1. In either Storyboard or Edit view, choose where you want the slide to be placed by selecting the slide just before the question. Captivate will insert the new slide immediately after the selected slide.

2. From the **Insert** menu, choose **Other Slide(s)** and then **Question Slide** to display the list of question types.

FIGURE 10-25   **Select from the list of question types.**

3. Click on the **Sequence** icon or text description to select it

4. Specify whether this question will be graded (that is, part of a quiz) or not by choosing either **Graded Question** or **Survey Questions**. Survey question results will be tabulated, but they will not be used to determine a score for the viewer. Once you've clicked either of these buttons, the window closes and the appropriate Edit Question window is displayed.

FIGURE 10-26   **Enter a question and multiple answers.**

5.   Enter a title in the Name box. This text will be displayed across the top of the slide when the movie is played. It won't be stored or tracked anywhere else.

TIP

You can type unique titles for each question, or you can use the title to categorize your questions for the viewer. For example, you might have the first few questions (regardless of question type) titled Navigation Tasks, the next few titled Message Board, and the final ones titled Feedback (or whatever categories fit your movie).

---

6.   Type the question, exactly as you want it to be displayed, in the Question box. You can include text, numbers, and special characters, including punctuation, and you may include instructions if necessary.

7.   If you specified a graded question, you can enter a number in the Points box to indicate the value or weight of the question within the context of the quiz. If you specified a survey question, this box is not available.

8. Type an answer into each of the rows in the Answers area. You must enter at least two answers, but you can enter as many as you need. You must enter them in the correct order—Captivate will scramble them at run-time. Highlight an answer and click the **Move Up** or **Move Down** button to rearrange the answers as needed. You can also delete answers by highlighting the answer and clicking the **Delete** button or the **Delete** key on your keyboard.

TIP

You can click in each row or you can use the up and down arrow keys to move from one answer to the next within the Answers area.

---

9. From the Style box, choose whether you want the viewer to choose the correct sequence by dragging and dropping the answers or by choosing from a drop-down list.

10. From the Numbering box, choose an option from the drop-down menu to indicate whether you want the answers to be listed with uppercase letters, lowercase letters, or numbers. The choice you make will be reflected in the answers that are currently displayed in the Answers area.

11. You may set options for this question as described in a later section in this chapter, or you can leave the default settings so that all your questions will act the same way.

12. You may set reporting options for this question as described later in this chapter.

13. Click **OK** when you are done to display the new question slide. Note that within the Captivate project, the slide displays the answers in the correct order. However, when you preview or run the movie, the appearance will vary depending on whether you chose drag-and-drop or drop-down in Step 9.

FIGURE 10-27   A sequence question using drop-down boxes.

FIGURE 10-28   A sequence question using drag-and-drop.

Defining Rating Scale (Likert) Questions and Answers

A rating scale (Likert) question asks respondents to rate a statement in terms of how strongly they agree or disagree with the statement. The Likert scale is usually five to seven possible responses, such as "strongly agree," "somewhat agree," "neutral," "disagree," etc. This is by default a subjective type of question, asking for the viewer's opinion, so there are no right or wrong answers.

Captivate gives you a lot of control over how your Likert question slide looks. You can control the number of possible responses on your scale. For example, for some questions you might want to include five options, to allow the viewer to select the middle one as a neutral response. For others you might want to list an even number of responses, to make sure that the viewer chooses one side or the other. You can label all of the elements on the scale or just some of them, and you can use whatever text you want for the labels.

Some possible scales are shown in Figure 10-29.

FIGURE 10-29   Sample Likert scales.

To add a Likert question slide, follow these steps:

1. In either Storyboard or Edit view, choose where you want the slide to be placed by selecting the slide just before the question. Captivate will insert the new slide immediately after the selected slide.
2. From the **Insert** menu, choose **Other Slide(s)** and then **Question Slide** to display the list of question slide options.

FIGURE 10-30   **Select from the list of question types.**

3. Click anywhere on the **Rating Scale (Likert)** icon or text description to select it.
4. Click the **Survey Question** button to display the appropriate Edit Question window.

FIGURE 10-31   **Enter the questions and scale you want to use.**

5.   Enter a title in the Name box. This text will be displayed across the top of the slide when the movie is played. It won't be stored or tracked anywhere else.

TIP

You can type unique titles for each question, or you can use the title to categorize your questions for the viewer. For example, you might have the first few questions (regardless of question type) titled Navigation Tasks, the next few titled Message Board, and the final ones titled Feedback (or whatever categories fit your movie).

---

6.   Enter a description that defines what you want the viewer to do on this slide. You may also want to include information about what you plan to do with the information, since it won't be part of the graded portion of a quiz.

7.   Type the questions, exactly as you want them to be displayed, in the Questions box. You can include text, numbers, and special characters including punctuation, and you may include instructions if necessary. You can click **Add** to add a new entry with default text, or you can simply click in the row to enter text. You can use the up and down arrow keys to the right of each list to move the entries within each list, or you can click the **Delete** key as necessary to remove entries.

> **TIP**
>
> You can click in each row or you can use the up and down arrow keys on your keyboard to move from one answer to the next within the Answers area.

8. Define the way you want your scale to look in the Answers area. You can modify the existing text by double-clicking on it and typing new text, or you can delete text with the **Delete** key. To add more answer types, click **Add** and type new text.

9. Click the check box next to each label that you want to display on the slide. Note that you don't have to display all the labels.

10. You may set options for this question as described in a later section in this chapter, or you can leave the default settings so that all your questions will act the same way.

11. You may set reporting options for this question as described later in this chapter.

12. Click **OK** when you are done to display the new question slide.

FIGURE 10-32 A Likert question slide.

Defining Question Slide Options

Like other interactive elements, question slides give you the option of defining what happens in the movie based on whether the viewer gets the question right or wrong. You can also specify whether the question should be graded (and specify which answers are right) or whether it is simply a survey question (no right or wrong, but the answers are stored). Finally, you can choose which buttons display on the bottom of the question slide (such as **Next** or **Back**).

TIP

Though you can define button display for individual slides, you may find it easier to define buttons through the Quiz Preferences window. This way, you'll ensure that the buttons are positioned consistently throughout the movie.

To define question slide options, follow these steps:

1. Open the question slide options window in one of the following ways:

   - If you're creating a new slide and already have the question window open, click the **Options** tab.
   - If you're editing an existing question slide, open the slide in Edit view, click the **Edit question** button that is in the upper-left corner of the slide, and then click the **Options** tab.

FIGURE 10-33 **Enter question slide options.**

2. Choose the type of question this slide will contain, either a graded question with one or more correct answers, or a survey question. The available options on the rest of the window will vary, depending on which question type you choose.

Note: The Type field is unavailable for Likert questions since they ask for opinions and cannot be graded.

3. Click the check boxes to specify which buttons you want to display across the bottom of the question slide. Available options include the following:

    ■ *Show clear button:* The viewer can click this button to remove any answers from the screen and start over.
    ■ *Show back button:* The viewer clicks this button to go to the previous slide.
    ■ *Show skip button:* The viewer can click this button to go to the next slide without submitting any answers to the current question.

Note: All question slides will also have a Submit button that the viewers must click in order for their responses to be recorded. The default text for these buttons is stored in the Quiz Manager, or you can edit the buttons directly on each slide.

4. If you chose a graded question type, choose from the **Action** drop-down list to specify what you want the movie to display when the viewer enters and submits a correct answer. Valid options include those listed in Table 10-2.

TABLE 10-2 Destination options based on viewer success (or failure) to perform certain actions.

Choose this option:	For this effect:	Also enter this information:
Continue	Continue playing the rest of the current slide and the rest of the movie.	None necessary
Go to previous slide	Display the previous slide, and then continue the movie from that point, even if all the actions for the current slide have not yet been performed.	None necessary
Go to next slide	Continue on to the next slide in the movie, even if all the actions for the current slide have not yet been performed.	None necessary
Go to last visited slide	Display the slide that was viewed immediately before the current one.	None necessary
Jump to slide	Display the specified slide and continue the movie from there.	Choose from the drop-down list of slides. Note that slide labels, if any, appear in the list instead of slide numbers. This makes it easy to find the slide you're looking for!
Open URL or file Open other movie	Display the specified URL or file in the viewer's default browser, or play another Flash movie. The viewer must have an active Internet connection to view URLs, and the specified file or movie must exist on the viewer's system. Note that the URL will not be visible on the finished movie.	Enter the URL or filename, or browse to the location of the file by clicking the button with three dots (. . .). For movies, you can also choose from a drop-down list. Click the black triangle button to choose the type of window in which the URL or file will display. Valid options are Current, New, Top, or Parent.
Send e-mail to	Create an e-mail message to a specified address in the viewer's default e-mail program. The viewer will still have to fill in the message and subject and hit Send.	Enter the e-mail address to which you want the e-mail sent. Click the check box to indicate whether or not the current movie should continue playing.

TABLE 10-2 Destination options based on viewer success (or failure) to perform certain actions (continued).

Choose this option:	For this effect:	Also enter this information:
Execute JavaScript	Run JavaScript commands.	Enter the JavaScript code you want to run.
Execute advanced action	Run a custom ActionScript that you've created through the Advanced Action feature.	Choose the name of the action.
Show	Display an element that had previously been hidden.	Choose the element on this slide that you want to display if the viewer successfully performs the required task. Similar to a success caption, this can be any element type. For example, you may want to show an additional button or display a different graphic.
Hide	Remove a displayed element from sight.	Choose the element on this slide that you want to hide if the viewer successfully performs the required task. This is particularly powerful when used in conjunction with the Show option (and Multiple Actions) to change the buttons available based on user interaction.
Enable	Activate a previously disabled element.	Specify the element you want to activate.
Disable	Cause an active element to become inactive. The element will still display, but none of the assigned interactivity will work.	Specify the element you want to inactivate.
Assign	Enter a value into a variable.	Choose from the list of variable names, and specify a value to assign to that variable.
Increment	Increase the value of a numeric variable.	Choose the variable from the drop-down list, then enter the number you want to add to the variable.

TABLE 10-2 Destination options based on viewer success (or failure) to perform certain actions (continued).

Choose this option:	For this effect:	Also enter this information:
Decrement	Decrease the value of a numeric variable.	Choose the variable from the drop-down list, then enter the number you want to subtract from the variable.
Multiple Actions	Choose this option to display a window that allows you to set more than one action for the current element. The available actions are the same as in the properties drop-down box.	Click the **More** button (. . .) to display the Set Multiple Actions window. Choose the actions you want and specify additional information as necessary, then click **OK** to return to the properties window.
No Action	Take no action, not even continue the movie.	None necessary

5. Select **Show correct message** if you want the slide to display a message when the viewer answers the question correctly. This option does not display if you chose a survey question type.

6. *If you chose a graded question type,* determine the number of incorrect answers the viewer can enter. By default, Captivate allows the viewer an unlimited (infinite) number of tries to get the correct answer. If you want to limit the number of attempts, click the **Infinite attempts** check box to deselect it, then specify the number of attempts you want to give to the viewer. If you leave Infinite attempts selected, the movie will pause until the viewer gets it right. If you specify a number of attempts, choose an option from the Action drop-down list to specify what you want the movie to display after the last unsuccessful attempt. Valid options are the same as for successful actions and are listed in Table 10-2.

7. *If you chose a graded question type,* specify the messages that you want to display (if any) when the viewer submits an incorrect answer. Click the check box to turn on or off the display the following possible messages:

   ■ *Show retry message:* Displays when the viewer enters an incorrect answer and has not yet reached the limit set in Step 6.

- *Show incomplete message:* Displays a message when the viewer does not enter any answer by the time limit set in the reporting options.
- *Show time out message:* Displays a message after a set length of time. Set the maximum time for each question in the properties window Reporting tab.

Note: The default text for these messages is stored in the Quiz Manager, or you can edit the message in the success caption on each slide.

8. *If you chose a survey question type,* you'll only have one Action drop-down list. Choose from this list to specify what you want the movie to display after the viewer enters and submits an answer. Valid options are the same as those for graded questions and are listed in Table 10-2.
9. *If you chose a graded question type,* click the check box to **Show correct message** when the viewer enters a correct answer.
10. You may set reporting options for this question as described later in this chapter.
11. Click **OK** when you are done to display the question slide with the options you've set.

Tracking Results with Reporting Options

To set an e-learning system to track the results of the viewer's actions, you'll need to first set the reporting options within Captivate. These options are the same for individual interactive elements on a standard slide and for question slides. To specify a destination and format for the results, use the Quiz Preferences.

To report results, follow these steps:

1. Open the element or question reporting window in one of the following ways:
    - If you're creating a new slide and have the element or question window open, click the **Reporting** tab.

- If you're editing an existing element, open the slide in Edit view, double-click the element on the slide, and then click the **Reporting** tab.
- If you're editing an existing element or question slide, open the slide in Edit view, click the **Edit question** button in the upper-left corner of the slide, then click the **Reporting** tab.

FIGURE 10-34   **Set the reporting options for interactive elements and question slides.**

2. *For interactive elements only,* choose whether or not you want the results of the viewer's actions included in the quiz by selecting (or deselecting) the **Include in Quiz** check box. This check box must be selected in order to store the viewer's answers and access the other options on the Reporting tab.

3. Click the **Report answers** check box to store the viewer's answers and add to the overall score for all questions and interactive elements that have this option checked. The answers will be handled as specified in the Quiz Manager. If you don't check this box, the viewer can still work through the questions or perform interactive tasks, but you will not get a record of them.

TIP

If you want to track the answers for a quiz without adding to the overall score, you can always set the points for a correct response to zero.

---

4. You can change either or both of the following additional items:

    ■ *Objective ID:* Enter the ID for the objective, if you have one. If you're exporting to a learning management system, use the ID set in that system. If you're just going to be reviewing answers without a coded system, you may want to change this item to a text ID. For example, for our sample movie, we may have objectives of Navigation, Message Board, and Books. You can use the same objective ID for more than one question or interactive element.

    ■ *Interaction ID:* This is the unique code that identifies this particular question or interactive element. If you're using a learning management system, enter the ID assigned by that system. If you're not using a learning management system, you can set whatever ID you want for each question. For example, you could use straight numeric coding (questions 1, 2, 3, etc.), or you could enter coding for category of question, type of question, or however you want to track items. You can use text or numbers in your Interaction ID. Note that the system will assign a subcode to questions that have multiple sections. For example, in a Likert question with an Interaction ID of 22934, each statement would be given an Interaction ID such as 22934_1, 22934_2, etc.

5. *For question slides only,* you can set a time limit in which the viewer must specify the answer. The time limit is in hours, minutes, and seconds, and defaults to 5 minutes (00:05:00). Remember that you need to allow enough time for the viewer to read and understand the question, then enter the answer or answers.

> **TIP**
>
> The timer ends when the viewer clicks the Submit button, and the movie goes on to the next thing specified by either the correct or incorrect answer. If you're using time limits, make them longer than you think the average viewer will need.

6.   Click **OK** when you are done to close the reporting window.

WORKING WITH QUESTION POOLS

If you want to randomize the questions in your movie—that is, specify that a random question should appear at specified points throughout the project—you can use the Question Pools function. This function allows you to create sets or pools of questions, and then instead of entering a question slide in the movie, you can enter a placeholder slide that will be replaced with one of the question slides from the specified pool. You can have multiple pools. For example, if your project has different sections, such as one on navigation and another on history, you would create two separate pools (one for navigation and one for history). This way, you could ensure that the questions that display in each section apply to that section. Similarly, you could have beginner, intermediate, and advanced level pools, then display questions from each at appropriate points in the movie.

There are three ways to add a question pool to your project:

- Create the pool and the questions in it from the Question Pools Manager.
- Create your question slides, then import them into a question pool.
- Import a question pool from a different Captivate project.

Creating a Pool of Questions

The first step in creating a pool of questions is to create the pool file. You do this through the Question Pools Manager.

1. From the **Quiz** menu, choose **Question Pools Manager**. The Manager window displays a lot of information about the questions in each pool and the pools in the project.

FIGURE 10-35   **Display the Question Pools Manager.**

2. To work with a pool, click on the line that contains the pool name. Note that Captivate starts you off with one empty pool file called "Pool1."

3. To rename a pool, double-click on the pool name, then type a new name. You can use up to 100 letters or numbers, but no special characters or spaces.

TIP

Use a name that identifies the type of questions you intend to store in the pool. Names like "AdvancedNavigation" or "HistoryQuestions" are more descriptive than "Pool1."

---

4. Click the **plus symbol** above the large white question area to display the list of available question types (such as true/false, multiple choice, and hot spot questions), then choose from the list of question types to create each question as described in the earlier sections of this chapter. As you add questions, the questions display in the Question Pools Manager. Different

symbols indicate the type of each question, and the question itself is displayed.

FIGURE 10-36   **The Question Pools Manager displays the questions in the pool.**

5. To remove a question from a pool, select the question and click the **minus symbol** above the question list.
6. Click the **Close** button to return to the main Captivate window.

Importing Questions into a Pool

Once you've created a pool, you can import questions to the pool in one of the following ways:

- Move existing question slides from the project into the pool.
- Copy questions from another pool in the project.

Move a Question Slide into a Pool

If your movie project already contains question slides, you can move those slides into a pool. Note that this will remove the questions from the original location in the movie. Follow these steps:

1. Display the question slide you want to import into a pool in the Edit view.

2. Right-click on the slide in either the filmstrip area or the main area of the Edit view, then choose **Move Question to Pool Navigation** to display a list of existing pool names.

FIGURE 10-37 Move a slide into a pool with the right-click menu.

3. Choose the name of the pool into which you want to move the question. The question is removed from the Edit view and stored in the specified pool. In Figure 10-38, the two available pools are called Navigation and History. You can access the slide for further editing through the Question Pools Manager.

Copy Questions from Another Pool

If you have several pools in your project already, you can copy or move questions from one pool to another. For example, you may want to include all the "Easy" questions in the more difficult pools. You can also copy a question slide (including all the graphics, fonts, links, elements, placements, etc.) and then just change the text to create new questions. Rather than recreate every question slide from scratch, you can create them once and then just copy them as needed. To do this, follow these steps:

1. From the **Quiz** menu, choose **Question Pools Manager**. The Manager window displays a lot of information about the questions in each pool and the pools in the project.

FIGURE 10-38   **Display the Question Pools Manager.**

2. Click on the name of the pool that contains the questions you want to copy or move to display the available questions in that pool.

3. Move the question to another pool in one of the following ways:

    ▪ Copy a slide by right-clicking on the question and choosing **Copy Question Slide** (or press Ctrl+C). Then open the destination pool, right-click, and choose **Paste Question Slide** (or press Ctrl+V).

    ▪ Drag the question from the list on the right side of the screen to the destination pool name on the left side of the screen. This will remove the question from the original pool (and from the displayed list of questions).

4. Click **Close** when you're done.

Importing an Entire Question Pool

If you have an existing question pool in one movie, you can copy the entire pool or specified questions from that pool into another movie. This can be useful if you want consistency across your movies, or if you have a core set of questions about your navigation or company that you want to include in all your output.

> **TIP**
>
> Be careful when importing question pools from one movie to another. If large questions are imported into a movie with a smaller size, the question slides may lose navigation buttons or other important elements.

To import a pool, follow these steps:

1. Open the project to which you want to copy the questions (the destination project.
2. From the **Quiz** menu, choose **Import Question Pools** to display a list of other Captivate projects.
3. Choose the project that contains the existing question pools and click **Open** to display the question selection screen.

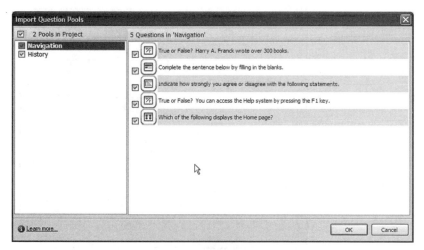

FIGURE 10-39   Import questions from one movie to another.

4. When you begin the import process, Captivate has all pools and all questions in each pool selected by default. Click on the pool name to display the questions in each pool. Click on the check box next to any question to deselect it if you don't want to import that question. Click on the check box next to the pool name to deselect an entire pool of questions.

5. Click **OK** when you've finished identifying the questions that you want to import. Captivate copies all of the selected pools and questions to the current project file.

Incorporating the Questions from Pools into Your Movie

Once you have defined the question pools, you still have to specify where the questions will display in your movie. Do this by inserting one or more random question slides. Captivate will insert one random question from the specified pool for each random question slide in the movie. The number of questions that actually appear in the movie is determined by the number of random question slides you include, not by the number of questions in the pool.

1. From the **Insert** menu, choose **Other Slide(s)** and then **Random Question Slide**.

FIGURE 10-40   **Create a random question slide.**

2. Enter a title in the Name box. This text will be displayed across the top of the slide when the movie is played. It won't be stored or tracked anywhere else.

3. You can enter a number in the Points box to indicate the value or weight of the question within the context of the quiz. Note that this may not apply if the randomly selected question is a survey-type question.

4. Choose a pool from the drop-down list.

5. Click **OK** to display the random question slide. Note that most of the elements for a random question slide are defined by the question slides in the specified pool. Therefore, this random question slide will not have timeline information or any elements other than placeholder information such as the name of the pool.

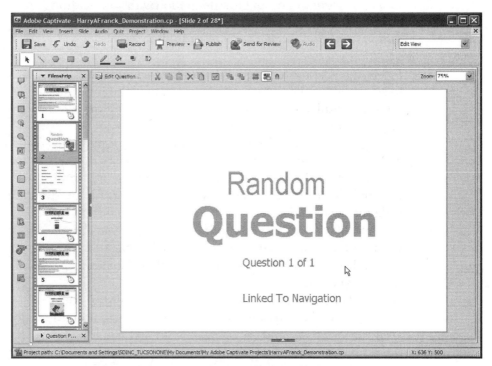

FIGURE 10-41   **The random question slide is a placeholder.**

6. If necessary, repeat Steps 1 through 5 to add more questions. The number of questions that actually appear in the movie is determined by the number

of random question slides you include, not by the number of questions in the pool. If, for example, you want to include a five-question quiz in your movie, you'll need to add five random question slides.

SETTING QUIZ PREFERENCES

As you create interactive elements and question slides, you specify which ones will be part of the quiz for the current movie. The Quiz Preferences apply to all questions in the quiz. For example, use the Preferences window to control the overall scoring of a quiz, specify what the viewer will see based on the overall score, and define the default text for question slides and quiz results. You can also define the format of output for integration with your learning management system or other software package.

There are several categories of Quiz Preferences:

- *Reporting:* Captivate lets you define the format that will be used to store the results of each question and how the individual question results will be compiled into an overall quiz score and/or passed to an external learning management system.
- *Settings:* This section lets you specify whether or not the viewer will be allowed to review the quiz answers, how to display progress, and whether or not to display a total score for the viewer. This section also contains the default text for question slide messages and captions.
- *Pass or Fail:* Just as you can define different actions based on whether the viewer passes or fails a specific question, you can also define what happens based on whether the viewer passes or fails the entire quiz.
- *Default Labels:* This section contains the default text for question slide buttons and the messages that appear on the slide after the viewer submits an answer. Note that you can change these for each slide; this section defines the default values only.
- *PENS (Package Exchange Notification Services):* If your movie contains e-learning components that you want to integrate with an external learning management system, you must set the PENS preferences to define the way the two systems will

communicate with each other. Note that these preferences define how you send the data; you define the format of the data in the Quiz Reporting area.

Setting Reporting Preferences

To define the way that the movie will store, display, and/or output overall quiz results, follow these steps:

1. From the **Edit** menu, select **Preferences**, or from the **Quiz** menu, select **Quiz Preferences** to display the reporting options window.

FIGURE 10-42   **Set the reporting preferences for the entire quiz.**

2. If you want to store the quiz results for each learner, click the **Enable reporting for this project** box. You must check this box in order to set the other output options.

3. Choose what you want the system to do with the results of your quizzes by choosing from the Learning Management System (LMS) options. See Table 10-3 for the available options.

TABLE 10-3 Quiz results output options.

Click this:	To store results in this format:	You'll also need to:
Standard: AICC	Aviation Industry CBT Committee approved format, commonly used by learning management systems	Import the published Captivate files into your AICC-compliant learning management system and specify a template.
Standard: SCORM	Sharable Content Object Reference Model format	Define the options for a manifest file (see Step 4), import the generated imsmanifest.xml file and the associated .swf file to your SCORM-compliant learning management system, and specify a template.
Adobe Acrobat Connect Pro	Published directly to a server running Adobe Acrobat Connect Professional	Import the project from the Adobe Connect library to an available Adobe Connect meeting.
Questionmark Perception	Compatible with Questionmark Perception	Import the published Captivate .swf file and the associated .qml file into your Questionmark Perception software.
E-mail	An e-mail containing the quiz results in comma-delimited format	Type a complete e-mail address into the text box and specify whether you want the results in the body of the e-mail or as an attachment. When you get the results by e-mail, you can copy and paste them into other programs, such as spreadsheet or database software packages.

4.   *For SCORM-compliant output only,* click the **Manifest** button to display the SCORM Manifest options window.

FIGURE 10-43   **Enter the manifest options for use with a SCORM-compliant learning management system.**

Complete the manifest file information as described in Table 10-4, and then click **OK** to close the Manifest options window.

TABLE 10-4 Manifest file options for SCORM-compliant output.

In this field:	Do this:
Version	Choose the version number from the drop-down menu.
Course Identifier	Type a unique identifier for the Captivate movie.
Course Title	Enter a title that the viewers will see when they're within the learning management system.
Course Description	Enter a description that the viewers will see for this movie from within the learning management system.
Course Version	Enter a number that indicates the version of this movie. By default, the version number is 1.0.

TABLE 10-4 Manifest file options for SCORM-compliant output (continued).

In this field:	Do this:
Course Duration	You can specify the approximate time it takes to complete the Captivate movie. Type in the estimated time in hours, minutes, and seconds (hh:mm:ss).
Course Subject	You can enter keywords that identify the movie by typing them into the Subject field.
SCO Identifier	Type the identifier that the learning management system will use to distinguish this movie from other Sharable Content Objects (SCO).
SCO Title	Enter a description that the viewers will see for this movie from within the learning management system.
SCO Mastery score	If desired, you can enter the minimum passing score by typing a number from 0 to 100, where 100 means the viewer must get every question correct in order to pass. Be sure this score matches the score you set in Pass or Fail. The Pass or Fail score is used to indicate a score to the learner, but this SCO Mastery score is used to communicate a score to the LMS.
SCO Time allowed	If you want, you can enter a time limit for the viewer to complete the entire quiz. If you enter a time limit, you must also enter a time-limit action (see below).
SCO Time limit action	If you entered a Time allowed value, choose from the list of possible actions to take if the viewer exceeds the time limit. Valid options include the following: ■ Exit with message (stop the movie and display a time limit exceeded message) ■ Exit without message (stop the movie) ■ Continue with message (continue the movie and display a time limit exceeded message) ■ Continue without message (continue the movie)
SCO Launch data	If the learning management system requires initialization data, enter it here.

5. In the Report Status area, choose **Complete/Incomplete** to tell the movie viewer when the quiz is complete but not whether they passed or failed. Choose **Pass/Fail** to let the viewer know the status.

6. In the Report to LMS as area, choose **Score** to send the number of questions right (as in 6 out of 10), or choose **Percent** to send the results as a percentage (for example, 75% correct).

7. From the Choose Report Data section, specify the information you want to store. See Table 10-5 for available options.

TABLE 10-5 Data output by quizzes.

Select:	To perform this data transfer:
Adobe Acrobat Connect Pro	Passes the quiz reporting data to the Connect Enterprise Server.
Quiz results only	Reports quiz results.
User access only	Reports each time a viewer opens at least one slide, but doesn't track the quiz answers.
Quiz results and slide views	Displays both the quiz results and the number of slides the viewer displayed.
Slide views only	Reports how many individual slides users viewed as a percentage. For example, if a viewer displays 8 out of 10 slides, a slide view of 80% is reported.

> **TIP**
>
> If you're working with a learning management system, check to make sure the system can import individual interactions before setting this option.

8. Set Reporting Level to specify **Report score** to send the number of questions right (as in 6 out of 10), or choose **Interactions and score** to send more detailed results.

9. Click the **LMS Customization Settings** button to define advanced LMS options for Resume Data and Escape Version and Session ID. See your LMS documentation for appropriate escape characters for your system. Click **OK** when you are done with the customization settings.

FIGURE 10-44   Set LMS customization settings.

10.   Click **OK** when you are done to close the reporting options window.

Defining Overall Quiz Settings

If you chose to display the score after the viewer completes the quiz, Captivate will create a special slide that displays the results. To specify quiz settings, follow these steps:

1.   From the **Edit** menu, select **Preferences**, or from the **Quiz** menu, select **Quiz Preferences** to display the reporting options window.
2.   Select **Settings** to display the quiz settings options.

FIGURE 10-45   Define quiz settings.

3.   Type a unique name for the quiz.

4.   From the Required drop-down list, choose whether or not you want to allow the viewers to skip the quiz.

5.   Enter the Objective ID from your learning management system if you have one.

6.   (optional) Each user action is automatically assigned a unique ID. You can customize this ID by adding a prefix. Enter the prefix you want to use in the **Interaction ID prefix** field.

7.   Click the check box next to each of the options in the Settings area to select it. (See Table 10-6.)

TABLE 10-6 Quiz navigation and display settings.

When you choose this:	This happens:
Shuffle Answers	Displays answers in random order.
Show progress	Select this option to display the number of the current slide.
Allow backward movement	Displays the Back button and lets viewers see slides that contain questions they've already answered.
Show score at end of quiz	Select this option to display a summary slide at the end of the quiz. See the following section in this chapter for more detail on defining this summary slide.
Allow user to review quiz	Allows viewers to go back to see how they did on each question after they've completed the quiz. Their answer and the correct answer for each question displays in the review area for each slide while the viewer is reviewing the quiz.

8.   If you chose to let the viewers go back and review the quiz after they've completed it, you can click the **Question Review Messages** button below the review check box to display the default review messages. You can edit the text or type new text in any of the message boxes.

FIGURE 10-46   **Change the default review feedback messages.**

9.   Click **OK** when you are done to close the Question Review Messages window.

10.   Click the **Quiz Result Messages** button to display or edit the default messages.

FIGURE 10-47   **Change the result slide messages.**

11. Click the check box next to each feedback message that you want to display. Note that the summary/review slide is generated by the Flash movie and does not appear in your Captivate Storyboard view. Available feedback message options are listed in Table 10-7.

TABLE 10-7 Feedback message options.

This message:	Displays when:
Pass message	The viewer answers the question correctly. This is also called a "success message."
Fail message	The viewer answers the question incorrectly. This is also called a "failure message."
Display score	Check this box to display the number of points on the summary slide.
Display maximum possible score	Displays the score for 100% correct answers.
Display number of correct questions	Displays the number of questions the viewer answered correctly.
Display total number of questions	Displays the total number of questions displayed. Note that if the quiz includes branching, this number may vary for each movie.
Display accuracy	Displays the percentage of correct answers.
Display number of quiz attempts	Indicates how many times the viewer has taken the quiz.

12. When you finish, click **OK** to close the Quiz Result Messages window.
13. Click **OK** to close the quiz settings window.

Defining the Pass/Fail Options

To specify the actions that occur when a viewer passes (or fails) a quiz, follow these steps:

1. From the **Edit** menu, select **Preferences**, or from the **Quiz** menu, select **Quiz Preferences** to display the reporting options window.
2. Select **Pass or Fail** to display the available options.

FIGURE 10-48   **Change the default review feedback messages.**

3. Specify the lowest percentage that will be considered a passing score OR specify the total number of points that constitute a passing score.

4. Specify what you want the movie to display when the viewer passes the quiz by choosing from the If passing grade Action drop-down list. Valid options are given in Table 10-8.

TABLE 10-8 Action options for passed (or failed) quizzes.

Choose this option:	For this effect:	Also enter this information:
Continue	Continue playing the rest of the current slide and the rest of the movie.	None necessary
Go to previous slide	Display the previous slide, and then continue the movie from that point, even if all the actions for the current slide have not yet been performed.	None necessary
Go to next slide	Continue on to the next slide in the movie, even if all the actions for the current slide have not yet been performed.	None necessary

TABLE 10-8 Action options for passed (or failed) quizzes (continued).

Choose this option:	For this effect:	Also enter this information:
Jump to slide	Display the specified slide and continue the movie from there.	Choose from the drop-down list of slides. Note that slide labels, if any, appear in the list instead of slide numbers. This makes it easy to find the slide you're looking for!
Open URL or file Open other movie	Display the specified URL or file in the viewer's default browser, or play another Flash movie. The viewer must have an active Internet connection to view URLs, and the specified file or movie must exist on the viewer's system. Note that the URL will not be visible on the finished movie.	Enter the URL or filename, or browse to the location of the file by clicking the button with three dots (. . .). For movies, you can also choose from a drop-down list. Click the black triangle button to choose the type of window in which the URL or file will display. Valid options are Current, New, Top, or Parent.
Send e-mail to	Create an e-mail message to a specified address in the viewer's default e-mail program. The viewer will still have to click Send.	Enter the e-mail address to which you want the e-mail sent. Click the check box to indicate whether or not the current movie should continue playing.
Execute JavaScript	Run JavaScript commands.	Enter the JavaScript code you want to run.
No Action	Take no action, not even continue the movie.	None necessary

5. Enter the number of times the viewer can attempt to take a quiz. By default, Captivate allows the viewer an unlimited (infinite) number of tries. If you want to limit the number of attempts, deselect the **Infinite attempts** check box, and then specify the number. If you leave Infinite attempts selected, the movie will pause until the viewer gets it right. If you specified a number of attempts, choose an option from the Action drop-down list to specify what

you want the movie to do after the last unsuccessful attempt. Valid options are the same as for successful actions and are listed in Table 10-8.

6.   When you finish, click **OK** to close the quiz properties window.

Defining the Default Buttons and Messages

To specify the default messages and the button text that display on question slides, follow these steps:

1.   From the **Edit** menu, select **Preferences**, or from the **Quiz** menu, select **Quiz Preferences** to display the reporting options window.

2.   Select **Default Labels** to display the default message options.

FIGURE 10-49   **Set the default button text and feedback messages.**

3.   If you have the movie review buttons displayed, Captivate automatically uses the text in these default button fields. You can type new text for the buttons if you like.

> **TIP**
>
> It's best not to get too creative with button names. You want to ensure that the viewers understand the intent of the buttons right away.

4. The default question feedback lists the text that displays for each type of feedback. You can edit the text in individual slides, or you can edit the text for each message here; all subsequent messages of that type will use your new text. Available feedback message types are listed in Table 10-9.

TABLE 10-9 Feedback message options.

This message:	Displays when:
Correct message	The viewer answers the question correctly. This is also called a "success message."
Incorrect message	The viewer answers the question incorrectly. This is also called a "failure message."
Retry message	The viewer answers the question incorrectly, but there are remaining attempts available.
Incomplete message	The viewer does not answer the question at all or does not answer all portions of the question.
Timeout message	The viewer does not answer the question in the allotted amount of time.

5. When you finish, click **OK** to close the default options window.

Defining PENS Options

If your movie contains e-learning components that you want to integrate with an external learning management system, you must set the PENS (Package Exchange Notification Services) preferences to define the way the two systems will communicate with each other. Note that these preferences define how you send the data; you must define the format of the data in the reporting options window.

To define the way that the movie will send PENS data, follow these steps:

1. From the **Edit** menu, select **Preferences**, or from the **Quiz** menu, select **Quiz Preferences** to display the reporting options window.

2.   Select **PENS** to display the PENS options.

FIGURE 10-50   **Set the PENS options.**

3.   Set the desired options. (See Table 10-10.)

TABLE 10-10 PENS options.

In this field	Enter this information
Package (information about the data that you're sending)	
Source URL	The location where the learning content package is stored.
User ID and Password	User ID and password for the current system (if any).
URL Expiry	Expiration date and time for the learning content package. Default date and time is 24 hours from the time that you set PENS data.
LMS (information about the receiver)	
Target URL	Location of the publishing/management server.
User ID and Password	User ID and password required by the publishing/management server.
Send using	The method (HTTP-GET or HTTP- POST) that the LMS uses to transmit the package.

TABLE 10-10 PENS options (continued).

In this field	Enter this information
Command	Select one of the following commands: ■ **Collect:** Uploads a new project to the LMS. ■ **Delete:** Deletes a project from the LMS. ■ **Revise:** Updates the existing project in the LMS with the new version. **Note:** The PENS protocol currently supports only the Collect command.
Receipt Email	Choose E-mail or URL. If you choose E-Mail, you must also specify an e-mail address that will receive notification after the source package is uploaded to the LMS. If you choose URL, you must specify the location of a Web page that will display when the package has been sent successfully.
Receive alerts while LMS is processing the package	Select this option if you want to be informed of any alerts when the package is being uploaded to the LMS. The alert is sent to you using the option you have set in the Receipt Email field.
Preview	Click this button to see a summary of the PENS information.

4. When you finish, click **OK** to close the PENS options window.

EDITING QUESTION SLIDES

Captivate question slides are like other types of slides in that they have a background and a variety of elements placed on top of the background. You can add elements such as text captions or images, and you can move any of these elements around as needed. You can also change the font, reenter text, or align the elements with other objects on the slide as described in Chapter 7.

The true power of question slides, though, is that you don't have to create all the elements individually. When you create a question slide, Captivate automatically creates text elements, boxes, captions, and a variety of other elements required for each question slide format. For example, a matching slide automatically includes text captions that are designated as a slide title, a question, and titles for each column. This type of slide can include success and failure captions like other interactive elements, plus additional types of captions (incomplete and timeout). There are predefined buttons that allow the viewer to work through a question slide, and there is a special category of captions that are only displayed after the viewer has completed a quiz.

Although you can edit each element individually, it's easier and more efficient to use the Edit Question button that is displayed in the upper-left corner of each question slide. This button displays the same windows that you used to create the question slide (described in the earlier sections of this chapter) and allows you to access most of the element properties. However, if you want to change the placement of a question slide element or the font or size of the text that displays in captions or messages, do this from the Captivate Edit view.

Setting Font Properties on Question Slides

1. In Edit view, select the slide you want to edit.
2. Double-click on the message that you want to change. Figure 10-51 shows the Success Caption window that contains the default text and default settings for caption type and font and other properties.

FIGURE 10-51   Edit font or size or style in the caption window.

3. Type the text you want to display in the text caption area. Remember that you can include system or user-defined variables by clicking the Variable icon.

4. The changes you make to the properties will be applied to all subsequent messages of that type. If you want to apply these changes to all messages that are already in the movie, click **Apply to all** to apply the current settings as defined in the properties settings window. To view or change the properties settings, click the **Settings** button.

FIGURE 10-52   **Apply settings to previously created captions.**

5. If necessary, you can change the look of the text by editing the properties listed in Table 10-11.

TABLE 10-11 Text caption properties.

To change this:	Do this:
Caption type	Choose a caption type from the list. The caption type defines the shape and color of the outline that will be placed around the text, as well as the default text color (although you can change this). The icons below this field display the look of each caption type.
Font	Choose a font for the text from the list. The list of fonts will be determined by the fonts available on your system.
Size	Choose a size for the text from the list.
Color	Click the down arrow next to the color icon (large letter A) to choose a new color for the text. The text color does not change the color of the caption type outline.
Caption style	Many of the caption types include outlines that point in different directions. In Figure 10-51, the "adobe green" type has options that point in four different directions as well as an option with no direction. Click any one of the type icons to select it for the current text caption.
Text style	If desired, set additional display options such as bold, italic, or underlined text, and text justification.

Note: Selecting the Apply to all check box applies the caption style, font type, font size, font color, and transition properties to all messages in the movie. It does not change the wording of the text for messages of this type.

6.   Click **OK** to close the properties window.

Defining the Review Area

Another type of element generated by question slides is the review area. This is a type of highlight box that indicates where on the slide the results of each question will be displayed when the viewer reviews the answers after completing all of the questions in the movie.

The review area displays on the slide as a shaded box so that you can adjust its placement if necessary but does not appear on the slide. Only the review statements display in the final movie, and they will only appear when the viewer goes back to review the results of a completed quiz.

To move the review area, simply click and drag the shaded box to a new location.

To edit the content of the text that introduces the answers for the current slide, double-click in the review area to display the Review Area window. Note that changes you make here apply only to the current slide.

FIGURE 10-53   **The Review Area window.**

SUMMARY

This chapter reviewed the components that make up the Captivate e-learning functions. You learned about questions and quizzes and the reporting capabilities of Captivate. The following chapter describes how to work with the Branching view.

11

WORKING WITH THE BRANCHING VIEW

Branching (sometimes called "contingency branching") allows you to display different slides based on the way each viewer responds to interactive or question slides. For example, you could set up a question slide that indicates whether the viewer is a beginner, intermediate, or expert at the movie topic, then you can display the appropriate lessons for each level. Or you might set different slide sets (branches) for different job descriptions, different regions, or whatever category makes sense for your movie.

DISPLAYING BRANCHES

When you added interactivity (see Chapter 9) or created question slides (see Chapter 10), you had the option to specify an action based on how the viewer interacted with the slide elements or answered the questions. If you chose Jump to and specified any slide other than the next one, you created a branch within your movie.

For example, if you have inserted a click box on slide number 4, you can set the movie to skip ahead to slide number 12 if the viewer clicks in the box. If the viewer does not click in the box, the movie will continue with slide number 5.

FIGURE 11-1   **Branching based on a click box.**

The Adobe® Captivate® program can display the branches and links between slides in the Branching view. To display the Branching view, choose **Branching View** from the drop-down menu in the upper-right corner of the Captivate window. For example, the simple branch shown in Figure 11-1 would display as shown in Figure 11-2.

FIGURE 11-2 **A true and false question slide creates two branches.**

Note that there are now two lines coming from slide 4 (the slide with the click box). The green line points to the slide that is displayed when the box is clicked. The shorter red line points to the slide that is displayed if the box is not clicked.

A slide that doesn't use correct and incorrect designations (such as a slide with a series of buttons on it) displays branch lines in black (for "Jump to slide" settings) or blue (for "Next slide" settings).

FIGURE 11-3   **Multiple branches show slide navigation options.**

In Figure 11-3, slide 4 has three buttons that each begin a new path (starting with slides 5, 9, and 20). Slide 23 shows several possible navigation paths. There is a button that links to an outside URL (the square icon under slide 23). There is also an interactive element that, if performed correctly, returns the viewer to slide 1, or, if done incorrectly, displays slide 24.

The left panel of the branching display shows three additional sets of information:

- The Properties area displays the navigation panels for the selected slide or link. At the page level, this is the same as the properties that display while editing a slide or element. At the link level, the Properties area shows the object (button, click box, etc.) properties.

- Overview shows a miniaturized representation of the entire movie, with a square around the slides that are currently displayed.
- The Legend area displays a reminder of meanings of the colors and icons on the Branching view.

CHANGING BRANCHING DISPLAY

If you have a lot of slides in your movie, you probably won't be able to see them all at once on the branching display. There are several options for displaying slides in the Branching view:

- Use the Overview panel to display different areas of the movie.
- Zoom in or out to display the slides larger or smaller, to the left or to the right, or up or down, depending on the size and complexity of your movie.
- Group the slides and then view the groups at the same size as one individual slide.
- Click **Browse Into** to hide all slides before the specified slide.

Overview

The Overview shows a miniaturized representation of the entire movie, with a square around the slides that are currently displayed. A quick way to change the display is to click on the square in the Overview panel and slide it to a new position in the movie.

Zooming

You can view other parts of your movie using the scroll bars across the bottom and side of your window, or you can use the zoom buttons on the menu above the branching display. There are four zoom buttons, identified by small magnifying glass icons:

- *Zoom In (+):* Click (or click and hold) this icon to make the displayed slides appear larger. The larger your slides, the fewer that will fit on the current display area.

- *Zoom Out (-):* Click (or click and hold) this icon to make the displayed slides appear smaller. The smaller your slides, the more that will fit on the current display area.
- *Zoom Left (←):* Click (or click and hold) this icon to display the earlier slides in the movie. Note that this particular Zoom icon does not change the size of the displayed slides.
- *Zoom Right (→):* Click (or click and hold) this icon to display the later slides in the movie. Note that this particular Zoom icon does not change the size of the displayed slides.

Captivate also offers a zoom slider that allows you to set the Branching view from 25% (very small) to 400% (huge) of the original size. You can either slide the rectangular control in the center of the slider or type (or select) a percentage in the Zoom percentage box on the upper-right side of the window.

Grouping

If your movie has a lot of slides, you can create slide groups to make them easier to manage. A slide group can display as either collapsed (taking up the space of a single slide) or expanded (each slide in the group taking up a full slide space).

> **Note:** Grouping slides is a tool for managing within Captivate. Group functions do not carry over to the finished movie.
>
> You can perform functions on a slide group just as you do on a single slide (such as moving, deleting, or hiding). In addition, you can assign a border color to all slides in a group for easy identification.

Creating a Slide Group

To create a slide group, follow these steps:

1. Select the slides that you want to group, either by using the mouse to draw a box around the selected slides, or by clicking one slide and then holding down the Shift key to select additional slides.

> **Note:** Slides must be concurrent in order to group them. For example, you can group slides 8, 9, 10, and 11, but you cannot make a group of just slides 8, 10, and 12.

2. Once the slides are selected, you can create a group in any of the following ways:

-   Click the **Create Group** (a square with a dotted outline) icon at the top of the Branching View window.
-   Right-click, choose **Slide Group**, and then choose **Create**.
-   From the **Slide** menu, choose **Group**, and then choose **Create**.
-   Hold down **Ctrl** and **Alt**, then type the letter **G**.

3. The selected slides are grouped into a single group slide with their numbers and descriptions displayed on it.

FIGURE 11-4   Grouped slides collapse into a smaller space than individual slides.

4. To rename the group to something meaningful, open the properties window in one of the following ways:

- Click the **Edit Group** icon (a square with a pen symbol on it) at the top of the Branching View window.
- Double-click on the icon of the new group.
- Right-click, choose **Slide Group**, and then choose **Edit**.
- From the **Slide** menu, choose **Group**, and then choose **Edit**.
- Hold down **Ctrl** and **Alt**, then type the letter **E**.

FIGURE 11-5   Slide group properties window.

5. From the Color menu, select a color. This color will be displayed on the border of all the slides in the group when the group is expanded. It will NOT appear in the finished movie.
6. In the Title box, type a name for the group. The name will be displayed on the Branching view at the top of the grouped slides, and at the bottom of the collapsed group in the Edit and Storyboard views.
7. Click **OK** to close the properties window.

Expanding or Collapsing a Slide Group

Once you've created the groups, the group icon will be displayed instead of the individual slides in all three views (Storyboard, Edit, and Branching). To see the individual slides instead of the group icon, do any one of the following:

- Select the group you want to expand, then click the **Expand** icon (an image of a slide with a plus sign) at the top of the Branching View window.
- Click the **Expand All** icon (an image of a slide with a plus sign and an arrow) at the top of the Branching View window to expand all groups.

- Hover the mouse over the slide group icon to display small images of each slide in the group.
- Click the small triangular button beneath the group icon (and above the list of slide names).
- Right-click on the group icon, choose **Slide Group**, and then choose **Expand** or **Expand All**.
- From the **Slide** menu, choose **Group**, and then choose **Expand** or **Expand All**.

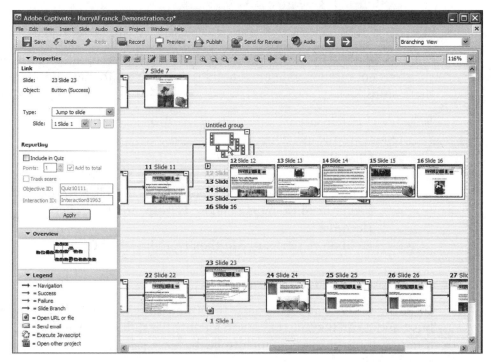

FIGURE 11-6   **Display slides in a group with the mouse.**

As you can see, there are many ways to expand a group. You can collapse an expanded group into the single group icon in similar ways:

- Select any slide in the group you want to collapse, then click the **Collapse** (an image of a slide with a minus sign) icon at the top of the Branching View window.

- Click the **Collapse All** icon (an image of a slide with a minus sign and an arrow) at the top of the Branching View window to expand all groups.
- Click the small triangular button beneath the first slide in the group.
- Right-click on any slide in the group, choose **Slide Group**, and then choose **Collapse** or **Collapse All**.
- From the **Slide** menu, choose **Group**, and then choose **Collapse** or **Collapse All**.

Ungrouping Slides

You can take slides out of a group by removing the group element. Note that this does not remove or delete the slides themselves! To ungroup slides, follow these steps:

1. Select a slide group.
2. Do one of the following:
   - Click the **Remove Slide Group** icon (a square with a minus sign) at the top of the Branching View window.
   - Right-click, choose **Slide Group**, and then click **Remove**.
   - From the **Slide** menu, choose **Group**, and then click **Remove**.
   - Hold down **Ctrl** and **Alt**, then type the letter **P**.

Hiding and Displaying Slides

In particularly complex layouts, the Branching View window can get very busy, and it can become difficult to identify the slides you want to see. You can temporarily clear space on the display by hiding slides either before or after a specified slide.

To Hide or Display Slides before a Specified Slide

The **Browse Into** option collapses all slides before the slide into which you're browsing. The slides aren't removed from the movie, just temporarily hidden when you work on other slides.

1. From the Branching view, select a slide.

2. Click the **Browse Into** icon (right arrow) in the Branching view toolbar, or right-click and then choose **Branch Into**. All slides that precede the selected slide will be hidden.

3. To redisplay the hidden slides, click the **Browse Back** icon (left arrow) or right-click on the first displayed slide and choose **Browse Back**.

To Hide or Display Slides after a Specified Slide

Each slide icon has either a plus sign (+) or a minus sign (−) in the upper-right corner. When the minus sign is displayed, all slides subsequent to that slide are also displayed. If you see a plus sign, that indicates that the subsequent slides are temporarily hidden. To hide or redisplay slides, follow these steps:

1. From the Branching view, select a slide. In the following example, slide 9 is selected.

FIGURE 11-7   The selected slide gets an orange outline.

2. Click the minus sign on the selected slide, or right-click the selected slide and choose **Collapse Slide Path**.

FIGURE 11-8 The small "plus" sign on slide 9 indicates that there are hidden slides.

3. To redisplay the hidden slides, click the plus sign on the selected slide or right-click the slide and choose **Expand Slide Path**.

EDITING NAVIGATION IN THE BRANCHING VIEW

In addition to changing the way the Branching view displays your slides, you can also make changes to the navigation right in the Branching view, either to an entire slide's navigation or to the properties for specific links within the slide.

To change properties for a slide, simply click the slide to display the current properties. For example, slide number 3 in Figure 11-9 simply goes to the next slide.

FIGURE 11-9   **Slide 3 navigates to the next slide.**

If you look at slide number 4 in Figure 11-9, you'll see that there are three possible navigation paths (to slide 5, 9, or 20). To view the navigation properties for any one of these paths, click on the path itself (not on the slide).

FIGURE 11-10   Display the navigation for a button in slide 4.

In Figure 11-10, the line that represents a specific button on slide 4 has been selected (on your screen, it would appear orange). The properties for that button display in the properties panel of the Branching view. You can change the navigation if you need to (see Chapter 9), or you can change the reporting functions (see Chapter 10). For example, if the button is strictly a navigation device, you may not want to include it in a quiz.

EXPORTING THE BRANCHING VIEW

The Branching view is a handy graphic representation of your entire movie. You can export the Branching view to a .bmp or .jpg file. The exported image will include only those slides currently displayed in your Branching view. This can be helpful, for example, if you want to ensure that reviewers or testers check all possible paths. If you have collapsed groups or other types of hidden slides, they will not be on the resulting image file. To export the displayed Branching view, follow these steps:

1. Ensure that the Branching view displays the slides you want in the exported image.
2. Choose one of the Export functions in any of the following ways:
   - Click the **Export Branching View** icon (a square with a curved arrow).
   - Right-click anywhere on the Branching view, then select **Export Branching View**.
   - From the **File** menu, select **Export** and then **Branching View**.

   The Save As window is displayed.
3. Type a name for the file in the File Name box.
4. Select either **JPEG** or **Bitmaps** from the File Type drop-down box. If you don't specify a type, the system will default to JPG format.
5. Click **Save**.

SUMMARY

This chapter described how to work with the Branching view, including grouping slides and changing the Branching view display. The next chapter will discuss how to use some of the software tools that come with Captivate.

Chapter 12 USING ADOBE® CAPTIVATE® TOOLS

Adobe® Captivate® software comes with a variety of useful tools that help you do better work and create better, more useful movies.

- *Spell Checker:* The spell checker in Captivate works just like spell checkers in other software packages. You can choose from a list of languages, or you can change the dictionary that the spell checker uses.
- *Slide Notes:* Add notes for your own use to any slide. You'll be able to see the notes from a variety of places within Captivate, but they won't be visible to the viewer once the movie is published. You can use these notes as references when editing or reviewing your movies, or as a guide when you're narrating. You can even print the notes.
- *Templates:* Once you've got a movie with all the settings you like, you can save it as a template. Then, when you start a new movie, use the template to ensure consistency across projects. You'll also save time because you won't have to reset all the movie parameters.
- *Sizing tools:* Anytime you're delivering electronic information, you need to be aware of your file size and the size of the images on the screen. Captivate has a couple of functions that help you manage your movie size.
- *TOC:* Table of Contents tool, described in Chapter 13.
- *Aggregator:* This tool allows you to create movies from multiple source files into one seamless output.
- *Reviewer:* Captivate Reviewer lets your reviewers comment directly on your movies as they're playing.

- *User Assistance:* Of course, Captivate comes with online documentation that you can access either as PDF files or online Help, including context-sensitive Help. In addition, there are a number of other resources that can answer your questions and help to solve problems you may encounter.

USING THE CAPTIVATE SPELL CHECKER

Captivate can check the spelling of most of the text in your movie. It does this by comparing the text you entered to valid words in the Captivate dictionary. To use the spell checker, follow these steps:

1. Do any one of the following to start the spell checker:
    - From the Edit view or Storyboard view **Project** menu, choose **Check spelling**.
    - From anywhere within Captivate, press the **F7** key.
2. If you want to specify a dictionary other than the United States English one, choose from the list of dictionaries on your system in the Main Dictionary language list. All of the dictionaries available on your system are displayed in the list.

FIGURE 12-1   Captivate finds misspellings.

3. If no spelling mistakes are found, a message is displayed, and you are done! If Captivate finds a word that isn't in the dictionary, the Check spelling window displays the suspect word and several words around it.

4. The misspelled word appears in the Not in dictionary box, and the sentence in which the word was found is displayed near the bottom of the window. If the spell checker identified a correctly spelled word as not being in the dictionary (common for proper names and technical words), follow the instructions in Table 12-1.

TABLE 12-1 Leave correctly spelled words alone.

Click this button:	To do this:
Ignore once	Leave the word as it is, this time only.
Ignore all	Leave the word as it is for this sentence and for every other instance of the word in this movie.
Add to Dictionary	Leave the word as it is, and add the word to the dictionary so that it will be recognized when you spell check other movies.

5. If the word is incorrect, click on the correct form of the word in the Suggestions box (or type the correct word in the Not in dictionary box) and then follow the instructions in Table 12-2.

TABLE 12-2 Fix misspellings.

Click this button:	To do this:
Delete	Delete the word from the movie.
Change	Insert the correction into this sentence in the movie.
Change all	Insert the correction into all places that use the misspelled word throughout the movie.

6. As you click to correct or ignore each word, Captivate automatically continues the check. If you want to stop the spell checker at any time, click the **Close** button.

7. When the check is complete, a message displays. Click **OK** to close the message window.

Setting Spell-Check Options

Captivate makes a few assumptions about the way you want to check your spelling. For example, words are checked against an English language (as spoken in the United States) dictionary, and words in all capital letters are ignored. To change any of these settings, follow these steps:

1. Do any one of the following to display the Spelling options window:

    ▪ If you have the spell-checker window open, click **Options**.
    ▪ From anywhere within Captivate, from the **Edit** menu, choose **Preferences**, display the General Settings tab (under Global) and then click the **Spelling Preferences** button.

FIGURE 12-2   **Set spell-checker preferences.**

2. Select the options you want to use the next time you run the spell checker.

TABLE 12-3 Spell-check options.

Select this:	To cause the spell checker to do this:
Ignore capitalized words	Skip over all words that start with an uppercase letter such as "Captivate."
Ignore all-caps words	Skip over all words that are all uppercase letters, such as acronyms.
Ignore words containing numbers	Skip over all words that contain numeric digits, such as phone numbers or zip codes.
Ignore mixed case words	Skip over all words that have a combination of uppercase and lowercase letters in positions other than the first letter. For example, select this to cause the spell checker to ignore words such as "JavaScript" or "RoboHelp."
Ignore domain names	Skip over all words that may be Internet domain names (or URLs) such as "www.harryafranck.com."
Report doubled words	Display instances where the same word appears twice in a row such as "the the."
Case sensitive	Consider the capitalization when determining if a word matches an entry in the dictionary. If the word in the dictionary is capitalized (as in proper nouns), then the word in your movie must be capitalized or it will be considered a misspelling.
Phonetic suggestions	List words in the Suggestions box that sound like the misspelled word.
Typographical suggestions	List words in the Suggestions box that use similar letters to the misspelled word.
Suggest split words	List word pairs in the Suggestions box for misspelled words that appear to be missing a space between two words, such as "twowords."

3.   When you finish, click **OK**.

WORKING WITH SLIDE NOTES

A note in Captivate is an organizational tool that you can see while you're working with the Captivate project, but that doesn't display in the finished movie. When you add notes to a slide, you can view the notes while editing the slide or while recording audio for the slide. For example, you can type the voice-over script into the notes area and then you can read it while recording the audio for that slide. Notes can also store information about the origins of imported objects or comments about what you plan to add to a slide. You can also print the notes as part of handouts if you wanted.

There are three ways to add notes to a slide:

- Use the Slide Properties window.
- Use the Slide Notes display in Edit view.
- Use the Slide Notes portion of the Record Audio window

Adding Notes with the Slide Properties Window

To add notes to a slide or to view existing notes, follow these steps:

1. Do one of the following to display the Slide Properties window:
   - From Edit view, double-click on the slide background.
   - From Storyboard view or the filmstrip in Edit view, right-click on a slide and choose **Properties**.
   - In either view, from the **Slide** menu, choose **Properties**.

FIGURE 12-3   **Enter notes from the Slide Properties window.**

2.   On the Slide Properties window, click the **Notes** button to display the Slide notes window.

FIGURE 12-4   **Type notes into the Slide notes window.**

3.   Type the notes you want to add to the slide. This is a free-form text box; you can type anything you want into it, and you can make the notes as detailed as you need them to be.

4.   Click **OK** to store the notes and close the Slide notes window.

> TIP
>
> You'll know when there are notes associated with a slide because the Notes button on the Slide Properties window will display as bold.

5.   Click **OK** to close the Slide Properties window.

Adding Slide Notes in Edit View

The Slide notes area of the Edit view displays the content of the note, and also indicates what the note will be used for. You can use slide notes in three ways:

- Simply store information (either as a script for your own audio later or as memos about the slide).
- Convert the typed notes to audio with the text-to-speech feature. This feature reads the entered notes in the voice that you choose, then plays that audio when the slide displays.
- Create closed captions that display the text of the note on the slide while the audio version of the note is playing.

To add slide notes in the Edit view, follow these steps:

1.   From the **Window** menu in Edit view, select **Slide Notes** to display the notes for any slide at the bottom of the screen. If the Slide Notes option is already selected, but you can't see the notes area, simply click the arrow icon at the bottom of the Edit view screen. You can resize the notes if needed by clicking and dragging the top edge of the notes display up or down.

Note: If you make the slide notes too big, you won't see much of the slide itself.

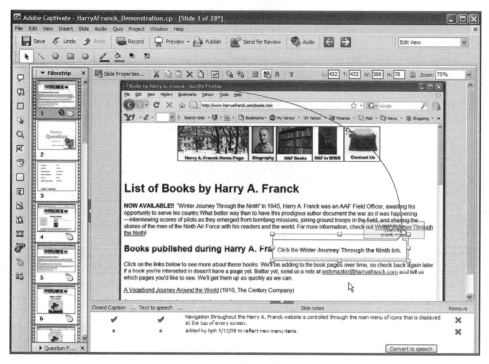

FIGURE 12-5 Slide notes in Edit view.

2.   Click on a line in the notes area and type the text you want to add. This
     may be text that you want to use later in the movie, or it may simply be
     comments that you want to store with the slide. For example, the first
     note in Figure 12-5 describes how to navigate the movie. This note, as
     you can see from the two green check marks, will be converted to speech
     and displayed in the final movie as a closed caption when the audio of the
     note is playing. The second note is a memo about the last change made to
     the slide. This note will not appear (or be read) in the finished movie.

3.   You can create multiple notes by clicking on the line below the last entered
     note, then typing more text.

4.   For each note for which you want to create an audio file, click in the **Text
     to speech** column to insert a check mark. Only notes with a check in this
     column will be converted.

5. Click the **Convert to speech** button to display the Speech Setting window.

FIGURE 12-6 **Choose a voice.**

> **TIP**
>
> If you haven't yet installed the text-to-speech feature, you'll see a Download Voice button. Click this button and follow the instructions on the screen to install this feature. If you're using the trial version, you'll need to return to the Adobe.com site to download the NeoSpeech Text-to-Speech voice databases.

6. Choose a voice from the drop-down box and then click **OK**. Note that you can click the **Do not show me again** box to use the specified voice for all subsequent note conversions. Once you've chosen a voice, the conversion process begins, and the progress window displays the filename and other information about the audio. All notes on this slide that have the Text to speech column selected will be stored in one audio file.

FIGURE 12-7 **Converting notes to audio.**

7.   When complete, Captivate stores the audio to the specified filename and inserts it as audio for the slide. You can view or edit this file as described in Chapter 8.

8.   If necessary, you can delete any notes in the Edit view by clicking the **X** next to the note.

TIP

While it is important to consider accessibility in your movies, don't go overboard—you only need one visual and one audio of each element. For example, if you have a text caption with an audio file that reads the caption, you don't need to include a closed-caption version of that audio (even though Captivate would allow you to create one).

Adding Slide Notes While Recording Audio

When you're recording audio (see Chapter 8), the Record Audio window allows you to display slide notes or add new ones. To access slide notes while recording, follow these steps:

1.   From the **Audio** menu, choose **Record** to display the Record Audio window.

2.   Click the **Slide Notes** tab at the bottom of the window. Notes that were added elsewhere will appear in the text box.

FIGURE 12-8 **Slide notes in the Record Audio window.**

3. You can type new text or edit existing text, if any.
4. Click **OK** to save the text to the Slide Notes tab.

TIP

While it is important to consider accessibility in your movies, don't go overboard—you only need one visual and one audio of each element. For example, if you have a text caption with an audio file that reads the caption, you don't need to include a closed-caption version of that audio (even though Captivate would allow you to create one).

WORKING WITH TEMPLATES

As you've seen throughout this book, Captivate gives you a lot of options for the way the individual slides look (and sound) and the way the movie runs. It can be very time-consuming to set all of these options, so Captivate gives you two ways to store settings and automatically use them in subsequent movies.

- *Design Templates:* Save settings for visual elements like button color, cursor movement defaults, caption size, animation speed, slide background, and more.
- *Project Templates:* Save layout and structure settings for the entire project. This can include background elements, or placeholders that indicate specific size and placement for required element types, as well as different slide types. A project template can also incorporate a design template.

Captivate 4 comes with several design templates and a large library of project templates that you can use. You can edit any of these and save it to a new name to create your own custom templates, or you can create a template from scratch.

Working with Design Templates

You can create or edit design templates whenever needed, and then you can apply those templates to existing projects to automatically assign visual components throughout the finished movie. You can apply a design template to a single slide or to the whole movie project.

Applying a Design Template

To apply a design template to an existing project, follow these steps:

1. Open the project and display any slide in Edit view.
2. From the **Window** menu, choose **Design Template** to display the Design Template panel.

FIGURE 12-9   **Display the Design Template panel.**

3.   The Design Template panel displays template icons in four areas:

- At the very top of the panel is a representation of the first slide in the most recently used or currently selected template.
- Used in Project displays icons for only those templates currently used in the project. Because you can apply different templates to individual slides, you may have more than one design template per project.
- Recently Used Templates displays icons for the templates you've used most recently. This is handy if you have a lot of template files but only use a few of them regularly.
- Available Templates displays icons for all templates in the system in alphabetical order.

Note: If you have already applied a template to one of the slides in your project, the icon for that template will appear in all four areas. Click any template icon to display the template options.

4. You can download additional design templates from the Adobe.com website by clicking the Adobe Captivate Exchange icon at the bottom of the panel (it's the second one from the left). You must be connected to the Internet for this to work.

5. Once you have selected a template, click **Apply** to apply the selected template to the displayed slide, or click **Apply All** to apply the selected template to the entire project. The buttons, click boxes, animations, and other visual elements will take on the properties as specified in the template.

TIP

If you apply a design template to just one slide, subsequent elements that you add to this slide or others in the project will not use the design template parameters. However, if you apply a design template to the entire project, all subsequently added slides and elements will use the design template parameters.

Creating or Editing a Design Template

You can create custom templates by editing existing templates or by creating a design template from scratch. To create or edit a design template, follow these steps:

1. Do one of the following:

    ■ To edit an existing template, from the **File** menu, choose **Open**, then browse to the location of your template files, and click the name of the template you want to edit. By default, design templates are stored in the Adobe Captivate 4\Templates\Design Templates folder.

    ■ To create a new design template, start at the Captivate Main menu and choose the **Design Template** option under Create Templates.

In either case, the design template opens in the Captivate window Edit view with all the template elements stored across seven slides.

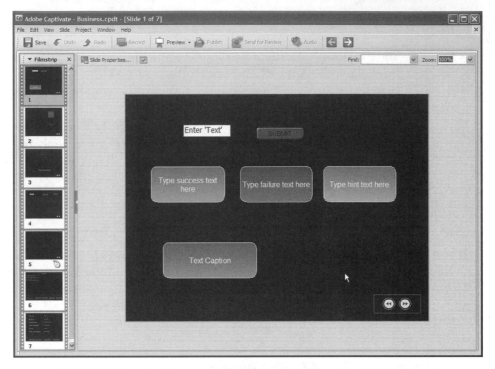

FIGURE 12-10   The Business design template is included with Captivate 4.

2.   Use the filmstrip on the side of the screen to display elements on the various slides, or use the Find drop-down list at the upper-right corner of the screen to specify and display the element type you want to edit. For example, the first slide in the Captivate 4 Business design template shows a text entry box, along with a stand-alone text caption.

3.   Change any of the elements in the same way that you would change an element in a regular project (see Chapter 7). Note that you won't be able to change all parameters for all elements. For example, in a text caption, you can change the color, size, alignment, and style of the text, but you cannot change the text itself (these are defined in the .rdl stored in the installation directory for each language, such as Adobe\Adobe Captivate 4\CaptureTextTemplate_English.rdl).

4. If needed, you can also change the slide properties, such as transition and background image, by clicking the Slide Properties button (or by double-clicking on the slide background). Remember that you have different types of slides, so a change to the background of the question slide in the template won't necessarily change the background of the standard slide.

TIP

Be careful with colors and contrast. If you change from a dark background (as in the Business design template) to a light background (as in Figure 12-11), you'll probably also want to change the text colors so that they are easily visible. In this case, you may want to change the text to black because the white text on a light background is hard to read.

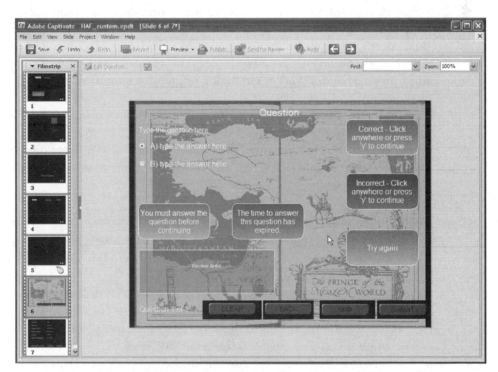

FIGURE 12-11   **A design template question slide with a new background image.**

5.   From the **File** menu, choose **Save As** to save the template to a new name, or click the **Save** icon to store the template changes to the current name. Note that if you're creating a new design template, the Save icon will prompt for a filename.

TIP

Use a name that is meaningful and indicates that the file is a template file. Though all design templates have the extension .cpdl, this extension does not show up on the Recent Files list.

Working with Project Templates

While design templates allow you to easily update visual elements, and they encourage consistency of design elements across projects, project templates take this a step further and allow you to design an entire project using placeholders where the content will be added later. You can also use project templates to store movie size, navigation elements, branching scenarios, and entire project outlines.

Captivate 4 comes with a wide variety of project templates designed for different output sizes (such as full screen 790x545 or mobile applications at 320x240) as well as for different types of movies (business presentations, quizzes, soft skills training, etc.). You can also download additional templates from the Adobe.com website.

Using an Existing Project Template to Create a New Movie

For the most part, creating a movie with a template is very similar to recording a new movie (as described in Chapter 4). There are a few minor differences:

- The size of the screen (and the recording area) is defined in the template. You can move the area around on your screen or resize a window to fit into the recording area, but you cannot change the size or shape of the recording area.
- There is at least one slide already in the template, and often many slides. Rather than inserting new slides, you're most likely going to be editing existing ones.

- Placeholders specify content type—thus, if the placeholder is expecting an image, you can't enter an animation in that placeholder.
- If the movie has a space for recorded slides, there will be a recording placeholder. Simply double-click this slide to create a new recording for the movie using the template defaults.

To create a new movie using a template, follow these steps:

1. Do one of the following:
   - From the Captivate Main menu, go to the **Create Project** area and click **From Template**.
   - From the **File** menu, choose **New**, then **Project**, then choose **From Template** in the window that appears.
2. Captivate displays the most recently used folder of templates. Click on the name of the template you want to use. If necessary, you can browse to different folders to display and choose the template. Captivate creates a new project based on the template and displays it in Storyboard view.

FIGURE 12-12 **A typical project template includes slides, navigation, and instructions.**

3. Some templates include instructions on the first slide and/or in the notes section (as shown in Figure 12-12). For this particular template, the first slide (with the instructions) is set to Hidden and will not be included in the finished movie.

4. After reading the first slide instructions, double-click the first non-hidden slide to display it in Edit view. In the example scenario template shown in Figure 12-13, the second slide contains two image placeholders, one text caption placeholder, and a text animation placeholder. The slide notes instruct the user to place a corporate logo in the left-side placeholder, an image that illustrates the subject in the right-side placeholder, the company name in the text caption, and the lesson title in the text animation placeholder.

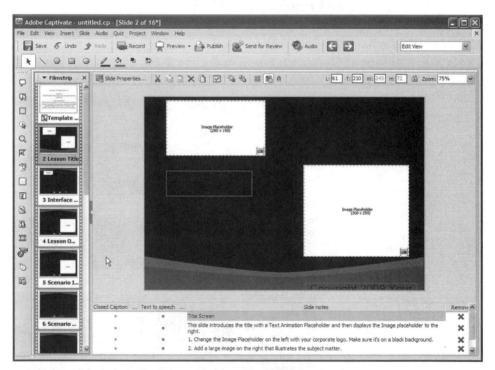

FIGURE 12-13   Working with placeholders.

5. Some templates include a recording placeholder slide. To record slides at that point in the movie, simply double-click the recording placeholder slide, then choose the window that you want to record.

FIGURE 12-14 Use the recording placeholder slide.

6. Continue editing each slide by adding the required elements or editing the placeholders. You can copy and paste slides as needed to create the length of movie that you need.
7. When finished, click **Save** to store the movie to a name you specify.

Creating a New Project Template

> **TIP**
>
> Before you decide to create a project from scratch, spend some time exploring the existing templates so that you'll see the range of options available to you. You may also find that an existing template just needs a few changes to make the movie you want (see "Editing an Existing Project Template").

To create a new project template, follow these steps:

1. From the Captivate Main menu, choose the **Project Template** option under **Create Templates** (or choose **New** from the **File** menu) to display the New Project window.

FIGURE 12-15   **The New Project window.**

2. With the Project Template item highlighted in the Create tab, specify the size of the movies that you'll create with the new template. You can do either of the following steps:

    ▪ Choose from the drop-down list of standard sizes.
    ▪ Enter a width and height in the appropriate boxes.

3. Click **OK** to create the template and display the first slide in Storyboard view.

FIGURE 12-16 **A blank project template.**

4. Insert slides, elements, notes, and navigation as you normally would (as described in Chapter 7). Standard elements that you place on slides in the template will be displayed exactly the same way in every movie that uses this template. You may want to use this for background images, logos, and other elements for which you want to ensure consistency. You can also

insert question slides, set up navigation, and view Edit, Storyboard, and Branching views.

5.   In addition to the standard elements, you can also choose from a list of element placeholders. To insert a placeholder, from the **Insert** menu, choose **Placeholder** and then click on the placeholder type you want to insert. Captivate will insert the placeholder (or prompt for needed information).

FIGURE 12-17   **Choose from a list of available placeholder types.**

For example, to insert a text caption placeholder, from the **Insert** menu select **Placeholder** and then **Text Caption** to display the New Text Caption Placeholder window.

FIGURE 12 18   **Inserting a text caption placeholder.**

6.   In the parameters window, you can edit the placeholder parameters (font, type size, position, alignment, etc.). Remember that the text of the caption will be replaced in the final movie, so you can use this space for instructions. Click **OK** to display the placeholder on the slide.

7.   You can move or resize the placeholder as necessary.

8.   Repeat for as many placeholders as needed.

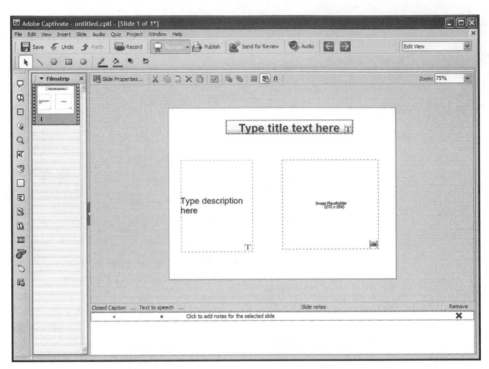

FIGURE 12-19   **A text caption placeholder on a slide.**

TIP

It's a good idea to document your templates in the slide notes area of each slide. You can also create an instructional slide at any point in the movie. Click **Hide Slide** from the Slide menu to prevent an instructional slide from being included in the final movie.

---

9.   From the **File** menu, click **Save As** (or click the **Save** icon) to name and store the template.

Editing an Existing Project Template

1. To edit an existing template, from the **File** menu, choose **Open**, then browse to the location of your template files and click the name of the template you want to edit. By default, project templates are stored in the Adobe Captivate 4\Templates\Project Templates folder.

2. Each template slide may have two types of elements:

    - Standard elements work the same as they do within the project, and they will appear in the finished movie exactly as they appear on the template.

    - Element placeholders appear with a small icon in the corner, and can be filled with content when a movie project is created from the template. For example, Figure 12-20 shows an image next to an image placeholder, a text caption next to a text caption placeholder, and an animated text element next to an animated text placeholder.

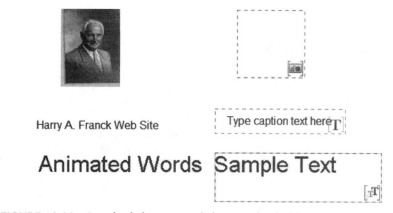

FIGURE 12-20   **Standard elements and element placeholders on a template slide.**

3. Edit any other elements as necessary (see Chapter 7).
4. Click the **Save** icon to store the template to the same name, or click **Save As** to store the file to a new name.

VIEWING AND CHANGING MOVIE SIZE

When we talk about the size of a movie, there are really two considerations.

- The size of the movie "screen"—that is, the dimensions of the recording area that determine the width and height of the displayed movie on a monitor. This is originally set when you record the movie but can be changed if needed.
- The size of the file, in bytes. This is determined by a combination of the resolution, number of slides, types of elements, and dimensions of the displayed movie. Depending on your delivery mechanism (such as on CD, as a download from a Web page, or stored on a server), you may need to be concerned with file size.

Viewing or Changing the Dimensions of a Movie

The specific height and width of your movie were set when you recorded or created it (see Chapter 4). For example, you may have specified a full-screen movie to be recorded at 640 pixels wide by 480 pixels tall. Or you may have dragged the recording area to a custom size. In general, the larger your movie dimensions, the larger the file size will be. Smaller dimensions, although easier to download, may be more difficult for viewers to see.

You can view the current dimensions of the movie in the Information area on the bottom of the left panel of the Storyboard view. For example, the movie in Figure 12-21 has a size of 920x685.

FIGURE 12-21 View the movie dimensions in Storyboard view.

TIP

Changing dimensions cannot be undone, so you should always make a backup of the movie before using this function.

TIP

When you reduce the dimensions of a movie, the image density is adjusted to be appropriate for the new movie size. If you are trying to enlarge a movie that had been reduced in the past, you may run into image quality problems. If you've saved the images (by themselves or in a backup of the original movie), you can import original quality images into the movie after enlarging it.

You can change the dimensions of a movie by following these steps:

1. From the **Project** menu, select **Rescale Project** to display the Rescale project window and to view the current movie dimensions.
2. To change the dimensions of the movie, choose either **User defined (custom)** or **Preset size**.
3. (Option 1) If you choose **User defined**, specify whether or not you want to maintain the aspect ratio. If you select this check box, the relative height and width of the slides will remain the same after resizing. If you don't select this check box, you may get some unexpected distortion. If you choose **User defined**, type either the number of pixels for each dimension or a percentage change. If you have selected **Maintain aspect ratio**, typing a new value in either the height or width dimension will automatically change the other dimension to maintain their relative sizes.

FIGURE 12-22   **Display the Rescale project window to change movie size.**

3. (Option 2) If you choose **Preset size**, choose from the drop-down list of available sizes. For example, you might choose 220x230 for a very small display or 1024x768 for a larger, full-screen display.
4. If the new size you've entered is larger than the original size, the If new size is larger area becomes active.

FIGURE 12-23   Define how Captivate will enlarge your movie.

- Choose whether you want to rescale each slide in the movie to fit the new size, or leave the slides the original size and insert a solid color to fill in around the slides.
- If you choose to keep the movie the same size, specify the color for the background by clicking the **Background color** box, and specify where on the new slide the original slide will be placed (such as top center or bottom right).
- Select the **Rescale captions** check box to enlarge the text captions and other elements so that they stay in the same proportion to the slide display.
- Skip to Step 9 when you are done.

5. If the new size you've entered is smaller than the original movie size, the If new size is smaller area becomes active.

- Choose whether you want to rescale each slide in the movie to fit the new size, or leave the slides the original size and just use whatever portion of the slide fits in the new movie space.

- Select the **Rescale captions** check box to reduce the text captions and other elements so that they stay in the same proportion to the slide display.
- Skip to Step 9 when you are done.

FIGURE 12-24   **Define how Captivate will reduce the movie dimensions.**

6. If you chose to crop the movie to a smaller size, the Next button becomes active. Click **Next** to display the Rescale project window with an area you can use to indicate which portion of each slide you want to include in the resized movie.

FIGURE 12-25 Specify the crop area.

7. Click and drag the highlighted window on the image of the original slide until it highlights the area you want to keep in the resized movie. Any part of the slide not highlighted will be cut away.

8. Do one of the following:
   - Repeat Step 7 for each slide by clicking the arrow to display the next slide or choosing a slide from the drop-down list.
   - Click **Apply to all slides** to crop the same area on every slide.

9. Click **Finish** (from either the Rescale project window or from the crop area window) to resize the movie.

10. A message displays, warning you that resizing cannot be undone. Click **OK** to complete the resizing process.

Viewing Movie File Size

Captivate can display the file size in bytes for the entire movie, and you can break it down to display the size of each individual slide and all the elements on it. You can also see a graphic that represents how long the movie will take to download at various connection speeds.

To display the movie file size, follow these steps:

1. From the **Project** menu, choose **Bandwidth Analyzer** to display the Bandwidth Monitor window. The first tab, Slide Summary, displays information about the size of each slide and the length of time it takes to play. The size of audio files, if any, is also identified.

Slide	KB per sec	Seconds	Video (KB, ...	Audio (KB)
Slide 1	27.4	8.7	237.6	103.7
Slide 2(Random Question)	-	-	-	-
Slide 3	0.0	3.0	0.0	0.0
Slide 4	40.6	4.3	174.6	32.8
Slide 5	75.0	3.0	225.1	0.0
Slide 6	56.1	4.6	257.9	0.0
Slide 7	490.4	1.8	882.8	0.0
Slide 8	40.8	6.3	257.1	0.0
Slide 9	26.0	10.0	259.9	0.0
Slide 10	25.7	10.0	256.9	0.0
Slide 11	26.0	10.0	259.9	0.0
Slide 12	25.9	10.0	259.3	0.0
Slide 13	96.3	10.0	962.6	0.0
Slide 14	24.8	10.0	248.0	0.0
Slide 15	227.3	2.3	522.7	0.0
Slide 16	51.3	4.2	215.5	0.0
Slide 17	73.9	3.0	221.8	0.0
Slide 18	77.0	4.2	323.5	0.0
Slide 19	54.3	4.1	222.7	0.0

FIGURE 12-26   **Display the size of each slide.**

2. Click the **Graph** tab to display a visual representation of how long it will take to display the movie over different types of connections. The vertical axis on the left of the graph represents the amount of bandwidth the movie requires. The bottom, horizontal axis represents the display time of the movie. In Figure 12-27 the jagged black line represents the actual size of each slide. The horizontal lines represent the amount of time for each bandwidth, identified by color.

FIGURE 12-27   **Display relative times for different bandwidths.**

3. Click the **Project Summary** tab to display a summary of the movie information. This is the same information that displays in the left panel of the Storyboard view.

FIGURE 12-28   **Display the summary.**

4. Click the **Slide Info** tab to display a list of slides with the approximate time it would take to download each of the elements on the slide at different network speeds.

FIGURE 12-29   **Display the slide info.**

5.   For any of the Bandwidth Monitor window tabs, you can click **Print** to print a complete bandwidth analysis, including the slide summary, graph, and project summary information.

6.   Click **OK** to close the Bandwidth Monitor window.

COMBINING FILES WITH AGGREGATOR

The Aggregator tool makes it easy to create a single movie from multiple .swf files. The Aggregator lets you specify which projects to include, which order you want them in, and how you want table of contents entries to look. Once you've created the Aggregator project, you can publish it to create a single .swf, .exe, .pdf, or .html file. The files that you're aggregating must meet these conditions:

■   The individual projects must be published by Captivate to SWF format.

■   All project files within a single Aggregator project must use the same version of ActionScript (either 2 or 3).

You can also use the Aggregator tool to combine .sco (scorable objects) files that you've created with Captivate's quizzing feature. The published Aggregator file can then be published to a .zip file that can in turn be uploaded to your LMS.

Combining Movies with Aggregator

To create and publish a movie using the Aggregator, follow these steps:

1. From the Captivate Main menu, click **Aggregator Project** under the **Others** category (or from the **File** menu, select **New** and then **Aggregator Project**) to display the Create New Project window.

FIGURE 12-30   Creating an Aggregator project.

2. Choose the version of Action Script for this project and click **OK**. Remember that all .swf files within the Aggregator project must use the same version of Action Script.

FIGURE 12-31   Start with the blank Aggregator screen.

3. Click the **Add Module** icon (plus sign) at the bottom of the screen to display a browser window.

4. Browse to and click on the name of the first Captivate project you want to include, and click **OK**. Repeat for each .swf file you want to include in the Aggregator project. As you add files, the movie name is displayed in the Module Title panel on the left of the Aggregator window, and the movie itself is displayed in the preview area on the right side. Note that Aggregator automatically creates a Table of Contents panel (shown in the preview area in Figure 12-32). You can click on the movie titles to run each movie, and you can use the controls at the bottom of the preview screen to play, fast forward, or pause the movie.

FIGURE 12-32   **Multiple movies on one Aggregator project.**

5. The currently selected movie is displayed in green in the Module Title panel. The controls at the top of the panel apply only to the selected movie. To rearrange the order in which the movies display, select a movie title in the Module Title panel, then click either the **Up** arrow or **Down** arrow icon at the bottom of the panel until the movie is in the position you want.

6. To remove a movie from the aggregated output, you have two choices:

- Select the movie in the Module Title panel, then deselect the check box under the eye icon to hide the movie. This leaves the movie in the project, but prevents it from being displayed in the finished output. Note that the movie is no longer displayed in the preview panel.
- Select the movie in the Module Title panel, then click the **Remove** icon (garbage can) at the bottom of the panel. This removes the movie from the Aggregator project altogether.

7. As you add, hide, or rearrange movies, the changes you make are automatically reflected in the preview panel Table of Contents, and Table of Contents files, if any, for each individual movie are displayed under the movie title. There are three additional ways to refine the Aggregator Table of Contents (TOC):

- To include a movie in the output but remove that movie's title from the Aggregator Table of Contents, select the movie in the Module Title panel and then deselect the **Include Module Title** check box.
- To ensure that the tables of contents for all included movies use the same parameters, select a movie in the Module Title panel and click the **Set as Master Movie** check box. All other movies in the aggregated project will use the same TOC settings as the selected Master Movie, and TOC information from the Master Movie is displayed above the Table of Contents in the output.
- To change the information that displays above the TOC in the finished movie, click the **Info** button at the bottom of the Module Title panel to display the TOC Info window. Select **Override TOC Info**, then fill in the information you want to display and click **OK**.

FIGURE 12-33   **Enter information for the table of contents.**

8.   Click the **Save** (or **Save As**) icon and enter a name for the Aggregator project. This will be stored with the extension .aggr.

9.   To publish the Aggregator project, click the **Publish** icon to display the publishing options.

FIGURE 12-34   **Aggregator publishing options.**

10. Select the parameters for the published file as described in Table 12-4.

TABLE 12-4 Aggregator publishing options.

For this option:	Do this:
File Type	Select the Flash (.swf) check box to create a single .swf file that incorporates the individual files in the Aggregator project.
	Select the Standalone (.exe) check box to create an executable file that incorporates the individual files in the Aggregator project.
Project Title	Enter a title for the output file.
Folder	Browse to the folder where you want to store the output file. Select **Publish files to a folder** if you want Adobe Captivate to create a default folder into which the files are published.
Output Options	You can choose one or more options here. Select **Zip files** if you want the final output to be compressed into a file with the extension .zip.
	■ Choose **Export HTML** to create a Flash file and an .html file that can be used to display the Flash file in a browser. The .html file will have the same name entered in the Movie Title field with the extension .htm.
	■ Choose **Export PDF** to include the .swf file in a PDF.
■ Exe Options	■ *For executable file output only.* You can select an icon that will be incorporated into the EXE output.

11. Click **Publish** to create the specified output.

GETTING FEEDBACK WITH CAPTIVATE REVIEWER

Adobe Captivate 4 comes bundled with an Adobe® AIR™ application that lets reviewers comment directly on the movie as it plays. This is a separate application that must be installed on the reviewer's computer in order for the reviewer to enter and store comments.

Using the Reviewer application requires three distinct steps:

1. You must create a .crev file for the review. Similar to other publishing options, Captivate can automatically create the needed file and e-mail it to the specified reviewer(s).

2.   The reviewers watch the movie, participate in simulations, answer questions, or whatever else is required by your output through the Reviewer application. They will then insert comments directly into the movie file. The reviewers do NOT need to have Captivate installed on their systems. The comments are saved to a common area.

TIP

You can copy and distribute the "Entering Review Comments" section (later in this chapter) to your reviewers who may not be familiar with the Reviewer software.

---

3.   As author of the movie, you can then review the comments, sort comments in different ways, and import or export comments as needed.

Creating and Sending a File for Review

To send a Captivate movie project to reviewers for comments, follow these steps:

1.   Create and save the Captivate project file.
2.   Click the **Send for Review** icon (or choose **Publish** from the **File** menu and click the **Review** tab) to display the review options.

FIGURE 12-35   Publish the project for review.

3.   Enter a name for the output file. Captivate will append the extension .crev.

4.   In the Publish folder field, type or browse to the folder where you want to store the movie. This could be a location that your reviewers can access directly, such as a shared drive, or it could be a local folder to store the file until you can e-mail it.

5.   In the Project comments folder field, type or browse to a folder where you want to store the reviewers' comments. This must be a shared folder to which all reviewers have access. If you do not have access to a shared folder, you'll have to instruct reviewers to export their comments to .xml files and e-mail them to you.

6.   Click the **Send Mail** check box to have Captivate generate an e-mail that you can send to the reviewers. Select the attachments you want to include in the e-mail:

   ■   Click the **Attach Review (.crev) file** check box if you want to e-mail a copy of the output movie to the reviewers. This is handy if they don't have access to a shared folder.

   ■   Click the **Attach "Adobe Captivate Reviewer"** check box to attach a copy of the Reviewer application to the e-mail. If all of your reviewers already have this application, this won't be necessary.

TIP

Reviewers can also download the Adobe Captivate Reviewer application from the Adobe website by browsing to http://www.adobe.com/cfusion/marketplace/index .cfm?event=marketplace.offering&marketplaceid=1&offeringid=11020.

---

7.   Click the **Publish** button to create the file for review and (if you've chosen to do so) create the e-mail that will be sent to reviewers. If you're sending e-mail, Captivate will open your default e-mail client and allow you to enter your reviewers' e-mail addresses.

Entering Review Comments

Adobe Captivate Reviewer is an Adobe AIR application that allows you to add comments directly onto a Captivate SWF movie. This could be a demonstration, an e-learning lesson, or any other type of Captivate SWF output. You do not need to have Captivate or Flash installed on your system to comment with Adobe Captivate Reviewer, but you must have both Adobe AIR and the Reviewer software installed.

Before You Begin: Installation

You must install the Adobe Captivate Reviewer software before you can open a movie file for review. To do this, follow these steps:

1. Do one of the following:
   - If you received the AdobeCaptivateReviewer.air application in an e-mail, download the file to your hard drive.
   - Download the application from http://www.adobe.com/ cfusion/marketplace/index.cfm?event=marketplace .offering&marketplaceid=1&offeringid=11020 by clicking the **Download from Publisher** button, and click **Save** to store the file to your hard drive.
2. Double-click on the **AdobeCaptivateReviewer.air** file to begin the installation wizard.
3. Click **Install**, then enter the folder location where you want the software to be stored.
4. Click **Continue** to install the Reviewer application.

Note: If you do not yet have the Adobe AIR software installed, the Reviewer application will prompt you through the AIR installation process.

Enter Your Comments on the Movie

To comment on a movie, you'll need to open it with the Reviewer software. To do this, follow these steps:

1. Open the file in one of the following ways:

    ▪ If you received the file in an e-mail, you can double-click the .crev file right in the e-mail.

    ▪ If you received a link to the file location on a stored server, browse to that file and double-click to open it.

    ▪ Open Adobe Captivate Reviewer, click **Load Captivate Movie**, and browse to the location of the .crev file.

2. Specify a location where your comments will be stored. If the person who sent you the movie set it up with a shared folder, the comments will automatically be stored to that location. If there is no defined shared comments folder, you will have to specify a local folder where your comments will be stored as an .xml file. When you're done, you'll have to e-mail this .xml file to the movie author.

3. Once the Reviewer software opens, you'll see a large Play button (with a triangle) in the center of the Reviewer screen. Click the **Play** button to begin the movie. The movie plays with a set of Reviewer controls along the bottom of the screen. The timeline stretches across the width of the screen and shows the progress of the movie as it plays. The controls on the left allow you to start over, play, rewind, fast forward, or control the audio. The controls on the right allow you to add, save, view, or export your comments.

FIGURE 12-36 **The Reviewer controls.**

4. At any point in the movie, you can add a comment by clicking on the timeline or on the **Add** icon (plus sign) and typing in the dialog box that appears. A white square indicates where you've added each comment.

5.   Use any of the other Reviewer controls as described in Table 12-5.

TABLE 12-5 The Reviewer controls.

This icon:	Is called:	And does this
	Add Comment	Opens the comment dialog box. Type the comment you want to make, then click **Add** to store the comment and mark the comment's location on the timeline.
	Open	Opens a browser window that allows you to point to a different movie file you may want to open.
	Save	Saves your comments.
	Refresh Comments	Updates the file with the latest comments. If you're working off a shared drive, this will show comments from all other reviewers.
	Show All Comments	Displays all comments in a text dialog box. Each comment will display the text of the comment, the name of the reviewer who made the comment, and the time that the comment was recorded by the system.
	Filter Comments	Allows you to display only those comments by a single reviewer that you specify.
	Import Comments	Reads an .xml file created by Reviewer and stores it as comments.
	Export Comments	Writes an .xml file that can be read by Reviewer and converted back to comments.

6. You can edit or delete any existing comment in either of the following ways:

    ▪ Click the **Show All Comments** icon, then click **Edit** or **Delete** in the comment you want to change.
    ▪ Click on the **white marker** on the timeline for the comment you want to edit. This will open the comment in a small dialog box, where you can click **Edit** or **Delete** as necessary.

7. When you're finished making comments, click the **Save Comments** icon. If you close the Reviewer application without saving comments, they will not be stored.

8. To close the file, click the **Close** icon (the small X in the upper-right corner of the Reviewer screen).

Reading Review Comments

Once reviewers begin entering and saving comments, you can easily view their comments through the Reviewer application (as described in the previous section). You can also view reviewer comments right in the Captivate project. The Captivate Comments panel gives you many more options for viewing, sorting, and responding to comments than the Reviewer application.

1. Open the movie for which you want to see comments.
2. To display the comments within Captivate, from the **Window** menu, click **Comments** to display the Comments panel.
3. If you're using a shared folder where reviewers can store their comments, the comments will already be associated with the movie. If you don't have a shared folder, instruct your reviewers to export their comments to .xml files. You'll then need to import the .xml files to the movie. There are three ways to do this:
    - In Reviewer, click the **Import Comments** icon.
    - In Captivate, from the **File** menu, choose **Import** and then **Comments**.
    - In Captivate, from the Comments panel, click the **Import Comments** icon.

FIGURE 12-37   **Comments panel within Captivate.**

4. You can view comments in several ways:

    ▪ Choose from the View by drop-down list to display comments in order by date entered, status, or reviewer name.

    ▪ Click the arrows to reverse the order of displayed comments.

5. You can use the Comments panel to keep track of the status of each comment, to indicate whether you're accepting or rejecting each comment, and to post replies to comments. Select a comment by clicking in the blank square next to the comment, then use the icons at the bottom of the Comments panel as described in Table 12-6.

TABLE 12-6 Comments Panel functions

This icon:	Is called:	And does this:
🗑	Delete Comments	Removes the selected comment(s). Note that you must respond to the comment first (either accept, reject, or reply) before you can delete it.
↻	Refresh Comments	Updates the comment display with all comments found on the shared drive (if any).
▤✗	Reject Comment	Indicates that you're going to ignore the comment. You can enter a reason for the rejection in a text box that appears. This will be visible to other reviewers.
▤✎	Accept Comment	Indicates that you're going to take action on the comment. You can enter a reason or explanation in a text box that appears. This will be visible to other reviewers.
💬	Reply to Comment	Allows you to post a comment or question about the comment without indicating whether you will accept or reject it. Type the reply in the text box that appears. This will be visible to other reviewers, including the one who made the initial comment to which you're replying.
▤	Import Comments	Import comments from an .xml file. You'll need to specify a filename.
▤	Export Comments	Export comments to an .xml file. You'll need to specify a filename.

USING USER ASSISTANCE

Captivate comes with a number of tools that you can use when you aren't sure about a function or need additional information about something within Captivate. There are three main areas of available user assistance:

- Help files
- Captivate movies
- Captivate online support

Viewing Help Files

To display the included Help files, click the **Help** menu option and choose **Adobe Captivate Help** (or press **F1** from anywhere within Captivate).

> **TIP**
>
> The Help menu can be accessed from anywhere in Captivate by pressing **F1**.

FIGURE 12-38   Captivate Help window.

You can find information in several ways:

- Enter a word or phrase in the search box at the top of the Help window.
- Click on the menu options on the left side of the screen to display categories of information.
- From within each displayed topic, click any underlined word to display more information on that word or phrase.

When you're finished, close the online Help window by clicking the **close** icon in the upper-right corner of the Help window.

Viewing Helpful Movies

In addition to traditional Help systems, Captivate comes with a variety of Captivate movies that you can view. These movies step through some of the Captivate processes and are most useful for those who are just getting started. When you first start Captivate, the list of available movie topics is displayed on the right side of the screen, or you can open the list from the Help menu by choosing **Getting Started Tutorials**.

Use the playback controls along the bottom of the movie screen to start, stop, pause, or otherwise navigate through the movie. When you're finished, close the movie window by clicking the **close** icon in the upper-right corner.

Captivate Online Support

Adobe hosts a variety of online support areas from which you can find answers to your Captivate questions. You can use any browser to view the support pages at http://www.adobe.com/support/captivate/ or you can go to the Help menu and choose **Support Center** (for most users), **Developer Center** (for more advanced users), or **Adobe Captivate Forums** (where you can communicate with the Captivate community of users).

From this site, you can ask questions, view articles, download files, look at documentation, and even participate in the Adobe online forums where other Captivate users share problems—and resolutions—with each other.

SUMMARY

This chapter reviewed the tools that help you work with Captivate and help you to make better, more efficient movies. The following chapter discusses how to set global properties that determine how your movie looks when it is finished.

REFINING THE MOVIE

Chapter **13**

Up to this point, we've been working with individual slides and the elements on those slides. You also need to take a look at your movie as a whole. This chapter describes some of the features that help you refine your movie, including moving slides around within the movie and managing the movie files.

WORKING WITH MULTIPLE SLIDES

The Storyboard view allows you to do some of the tasks that you can do in Edit view. The main difference is that, in Storyboard view, you can apply your changes to multiple slides at once.

As you've already seen, the Storyboard view displays all of the slides in your movie. When you first open a movie in the Adobe® Captivate® program, the movie is automatically displayed in Storyboard view.

The left side of the Storyboard view displays a menu of tasks you can perform on the slides and some information about the movie as a whole, such as the running time, movie size, and resolution. This information only displays after you've published the movie at least once.

The right side of the Storyboard view displays miniature versions of each slide called thumbnails. If you've entered slide labels, they are displayed beneath each slide next to the slide number; otherwise, just the slide number is displayed. There are also icons that indicate the type of components that are associated with each slide.

FIGURE 13-1   Display a movie in Storyboard view.

TABLE 13-1 Storyboard view icons.

This icon:	Indicates this:
	The slide contains a full-motion recording, usually a small, high-resolution movie of scroll bar movement or a drag-and-drop action.
	The slide contains an audio element. Note that this icon only displays for slide-level audio, not for audio associated with individual elements such as click boxes or captions.
	The slide is locked so that the elements on it cannot be changed.
	The slide is hidden, so that although it is displayed in Captivate, it will not be displayed in the published movie. The hidden icon is displayed over the slide number.
	The slide contains information for cursor movement (the beginning and end points of the track along which the cursor moves).
	The slide represents a group of slides. The numbers of the slides in the group appear in the upper-left corner of the slide icon.

These icons are also displayed on the filmstrip in the Edit view (see Chapters 5 and 6 for details about working in Edit view) and Branching view (see Chapter 11). Most of the tasks that you can do in the Edit view filmstrip can also be accomplished in the Storyboard view.

Changing the Storyboard View Display

In Storyboard view, you can specify which elements of the Storyboard view are displayed and the size of the slide thumbnails.

Modifying the Thumbnail Display

By default, the thumbnail images of each slide start out as medium-sized images, but you can change the size of each slide icon (called thumbnails) at any time. You can either make the icons smaller (so you can see more slides at once), or make them larger to display more detail on each one. Follow these steps:

1. From the Storyboard view screen, click **Window** to display the viewing options.
2. Click **Filmstrip Size** to display the available options (small, medium, or large).
3. Click the size you want for your thumbnails.

FIGURE 13-2   Display the storyboard with small icons.

Displaying or Hiding the Left Panel Information

The left panel of the Storyboard view contains two elements. The top of the panel contains a list of common tasks that you can perform on the selected slides. The bottom shows information about the movie. You can hide or redisplay either at any time by clicking on the title of each section (Slide Tasks or Information). For example, if the movie information is displayed, click on the word **Information** to hide it. If the information is already hidden, click on the word **Information** to redisplay it.

You can also hide or redisplay the entire panel by clicking the **arrow** icon between the left and right panels. This is a narrow arrow in the center of the dividing border between the two elements. The direction of this arrow will vary depending on whether or not the panel is currently displayed.

FIGURE 13-3   Display or hide the left panel with the arrows.

Selecting Slides

One of the most useful features of the Storyboard view is the option to make changes to many slides at once. For example, if you want to display a series of slides for exactly 10 seconds each, you could go into the properties for each slide and set the display time for each one. Or you can select them all in Storyboard view and change the setting just once.

To select slides, do any of the following:

■   Click on a slide once to select it.

TIP

Don't double-click; that will open the slide in Edit view. If you double-click by accident, simply click the Storyboard tab to return to Storyboard view.

■   Click on one slide; then hold down the **Shift** key before clicking another slide. Both slides you clicked and all of the slides between them will also be selected. Use this method to select a consecutive series of slides.

- Click on one slide, and then hold down the **Ctrl** key before clicking on another slide. Each additional slide you click while holding down the **Ctrl** key will be selected. Use this if you want to select every fifth slide, or only those slides with questions on them, or some other set of slides that aren't next to each other.
- Hold down the **Ctrl** key and press the **A** key (**Ctrl+A**) to select all slides. You can also choose **Select All Slides** from the **Edit** menu.

FIGURE 13-4   **Select multiple slides.**

Selected slides are displayed in the Storyboard view with a shaded background. Any task you choose from the Slide Tasks panel on the left of the Storyboard view will be applied to all of the selected slides. For example, in

Figure 13-4, you can see that slides numbered 6 through 15 have been selected. The other slides above and below them are not selected. You could delete them all by choosing **Delete Slide** from the Slide Tasks list, or copy them all, or modify the slide properties such as transitions or timing.

> **Note:** When you have multiple slides selected, some functions will not be available (such as adding a label). These functions will be displayed in pale gray, and you won't be able to click on them.

Rearranging Slides

After you've recorded a movie, you may decide that a particular set of slides belongs in a different part of the movie. Or you may want to set all the animation, transitions, and interactive elements for one section, then copy and paste those slides for modification in another section. These sorts of tasks are easy to do in Storyboard view.

> **TIP**
>
> When you move slides, all the slides will be renumbered so that the numbering remains sequential—that is, if you cut slide number 3, the old slide number 4 becomes the new slide number 3, and all subsequent slides are renumbered. You may want to assign a label to slides you're moving so that you can keep track of them more easily.

There are several methods you can use to move slides around within your movie:

- Select the slides or slides you want to move, click and hold down the left mouse button, and drag the slides to a new location in the Storyboard.
- Select the slide or slides; then copy them to the clipboard with the **Copy** command in the Slide Tasks panel, the **Copy** function in the **Edit** menu, or the **Ctrl+C** key combination.

- Cut slides from your movie and copy them to the clipboard with the **Cut** command in the Slide Tasks panel, the **Cut** function in the **Edit** menu, or the **Ctrl+X** key combination.
- Paste slides from the clipboard to wherever the cursor is by choosing the **Paste** command in the Slide Tasks panel, the **Paste** function in the **Edit** menu, or the **Ctrl+V** key combination.

CHANGING MOVIE-WIDE SETTINGS

Some of the Captivate functions apply to the entire movie, not just individual slides. For example, you can set a background color that is displayed if the content of a slide doesn't fill the whole screen, or you can change the movie speed or color quality.

Choosing a Background Color

The background of a movie is the portion of the screen not covered by the content of a slide. For example, if you import an image that does not fill the entire screen, the background of the slide will show through around the border of the image. Note that the background color won't show through on all slides: If your slide content, such as a screen capture, covers the entire screen, the background won't show.

To set the background for a movie, follow these steps:

1. From any view, open the **Edit** menu, and then select **Preferences** to display the Preferences window.
2. Under **Global**, click **Defaults**.

FIGURE 13-5   Set the background color in the Preferences window.

3.   The current background color is displayed in the box next to Background color. The default is white. Click on the color box to display a set of pre-defined colors. You can also click on **More Colors** to display the Color window.

FIGURE 13-6   Choose a background color.

4. Select the color you want for the background in any of the following ways:

   - Click on a color in the Basic colors grid.
   - Type the Hue, Saturation, and Luminosity values in the appropriate boxes.
   - Type the Red, Green, and Blue values in the appropriate boxes.
   - Click anywhere on the color chart on the right side of the window.
     - Use the arrow keys to move the color selection indicator.
     - Slide the arrow on the far right of the window up or down to increase or decrease the intensity of the current color.

5. Click **OK** to close the Color window.
6. Click **OK** to close the Preferences window.

Changing Display and Audio Quality

When you first recorded your Captivate movie, you specified the quality you wanted for both the video and audio. You can override those settings in the Preferences window.

1. From any view, open the **Edit** menu, and then select **Preferences** to display the Preferences window.
2. Under **Project**, select **SWF Size and Quality**.
3. You can choose to let the settings you entered for each slide determine the overall quality for the movie. For example, you may have one audio file that you want stored at the highest-quality settings, but you may not need that for every file. To let the slide settings determine output quality, select the **Retain slide quality settings** check box.

> **Note:** This check box must NOT be selected if you want to access all of the movie-wide quality settings in the Properties window.

4. Set the image quality as a percentage of the original input quality. Thus, if you start with very high-quality JPEG graphics, you can probably reduce the quality and still get decent images. However, if your graphics start out

at low quality, you want to leave this setting high. You can set different quality levels for JPEG and for BMP images.

FIGURE 13-7   **Set image quality in the Preferences window.**

5.   Set the audio quality by clicking on the displayed audio quality description to display the audio options. For example, in Figure 13-7, the audio quality is MP3, 96kbps, 44.10 KHz.

FIGURE 13-8   **Set audio quality in the Audio settings window.**

You can choose a variety of audio settings—see Chapter 8 for more information about audio options. Remember, your audio input must start out at high quality in order to get high-quality output.

Correcting Colors in Slides

In general, color should appear correctly in Captivate movies. However, there are cases in which colors may appear inaccurately, such as when the color scheme varies radically between slides. So if slide A uses color palette ABC, and slide B uses color palette XYZ, and the two palettes are radically different, slide B might resort to using palette ABC.

Most of these problems can be fixed by changing the video quality of the slide. Captivate provides four levels of video quality, even though the Low option is suggested for most uses.

To change video quality in a slide:

1. Open a Captivate project.
2. Double-click on the slide containing the colors you want to correct.
3. From the **Slide** menu, select **Properties** to display the slide properties.

FIGURE 13-9   Set color quality in the Slide Properties window.

4.   Select one of the video options from the **Quality** drop-down menu:

- *Low (8-bit):* The default format for slides. Low is the most efficient choice for the majority of screen shots because it uses 256 optimized colors. Slides in this format also compress well, which results in smaller file sizes.
- *Optimized:* Better resolution than the Low option.
- *JPEG:* This option is best used when the slide contains a photograph. You can change the quality and compression ratio for JPEG images in the Preferences window.
- *High (24-bit):* Compared to the low-quality format of 256 colors, this format uses 16 million colors for the slides. This option should only be used if the Low and JPEG options do not offer the correct color depth. The file size increases dramatically using this option.

Note: Selecting the JPEG or High options may increase the file size and the time it takes to download your movie. You should only use a format other than Low when necessary and appropriate.

ADDING CUSTOM COMPONENTS

For each project, you can add a variety of special components to polish the finished movie. For example, you can add a loading screen at the beginning of the movie, and you have the option of including playback controls to allow the viewer to start, stop, or "rewind" the movie. You can also include a custom information screen that the viewer sees when the Information button is pressed.

Movie Start Options

You can specify a variety of options for the beginning of your movie through the Preferences window.

- *Auto Play:* The movie will begin playing as soon as the movie is downloaded.

- *Preloader:* This displays an image (such as a clock or an icon that says "Loading. . . ") while your movie is being prepared for the viewer. For short movies displayed from a hard drive, the loading process may be so short that you don't even see the loading screen. For longer movies, particularly those distributed over the Internet, you may want to include a loading screen to indicate that the movie will start soon.
- *Password protect project:* You can limit the viewers of a movie by requiring that a password be entered before the movie plays. You can set one password for each movie.
- *Project expiry date:* Depending on the content of your movie, you may want to limit the number of days that viewers can access your movie. Do this by setting an expiration date for the movie.
- *Fade in on the first slide:* Rather than have the first screen on your movie appear suddenly, you can specify a fade-in effect.

TIP

Always test your movie from the final location—with all files and folders in place. Sometimes, if you're running in a development environment or on a local hard drive, the movie start options (particularly the loading screen) may not display as they will on the finished project.

To define the way your movie begins, follow these steps:

1. From any view, open the **Edit** menu, and then select **Preferences** to display the Preferences window.
2. Click the **Start and End** option under the **Project** menu on the left side of the screen.

FIGURE 13-10   **Set movie start preferences.**

3.   If you want the movie to begin playing as soon as it is downloaded, select the **Auto Play** check box. If you want to require that the viewer click Play to begin the movie, deselect this box. If you require the viewer to click Play, you can also specify an image that will display behind the Play button. This image must already be part of the movie (i.e., a background or imported image). If you don't specify an image, the movie will simply display the first slide while waiting for the viewer to click Play.

4.   To specify a loading screen, click the **Preloader** check box, and then type the location and filename of the file you want to use into the Preloader text box. You can also click the **Browse** button to browse to the file location. Loading screens, icons, and/or animations must be in one of the supported formats (JPG, JPEG, GIF, PNG, BMP, ICO, EMF, WMF, or SWF). If you're using a small SWF as a preloader, you can also specify how much of the file must be downloaded before the preloader begins to play. Enter a percentage in the **Preloader %** box.

> **TIP**
>
> Captivate comes with a variety of animations that you can use as loading screens. By default, they're stored in the Adobe Captivate 4\Gallery\Preloaders folder.

5. If you want the viewer to enter a password before viewing the movie, click the **Password protect project** check box. If you select this option, you must also enter a password, either by typing it into the text box or clicking the button to the right of the box to display the Password options window. Passwords may contain any combination of letters and numbers, and may also include the underscore character (_) but no other punctuation or spaces.

FIGURE 13-11   **Password options control access.**

6. (*Optional*) If you chose to open the Password options window, you can type a password in the Password text box. You can also change the text that displays on the Password screen by entering text in the appropriate fields. Click **OK** when you are done to return to the Preferences window. You may leave the default text (shown in Figure 13-11) or edit any or all of the following:

    ▪ *Message:* This text appears on the screen along with a text entry box.

    ▪ *Retry message:* This text appears only if the viewer enters an incorrect password.

    ▪ *Button text:* This text appears on the button that the user must click after typing in the password.

7.   If you want to set a movie expiration date, click the **Project expiry date** check box and then enter a date. Viewers will be able to view the movie up through the end of the day you've specified.

> **Note:** Captivate compares the expiration date of the movie to the date as set on the viewer's system. If the viewer's system has an incorrect date, the viewer may not be able to see the movie (or may be able to see a movie after you've set it to expire).

8.   (*Optional*) If you've set an expiration date, you can also modify the text that appears on the screen when the viewer attempts to open an expired movie. You can have up to two lines of text.

9.   Click the **Fade in on the first slide** check box to have the beginning of your movie appear on the screen gradually.

10.   Click **OK** when you are finished to close the Preferences window.

Movie End Options

You can also specify what happens at the end of the movie. There are a variety of options, including simply stopping or closing the movie, replaying the movie again from the beginning, and starting some other movie. To set the movie end action, follow these steps:

1.   From any view, open the **Edit** menu, and then select **Preferences** to display the Preferences window.

2.   Click the **Start and End** option under the **Project** menu on the left side of the screen.

FIGURE 13-12   Set movie end preferences.

3.   Choose an action from the drop-down list. Available options are shown in Table 13-2.

TABLE 13-2 Options for the end of a movie.

Choose this action:	For this result:
Stop project	The movie simply stops at the last slide.
Loop project	The movie restarts from the beginning. This is often useful for kiosk-type delivery.
Close project	The movie stops at the last slide and closes the movie viewer.
Open URL or file	After the last slide plays, either a new file or a Web page will display. You must enter the name of the file or URL of the page by typing it in the box or by browsing to the file location or URL. You can also click the drop-down menu to select the window in which the URL or file should appear (Current window, New window, Parent window, or Top window).

TABLE 13-2 Options for the end of a movie (continued).

Choose this action:	For this result:
Execute JavaScript	Run specified JavaScript when the movie ends. Click the Browse button to enter the JavaScript code you want to run.
Open other project	Play another movie as soon as this one ends. You must enter the movie by typing it in the box or by browsing to the file location. You can also click the drop-down menu to select the window in which the movie should appear (Current window, New window, Parent window, or Top window).
Send e-mail to	Send an e-mail as soon as the movie has finished. You must type the full e-mail address (for example, bphuettner@p-ndesigns.com).

4. Click **Fade out on the last slide** to display the last slide and then gradually have it fade from view. This fading will happen immediately before other actions you may have specified in Step 3.
5. Click **OK** to close the Preferences window.

Movie Skins

You can control the final look and feel of your movie using Captivate "skins." A skin defines the playback controls, the background that is displayed behind your slides, and the information that is displayed when the viewer presses the information (i) button on the playback controls. You can also use skins to define a table of contents that will be displayed on the finished movie in addition to the playback controls.

Captivate comes with a variety of predefined skins. You can edit any of these skins, or you can create your own skin so that you can reuse it in other movies.

FIGURE 13-13 Different skins change the look of your movie.

Changing the Skin

To change the look and feel of your movie, you can use any one of the predefined skins that are shipped with Captivate.

1. From any view, open the **Project** menu, and then select **Skin Editor** to display the Skin Editor.

2. Click the **Playback Control** tab to display the playback control options.

FIGURE 13-14 **Different skins change the look of your movie.**

3. Choose a skin from the drop-down menu at the top of the Skin Editor. The preview of the movie with the new skin displays on the right side of the screen.

4. You can make changes to any skin as described in the following sections; then click the **Save As** button to store your changes. Or you can just use the predefined options.

5. Click **OK** when you're finished changing the skin.

Changing Playback Controls

For each movie, you have the option to include playback controls that determine which buttons are displayed while the viewer is playing the movie. You can choose from a variety of playback control styles that come with Captivate. Some have many buttons, such as forward one slide, forward to the end of the movie, go back one slide, go back to the beginning, pause, stop, etc. You can also specify where the playback controls will be displayed.

FIGURE 13-15   **A variety of playback controls.**

Note: These are not the same as the controls that are available when you're previewing a movie. Playback controls usually (though not always) have an Info button (designated by the letter i).

To select the playback controls for the current movie, follow these steps:

1. From any view, open the **Project** menu, and then select **Skin Editor** to display the Skin Editor.
2. Click the **Playback Control** tab to display the playback control options.

FIGURE 13-16   **Set playback control options in the Skin Editor.**

3.   Click the **Show playback control** check box to display the controls and activate the playback options. If this check box is not selected, no playback controls will be displayed on the finished movie.

4.   Choose a set of playback controls from the drop-down Playbar list to display a preview of the selected playback controls in the preview area. Note that as you scroll through the options, some controls have more buttons than others, and a few are oriented vertically. The buttons may include some or all of the following functions:

   ■   *Play/Pause:* Plays the movie (or restarts the movie after the viewer pauses it).

   ■   *Back:* Displays the previous slide.

   ■   *Rewind:* Restarts the movie from the beginning.

   ■   *Forward:* Displays the next slide.

   ■   *Closed Captioning:* Displays an icon that activates text descriptions of the movie as it plays (if you've created them)

- *Close/Exit:* Closes the movie window.
- *Mute:* Displays an audio control icon.
- *Progressbar:* This is the visual representation of where the viewer is within the movie. For example, if the viewer is looking at slide 10 of 100, the progress bar will display across one-10th of the available bar length. If the viewer is looking at slide 80 of 100, the progress bar will show that the movie is 8/10ths of the way complete.
- *Fast Forward:* Displays a button that allows the user to skip through parts of the movie.

5. Choose the location for the playback controls by clicking on one of the Position icons. You can place the controls on the left, top, bottom, or right side of the movie viewer screen.

TIP

Make sure you preview your movie with the playback controls to ensure that your controls don't cover important captions or other buttons. Some playback controls are much larger than others, and switching controls without testing can give unexpected results. You'll also want to think carefully about choosing controls that omit, for example, an exit button, particularly for a full-screen movie that may have no other way of ending early if the viewer needs it to.

---

6. Choose the layout of the playback controls within the location you specified by choosing from the Layout drop-down list. These options will vary depending on the location you chose. For example, if you chose a vertical orientation (left side or right side), you'll be able to specify whether the controls should be on the top or bottom of that side. You also have the Stretched option, which displays the controls from one edge of the screen to the other. As you specify these options, the preview panel reflects the changes as you make them.

7. You can choose which buttons to include by selecting the buttons from the center of the **Playback Control** tab. Your choices here override the default settings for each Playbar style.

8. If you choose to display closed captions, click the **Settings** button to display the Closed Captioning settings window. You can define the number of lines on which the captions display, as well as the font, size, background,

and transparency of the displayed text. Remember, you must create the captions for each audio file as described in Chapter 8. Click **OK** to close the Closed Captioning settings window.

FIGURE 13-17   **Define how the closed captions will display.**

9. You can set the transparency of the playback control background by either using the up and down arrows to increment the transparency by steps of 10 percent or typing a specific transparency number. Note that a transparency of 0 is solid (nothing shows through) and a transparency of 100 removes the control background entirely (the playback buttons appear to "float" on the movie).

10. (*Optional*) Predefined playback controls have predefined control colors. You can change these colors by selecting the **Playback Colors** check box to activate the color controls. As you choose new colors for each of the options, the colors are displayed on the preview.

11. Click **Save As** if you want to store your changes to the skin (to the current name or to a new custom name). If you don't save the changes you've made, they'll be applied to the current movie only. Click **OK** when you're done to close the Skin Editor.

Defining Borders

The borders on the final movie are the areas around the captured area. By enlarging the border behind the location you've chosen for the playback controls, you can ensure that those controls don't cover important areas of your movie.

1. From any view, open the **Project** menu, and then select **Skin** to display the Skin Editor.
2. Click the **Borders** tab to display the border options.

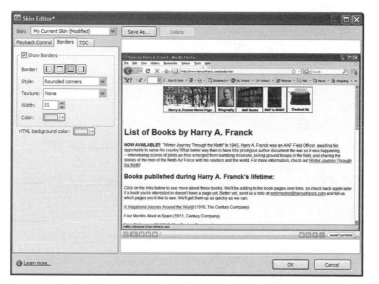

FIGURE 13-18   **Enlarge or shade around the edges of your movie.**

3. Click the **Show Borders** check box to display the defined borders and activate the border options. If this check box is not selected, no borders will be displayed on the finished movie.
4. Select which borders to display by clicking the Border icons. Note that unlike the Position option for playback controls, which allows you to select any one icon, this window lets you choose as many borders as you need. As you click on each icon, the selected border is displayed on the preview portion of the window.

5. Select a Style of either **Rounded corners** or **Square edges**. Note that this style applies to the outer edges of the borders around the movie, not the captured movie itself.

6. Choose either a Texture (by selecting a graphic from the drop-down list) or a Color (by clicking on the color box and choosing a color) for the borders. If you choose a texture, the selected graphic will be used as the selected border edges. For example, Figure 13-19 shows the texture "thatch" on all four sides of the movie (and a rounded-corner style).

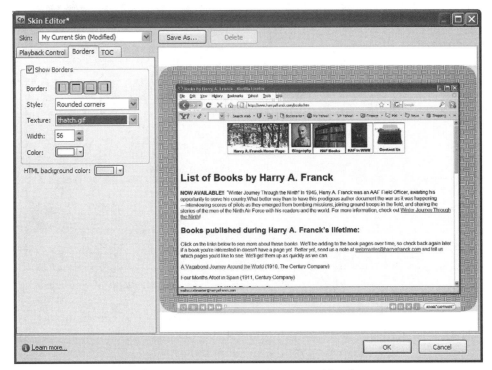

FIGURE 13-19   **A movie with textured borders.**

7. Specify the border width (in pixels). The border should be at least as large as your playback controls on the edge where the playback controls are displayed (the bottom edge in Figure 13-19).

8. Choose a color that will be displayed behind the movie (for example, show through the rounded corners).

9. Click **Save As** if you want to store your changes to the skin (to the current name or to a new custom name). If you don't save the changes you've made, they'll be applied to the current movie only. Click **OK** when you're done to close the Skin Editor.

TABLE OF CONTENTS

Captivate allows you to create a unique table of contents (TOC) that displays at run-time. You can define the appearance of the menu and the actions that occur when the menu subitems are selected.

Creating a Table of Contents

1. From any view, open the **Project** menu, and then select **Skin** to display the Skin Editor.
2. Click the **TOC** tab to display the TOC options.

FIGURE 13-20 Define a TOC that will be displayed at run-time.

3. Click **Show TOC** to display the table of contents in the preview area of the window.
4. The TOC tab panel displays a list of all slides in the movie. By default, they're all selected (and thus will appear in the TOC at run-time). To prevent slides from displaying in the TOC, click the check box next to the slide number to deselect it.

TIP

If you've grouped your slides in the Captivate project, the TOC will reflect those groupings by automatically creating submenus for each group.

---

5. You can create submenus as part of your TOC using the buttons at the bottom of the slide list. To do this, click the **Add Topic** button (a folder with a plus sign) to create an entry under which you want to put some slides, then move the slides so that they're under that entry. Use the following keys to move TOC entries around:
    - *Right arrow:* Puts the entry into a submenu.
    - *Left arrow:* Takes the entry out of the current submenu.
    - *Up arrow:* Moves the entry so that it displays toward the top of the TOC.
    - *Down arrow:* Moves the entry so that it displays toward the bottom of the TOC.
6. The default name for all new topics is "Topic Name." You can rename the topic by clicking on the topic name and typing a new name. You can also rename any of your slides this way. The name you type will be displayed on the TOC at run-time.

FIGURE 13-21   **Reorganize the TOC entries with the buttons at the bottom of the slide list.**

7.   You can remove a slide entry or topic heading from the TOC by selecting it and then clicking the **Trash** icon. Note that this does not remove the slide from the movie; it only removes the entry from the TOC.

8.   If you want to undo all of the changes you've made to the TOC, you can click the **Reset** icon (second from left, has a green arrow that points to the left).

9.   Click **Save As** to store the table of contents (and all skin settings) to a name you specify. You can apply this skin to any subsequent movie by choosing it from the Skin drop-down menu at the top of the Skin Editor.

Changing the Appearance of a TOC

You can modify the appearance of any TOC with the TOC settings. These options allow you to modify both the color and placement of the TOC and to control the actions that occur when the viewer is using the TOC.

1. From any view, open the **Project** menu, and then select **Skin** to display the Skin Editor.
2. Click the **TOC** tab to display the TOC options.
3. Click the **Settings** button to display the Skin TOC settings window.

FIGURE 13-22   **The Skin TOC settings window.**

4. Define the location of the TOC with the Style and Position radio buttons. Choose **Separate** if you want the TOC to appear just outside the movie as it plays. This is the default. Choose **Overlay** if you want the TOC to be hidden until the viewer clicks the TOC button on the playback bar. Choose **Left** or **Right** to indicate on which side of the movie to display the TOC.

FIGURE 13-23 The Overlay option covers the slides when the movie is played.

5. Define the colors for the TOC panel by setting any or all of the options shown in Table 13-3.

TABLE 13-3 TOC color settings.

Use this:	To set this:
Background	The color of the area behind the panel.
Default	The color of the panel itself—this is the color on which the TOC entries (in black) will be placed, so don't make it too dark.
Active	The color of the panel behind the name of the slide that's currently displayed at run-time.
Rollover	The color of the panel behind each entry as the viewer moves the mouse over the entries. This becomes the active color once the viewer clicks the entry.

TABLE 13-3 TOC color settings (continued).

Use this:	To set this:
Heading	The color of the panel behind the top heading (that describes the TOC columns for the viewer) and the bottom or footer area of the slide (where the info and search display, if included).
Outline	The color of the borders around the TOC panel.
Transparency	The amount of transparency that allows the background or slide (if Style is set to Overlay) to show through the TOC panel. A transparency level of 100% is clear; a transparency level of 0% is solid.

6. Set the run-time options by selecting any or all of the following:

TABLE 13-4 Run-time TOC options.

Click this check box:	For this result:
Self Paced Learning	Stores the status flags for each viewer. If the viewer stops in the middle of the movie, then returns later, this option will cause the movie to begin AFTER the last slide seen.
Show Duration	Displays the duration and status of the slides in the table of contents during run-time.
Enable Navigation	Allows viewers to use the TOC to move to different points in the movie. If this is not selected, the TOC becomes a display-only indication of where they are in the movie.
Show Search	Display a search field at the bottom of the TOC that allows the viewer to enter a word or phrase. You can specify whether or not the search will include quiz question slides by selecting or deselecting the Search Quiz check box.
Status Flag	Displays a check mark in the status column for each slide the viewer has already seen. If you use the status flag, you may also select the Clear Button check box to display a button at the bottom of the TOC that will allow the viewer to remove the status check marks.
Auto Preview	Displays the changes you make to the settings in the preview window. You can turn off the preview by deselecting this option.

7. You can control the appearance of the text on the TOC by clicking **Advanced** to display the font options. For EACH level of the TOC, specify the font, color, size, and style you want for the text.

FIGURE 13-24   **Set the TOC font options.**

8. Click **OK** to close the Skin TOC settings window.
9. Click **Save** to store your changes to the table of contents, or click **Save As** to store the TOC to a new name.

DISPLAYING MOVIE INFORMATION

If you display movie controls on the finished movie, the controls will always include an information button. The button itself will vary according to the style of controls you choose, but it will always be designated with the letter **i**. To specify the information that is displayed when the viewer clicks the information button, follow these steps:

1. From any view, open the **Edit** menu, select **Preferences**, and then click the **Info** option under **Projects** (or choose **Document Info** from the **File** menu).

FIGURE 13-25   **Enter information in the Preferences window.**

2. Type information in any or all of the text boxes.

Note: Though you can leave the information boxes empty, you must enter at least the project name and description for full compliance with the U.S. government Section 508 accessibility rules.

TABLE 13-5 Movie information fields.

This field:	Should contain this information:
Author	The name of the author of the movie (or department, if more applicable).
Company	The company name.
E-mail	An e-mail address to which people can write with problems, if they encounter any.
Website	The web address (URL) for your company or organization.
Copyright	The copyright information for your movie.
Project name	A unique name for the movie. If you're generating accessible movies, this name will be read by screen reader software at the beginning of the movie. Note that this does not display in the movie information window.
Description	A short description of the movie. If you're generating accessible movies, this description will be read by screen reader software at the beginning of the movie. Note that this does not display in the movie information window.

3.   Click **OK** when you're done to close the Preferences window.

MANAGING MOVIE FILES

You can set Captivate to automatically save movies with a global setting within Captivate. But if you want to rename or copy or delete a movie, the easiest way is to use Windows Explorer to manipulate your files. Captivate stores information about each movie in Captivate project files (with an extension of .cp). You can delete these files, if necessary, or copy them to create new files. Back within Captivate, you can also hide a movie so that it doesn't appear on the opening Captivate screen.

Saving Movies

As you've seen throughout this book, it is easy to save a movie periodically while you're working on it. There are three ways to save a movie:

■   Click the **Save** icon on the toolbar.

■   From the **File** menu, choose **Save**.

■   Press **Ctrl+S** on the keyboard.

Working with Movie Files in Windows® Internet Explorer®

You can view all of your movie projects, or delete or copy them, or perform any of the other tasks that are normally handled by the Windows operating system. To do this, follow these steps:

1.   Open Windows Explorer, then navigate to the location of the Captivate movie.

> **TIP**
>
> As you create movie projects, Captivate stores the files by default in the folder \My Documents\My Adobe Captivate Projects. If you've saved movies to a location other than this (using the Save As command) you'll need to browse to wherever your movies are stored.

2.   Captivate creates a number of files of various types while you're working within the project. Click the file icon (or name) to select it.

TABLE 13-6 Captivate file types.

This extension:	Indicates this file type:
.cp	The Captivate project files. All other files are created from this one.
.htm	An HTML file that is created specifically to play a Flash movie file.
.swf	The Flash movie file itself.
.mpg	MenuBuilder files that point to a variety of other files.
.cptl	Project template file.
.cpdl	Design template file.

3. Choose any of the displayed tasks (**Rename**, **Move**, **Copy**, **Delete**). You can also right-click on the file icon (or name) to display a drop-down menu of tasks.

TIP

It is easy to recreate deleted .htm or .swf files from your Captivate project file (.cp). However, if you delete the Captivate project file, you'll have to start all over again to create that particular movie. Make sure you are completely finished with a project file before you delete it—better yet, archive the project for future reference. You may be able to use tricks or slides from one movie in another movie later.

Hiding Movies

When you start Captivate, it displays a list of the most recently created movies. You can remove a movie project from this list. For example, if you've got several versions of a movie and only want the most recent one to be displayed, you can "hide" the older versions. To do this, follow these steps:

1. From the main Captivate opening window, right-click on the movie that you want to hide in order to display a menu.
2. Choose **Hide project** to display a confirmation dialog.
3. Click **Yes** to remove the movie from the list of recently viewed movies. The project remains in the folder and can still be accessed using the Open button.

SUMMARY

This chapter reviewed some of the tasks you might perform on movies and projects, including setting start and end options and managing movie files. The following chapter discusses the various output options for Captivate projects.

14 GENERATING ADOBE® CAPTIVATE® OUTPUT

After you've created your slides, added objects and interactivity, and defined the movie-level components, the final step is to generate the movie output. The Adobe® Captivate® program gives you a variety of output options, such as stand-alone executable files or .html files for web-based delivery.

Another type of Captivate output lets you specify just parts of the movie, such as pulling out the text captions (for translation or review purposes) or creating a variety of paper-based handouts.

There are also options that you can set to ensure your movie is compatible with the U.S. Section 508 accessibility rules.

PUBLISHING A MOVIE

There are a variety of output options available when you generate (or "publish") a movie project.

- *Flash file:* This option creates a standard Flash file (.swf) that can be played by a Flash viewer. You can have Captivate automatically generate an .html file that will use the default browser viewer, or you can create a zipped file for easier transportation between systems.
- *Adobe Acrobat Connect Pro:* Adobe Acrobat Connect Pro is a web-based meeting and presentation server software package. You can export Captivate projects directly to an Adobe Acrobat Connect Pro server.

- *Media:* This option can produce a Windows executable file (.exe) or an .avi video file. Viewers of the movie would not need to have any viewing software on their systems to run a stand-alone movie.

In addition, you can e-mail or FTP Flash files, executable files, or even the original project files directly from Captivate.

You can also publish Captivate files specifically for review with the Captivate Reviewer software as described in Chapter 12, "Using Adobe Captivate Tools."

Publishing Movies as Flash Files

When you publish Captivate movies as Flash .swf files, you can automatically create zip files (for easier distribution) or .html files for use with web pages. You can also specify whether the movie should play as a full-screen movie or at the size you specify when recording.

To publish a movie as a Flash movie file, follow these steps:

1. Click the **Publish** icon or select **Publish** from the **File** menu to display the Publish window.
2. Click the **Flash (SWF)** icon to display the Flash options.

FIGURE 14-1 Set the Flash publishing options.

3. The Project Title text box defaults to the name you entered for the project file. You can leave this as is or type a new name. It isn't necessary to include the file extension—Captivate will add .swf to the finished filename.

4. The Folder text box defaults to the folder that stores the project files. You can leave this as is, type a new folder location, or click the **Browse** button to browse to the output location.

5. Select any of the options in Table 14-1 from the Output Options area.

TABLE 14-1 Flash movie output options.

Select this option:	To create this:
Zip files	A .zip file containing your Flash file. The .zip file will have the same name entered in the Movie Title field with the extension .zip.
Full screen	A Flash file and two .html files that you'll use to play the Flash file in full-screen mode. The .html files both have the same name as the Movie Title (and the extension .htm), but one also has "_fs" appended to the filename. When you open *filename*_fs.htm, the movie will play full screen. Note that this option is not available if you have selected AICC or SCORM options (see Chapter 10).
Generate autorun for CD	A Flash file and an autorun file (called autorun.inf). If you copy both of these files to a CD, the movie file will play automatically when the user starts the CD (depending on the user's system).
Export HTML	A Flash file and an .html file that can be used to display the Flash file in a browser. The .html file will have the same name entered in the Movie Title field with the extension .htm.
Send PENS notification	Notification to the specified learning management system (if you've defined it in the Quiz Preferences area).
Export PDF	A .pdf file that includes the movie.
Flash Player Version	Output that can be read by the specified version of the Flash Player.

6. The Project Information area on the right of the screen displays the current preference settings for the movie, such as the size (resolution) and audio information. To change the options listed in this area, click **Preferences** to display the Preferences window. The publishing options on this window are

described later in this chapter; other preferences are described throughout this book.

7.   When you are done, click **Publish** to generate the output file or files.

Publishing to Adobe Connect

If you use the Adobe Acrobat Connect Pro collaboration and meeting application, you can publish your movie directly to the Adobe Acrobat Connect Pro server.

To send a Captivate movie directly to a Connect server, follow these steps:

1.   Click the **Publish** icon or select **Publish** from the **File** menu to display the Publish window.
2.   Click the **Adobe Acrobat Connect Pro** icon to display the server options.

FIGURE 14-2   Set the Connect publishing options.

3.   Click the **Change Server** button to display the list of Connect options available on your system.

FIGURE 14-3   **Choose a Connect server.**

4.   Select the server you want to use by clicking on the server name or URL. If the server isn't listed, you can click the **Add** button to enter information about a new server. You must enter both the name and URL of the server. Click **OK** when you are done to close the Connect window.

5.   Select the check boxes for the output options you want.

TABLE 14-2 Adobe Connect output options

Select this option:	To do this:
Publish project files (*.cp)	Copies the source Captivate file (along with the output SWF file) to the Connect server.
Zip Project file	Zips the Captivate source file before storing it on the Connect server.
Publish Video Files (*.flv)	Copies FLV files (if any) from the Captivate project to the Connect server.

6.   The Project Information area on the right of the screen displays the current preference settings for the movie, such as the size (resolution) and audio information. To change the options listed in this area, click **Preferences** to display the Preferences window. The output options on this window are described later in this chapter; other preferences are described throughout this book.

7. Set the preferences you want and then click **OK** to close the Preferences window.
8. When you are done, click **Publish** to display the Adobe Connect login screen.
9. Sign in to Adobe Connect using your login name and password.
10. Select a location on the server to store the Captivate movie.
11. Click **Publish to This Folder** to display the available options.
12. Type a title for the movie, choose a language, and enter a speaker name. When you are finished, click **Next**.
13. When the movie has been published to the server, a confirmation dialog displays. Click **OK** to close the confirmation dialog.

Publishing Movies to Media Files

Captivate can publish to either an executable file that does not require a browser for viewing or a video file (extension .avi).

To generate a stand-alone movie file, follow these steps:

1. Click the **Publish** icon or select **Publish** from the **File** menu to display the Publish window.
2. Click the **Media** icon to display the executable options.
3. Choose the type of output file you want (.exe or .avi) from the Select Type drop-down list.

FIGURE 14-4 Set the publishing options.

4.   The Project Title text box defaults to the name you entered for the project file. You can leave this as is or type a new name. It isn't necessary to include the file extension—Captivate will add the appropriate extension to the finished filename.

5.   The Folder text box defaults to the folder that stores the project files. You can leave this as is, type a new folder location, or click the **Browse** button to browse to the output location.

6.   If you've chosen EXE output, you may also specify an icon for the executable file. Type the name or browse to a graphic icon file (extension .ico) to select it. The specified graphic will be included in the executable file.

7.   Select any or all of the options in Table 14-3 from the Output Options area.

TABLE 14-3 Executable output options.

Select this option:	To create this:
Zip files	A .zip file containing your executable file. The .zip file will have the same name entered in the Movie Title field with the extension .zip.
Full screen	An executable file plays the movie in full-screen mode.
Generate autorun for CD	An executable file and an autorun file (called autorun.inf). If you copy both of these files to a CD, the movie file will play automatically when the user starts the CD. Depending on the user's system configuration, users can start the CD by putting the CD into their computer or by clicking on the CD drive icon.
Flash Player Version	Output that can be read by the specified version of the Flash Player.

TIP

If you're using the Generate autorun for CD option, keep your movies in separate folders. This prevents Captivate from overwriting prior autorun files with new ones you generate. They are all named autorun.inf; just the contents of the files will vary by movie title.

8.   The Project Information area on the right side of the screen displays the current preference settings for the movie, such as the size (resolution)

and audio information. To change the options listed in this area, click **Preferences** to display the Preferences window. The output options on this window are described in the following section; other preferences are described throughout this book.

9.   Set the preferences you want, and then click **OK** to close the Preferences window.

Note: This window is discussed in more detail in Chapter 13.

---

10.   When you are done, click **Publish** to generate the output file or files.

Setting Movie Preferences

During the publishing process, you can view the movie preferences on the right side of the screen. If you need to change these settings, click the Preferences button to display the Preferences window, as shown in Figure 14-5.

Refer to Table 14-4 to set the output, visual, and sound options on the Preferences window.

FIGURE 14-5   **Set the movie output, visual, and sound options.**

TABLE 14-4 Movie output, visual, and sound options.

Select this:	To cause this:
Frames per second	Determines the speed at which the movie will be played.
Publish Adobe Connect Server metadata	Add information to the project file (.swf) that makes it easier to integrate the project into Adobe Connect Enterprise.
Include mouse	Select this option to include any recorded mouse movement in the movie.
Include audio	Select this option to include any added audio files in the movie.
Play tap audio for recorded typing	This option plays tapping sounds in the final movie whenever keys are pressed as you record the movie. (For example, if you record an e-mail message being sent, you most likely type an e-mail address. Using this option, a tapping sound is played for each of the keystrokes.)
Enable Accessibility	Select this option if you need to deliver accessible Flash files. See the section "About Accessibility" later in this chapter.
ActionScript version	Choose **AS2 or AS3** to indicate which version this movie uses.
Externalize resources	Select the check box for the elements (Skin, Widgets, Full Motion Recordings, or Animations) that you want to store as separate files. This will greatly reduce the size of your movie file. However, you must ensure that the files remain together since the smaller .swf file will still reference these other components.

SENDING MOVIE FILES

Once you've published a movie to any of the available formats, you can send the files to other people by e-mail, on CD, over a website, or by any other method that works for you. In addition to sending files after they've been published, Captivate allows you to send a movie either by e-mail or by FTP at the same time as you publish it.

Sending Movies through E-mail

To publish a movie and send it through e-mail all at once, follow these steps:

1. Click the **Publish** icon or select **Publish** from the **File** menu to display the Publish window.
2. Click the **E-Mail** icon to display the e-mail options.

FIGURE 14-6   **Enter e-mail options.**

3. The Project Title text box defaults to the name you entered for the project file. You can leave this as is or type a new name. It isn't necessary to include the file extension—Captivate will add .swf to the finished filename.
4. Specify which of the file types you want to generate by choosing from the drop-down list under File type:

   - *SWF File:* Creates and sends a Flash format file.
   - *Windows Executable:* Sends a stand-alone executable file with the extension .exe that runs on any Microsoft Windows-based system.
   - *Project Files (.cp):* Sends the source Captivate files.
   - *XML:* Sends an XML version of the project.

5. (*Optional*) Select the **Zip files** option to compress all output files into a single file with the extension .zip.

6. (*Optional*) Select the **Full screen** option to create and e-mail a full-screen version of the movie.

7. (*Optional*) Select the **Export HMTL** option to create an .html file that will run the exported .swf file.

8. The Project information area on the right of the screen displays the current preference settings for the movie, such as the size (resolution) and audio information. To change the options listed in this area, click **Preferences** to display the Preferences window. The output options on this window are described earlier in this chapter; other preferences are described throughout this book.

9. When you are done, click **Publish** to create the specified files and open your default e-mail program. The files will automatically be attached to the generated e-mail message.

10. Type an e-mail address into your e-mail program and send an e-mail message with the attachment.

Sending Movies through FTP

You can publish your Captivate movies directly to a website using the standard file transfer protocol (FTP). You must have permission to access the destination site, which often means you'll need a user name and password.

To publish a movie and send it through FTP, follow these steps:

1. Click the **Publish** icon or select **Publish** from the **File** menu to display the Publish window.

2. Click the **FTP** icon to display the FTP options.

FIGURE 14-7 Enter FTP options.

3. The Project Title text box defaults to the name you entered for the project file. You can leave this as is or type a new name. It isn't necessary to include the file extension—Captivate will add the .swf extension to the finished filename.

4. In the Server box, enter the server that hosts the destination for the movie files. You must type the "ftp" and the extension. For example, you might send it to ftp.harryafranck.com.

5. Enter the directory on the server for the files you're sending. Remember, you must have access to this directory.

6. Enter your user name and password, if required. Once you've entered this information, you may click the **Test Settings** button to make sure that you do have access and all systems are working before generating and sending the movie files.

7. Enter the port for this system. Captivate defaults to Port 21 because it is the most commonly used.

8. Specify which of the file types you want to generate by choosing from the drop-down list for File type:

   ▪ *SWF File:* Creates and sends a Flash format file.

- *Windows Executable:* Sends a stand-alone executable file with the extension .exe that runs on any Microsoft Windows-based system.
- *Project Files (.cp):* Sends the source Captivate files.

9. Select any of the options shown in Table 14-5 from the Output Options area:

TABLE 14-5 FTP output options.

Select this option:	To send this:
Zip files	A .zip file containing your Flash file. The .zip file will have the same name entered in the Movie Title field with the extension .zip.
Full screen	A Flash file that plays in full-screen mode. Note that this option is not available if you have selected AICC or SCORM options (see Chapter 10).
Export HTML	A Flash file and an .html file that can be used to display the Flash file in a browser. The .html file will have the same name entered in the Movie Title field with the extension .htm.
Send PENS notification	Notification to the specified learning management system (if you've defined it in the Quiz Preferences area).
Flash Player Version	Output that can be read by the specified version of the Flash Player.

10. The Project Information area on the right of the screen displays the current preference settings for the movie, such as the size (resolution) and audio information. To change the options listed in this area, click **Preferences** to display the Preferences window. The output options on this window are described earlier in this chapter.

11. Click **Publish** to create the movie and send it by FTP to the designated server.

EXPORTING AND IMPORTING TEXT CAPTIONS

You can export text captions from an existing Captivate movie into a Word document (.doc) or into an XML localization translation file format (.xliff). The formatting from Captivate (font, color, size, etc.) will be preserved in the output document. You can then make changes using any of the Word features (such as global change and replace) or send your captions out for translation if necessary. Once you've made the changes, you can import the captions back into the original movie.

Exporting Captions to a Word File

Note: You must have Microsoft Word installed on your computer in order to export text captions to a Word document.

To export, edit, and import text captions using a Word document, follow these steps:

1. From the **File** menu, select **Export**, and then choose **Project Captions and Closed Captions** to display a standard Save As window.
2. Captivate defaults to using the same name and same directory as the project for your exported caption text. You can keep this name or type a new filename for the .doc file. You can also specify a different directory or folder.
3. Click **Save** to store the captions in a Word file (.doc format) and display a confirmation dialog.

FIGURE 14-8 **View the captions after exporting them.**

4. Click **Yes** to view the Word document containing the captions. The Word document contains information about all the captions in the movie (text captions, success captions, failure captions, etc.) in a table. The actual text is contained in two identical columns.

5. Make changes as necessary to your captions by editing the text in the Updated Text Caption Data column, as shown in Figure 14-9.

Note: Do not change anything in the first two columns (Slide ID and Item ID). Captivate uses this information when you import the captions back into the project. You can change the Original Text Caption Data if you like, though you may prefer to keep them as they are to track the changes as you make them. You can also use Microsoft Word change tracking features for this purpose.

FIGURE 14-9   The captions in a Word file.

6.   Save the Word document.

7.   Back in Captivate, determine whether you want to import the captions back into the same movie (as when correcting a product name) or into a copy of the movie (if, for example, you want to make copies of the movie in several languages).

TIP

When you import the captions, the original captions will be overwritten. You may want to store a copy of the movie as a backup before importing.

---

8.   Open the copy of the movie where you want the new captions.

9.   From the **File** menu, select **Import**, and then **Project Captions and Closed Captions** to display a window containing the files in the default folder.

Note: This option is only active for projects that have exported the captions already (or copies of projects that exported captions).

---

10.   Select the file containing the new captions, and then click **Open** to import the edited captions into the current movie.

11.   A message is displayed when the import is complete. Click **OK** to close the confirmation dialog.

Exporting Captions to an XML File

To export, edit, and import text captions using an XML localization interchange file format (.xliff), follow these steps:

1.   From the **File** menu, select **Export**, and then choose **To XML** to display a standard Save As window.

2.   Captivate defaults to using the same name and same directory as the project for your exported project text. You can keep this name or type a new filename for the .xml file. You can also specify a different directory or folder.

3. Click **Save** to store the captions in an .xml file and display a confirmation dialog.

Relevant objects in the project are converted into XML format. A dialog box appears, confirming that the XML export was successful. Choose whether you want to view the .xml file. If you click Yes, the .xml file is opened in your computer's default XML viewer.

PRINTING MOVIE COMPONENTS

Though you can't print animations, Captivate does allow you to print a variety of movie components:

- Handouts
- Lessons
- Step by step references
- Storyboards

Printing Slide Handouts

Handouts are created as a Microsoft Word file. You have the options of including a variety of components in your handouts and of determining the size of the slide images (much like PowerPoint handouts).

To publish a Captivate movie as a handout, follow these steps:

1. From the **File** menu, select **Publish** to display the Publish window.
2. Click the **Print** icon to display the print options.
3. From the Type drop-down list, choose **Handouts** to display the Handout options, as shown in Figure 14-10.

FIGURE 14-10   **Publish slides as handouts.**

4.   The Project Title text box defaults to the name you entered for the project file. You can keep this or type a new name. It isn't necessary to include the file extension—Captivate will add .doc to the finished filename.

5.   The Folder text box defaults to the folder that stores the project files. You can leave this as it is, type a new folder location, or click the **Browse** button to browse to the output location.

6.   Specify which of the slides you want to export by entering an export range. Choose one of the following:

   ▪   *All:* Export all slides.
   ▪   *Current slide:* Export only the one slide currently displayed in Edit view.
   ▪   *Selection:* Export all selected slides.
   ▪   *Slides:* Enter the numbers of the slides you want to export.

7.   Specify the layout options you want for the exported data. See Table 14-6 for available options.

TABLE 14-6 Options for printed handouts.

Select this option:	For this result:
Use tables in the output	Allows you to specify the number of slides that you want to print on each page. If you don't select this option, Captivate prints one slide per page, with other selected options (such as printing lines for notes or caption text) displayed beneath each slide.
Slides per page	This option is only available if you've selected Use tables in the output. Choose the number of slides you want to print on each page by choosing from the drop-down list. You can choose one, two, four, six, or nine slides per page. A graphic shows how the finished page will look based on the number of slides you specify.
Caption text	Exports the text of all captions and prints them below the slide on which they appear.
Add blank lines for notes	Several lines appear to the right of each slide image on which people can take their own notes if desired. This is similar to handout options in other software packages, such as PowerPoint handouts.
Slide notes	Exports the notes for each slide from the Slide Properties window. **Tip:** Before you actually hand out pages with your slide notes on them, proofread your handouts! You may not want a message that was intended for internal use to be distributed to other people.
Include objects and question slides	Exports a graphic representation of all objects on your slides (including captions and highlight boxes). Note that if you've got your captions stacked (that is, if the success, failure, and retry captions all display in the same location, then only the topmost one will appear on the slide). This option automatically includes the mouse movement for slides that have mouse movement turned on.
Include hidden slides	Exports the hidden slides. If you don't want the hidden slides on your handouts, make sure this option is not selected.
Include Mouse Path	Draws the mouse path on slides where a mouse movement is turned on.
Include question pool slides	Includes the question pool slides in the handouts. Note that this option is only available if you checked the Include objects and question slides option.

> **TIP**
>
> As you add options that display outside of the slides, such as slide notes, blank lines, or caption text, the slide image itself gets smaller. If you have a larger number of slides per page (six or nine) the images may be too small to read. Options that display on top of the slide, such as mouse path and include objects, can make the slides very busy and difficult to read. Always print and proof your handouts before distributing them!

8. Click **Publish** to create a Word file that contains your slides along with any selected options.
9. A confirmation dialog displays. Click **View Output** to open Microsoft Word and display the handout file.
10. You can edit any of the components in the Word document, including editing text captions and deleting slides if necessary, as well as editing the header and footer.

FIGURE 14-11   **A handout with six slides per page and blank lines for notes.**

> **TIP**
>
> By default, Captivate creates the handouts using the AdobeCaptivate.dot template that is stored in the folder Adobe\Adobe Captivate 4\. The name Captivate and the current date are in the header, and the page number is in the footer. You can make edits to this template to change the headers, footers, page size, and other elements.

Printing Slide Lessons

Lessons are created as a Microsoft Word file. There will be one page for each slide. If you've used (and included) question pools, these will be included at the end of the other types of movie slides. Finally, the lesson file will include a list of the answers for each quiz question. You have the option of including a variety of components in your lesson.

To publish a Captivate movie as a lesson, follow these steps:

1. From the **File** menu, select **Publish** to display the Publish window.
2. Click the **Print** icon to display the print options.
3. From the Type drop-down list, choose **Lesson** to display the lesson options, as shown in Figure 14-12.

FIGURE 14-12 Publish slides as a lesson.

4.   The Project Title text box defaults to the name you entered for the project file. You can keep this or type a new name. It isn't necessary to include the file extension—Captivate will add .doc to the finished filename.

5.   The Folder text box defaults to the folder that stores the project files. You can leave this as it is, type a new folder location, or click the **Browse** button to browse to the output location.

6.   Specify which of the slides you want to export by entering an export range. Choose one of the following:

   - *All:* Export all slides.
   - *Current slide:* Export only the one slide currently displayed in Edit view.
   - *Selection:* Export all selected slides.
   - *Slides:* Enter the numbers of the slides you want to export.

7.   Enter the header and footer text that you want to be printed on the top and bottom of each lesson page and select the options you want to be included in the output.

TABLE 14-7 Options for printed lessons.

Select this option:	For this result:
Include hidden slides	Exports the hidden slides. If you don't want the hidden slides in your lesson, make sure this option is not selected.
Include quiz question slides	Exports the question slides (and includes the answers at the end of the lesson file).
Include question pool slides	Includes the question pool slides in the lesson. Note that this option is only available if you checked the Include quiz question slides option.

8.   Click **Publish** to create a Word file that contains your slides along with any selected options.

9.   A confirmation dialog displays. Click **View Output** to open Microsoft Word and display the lesson file.

10.   You can edit any of the components in the Word document, including editing text captions and deleting slides if necessary, as well as editing the header and footer.

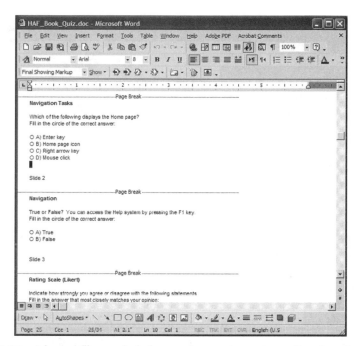

FIGURE 14-13   **A lesson file may include question pool questions after the other movie slides.**

Printing Slides Step by Step

This function creates a Microsoft Word file that contains one line for each interactive item in the movie (such as buttons or click boxes).

To publish a Captivate movie as a step-by-step reference, follow these steps:

1. From the **File** menu, select **Publish** to display the Publish window.
2. Click the **Print** icon to display the print options.
3. From the Type drop-down list, choose **Step by Step** to display the step-by-step reference options, as shown in Figure 14-14.

FIGURE 14-14   **Publish slides as a step-by-step reference.**

4.   The Project Title text box defaults to the name you entered for the project file. You can keep this or type a new name. It isn't necessary to include the file extension—Captivate will add .doc to the finished filename.

5.   The Folder text box defaults to the folder that stores the project files. You can leave this as is, type a new folder location, or click the **Browse** button to browse to the output location.

6.   Specify which of the slides you want to export by entering an export range. Choose one of the following:

   - *All:* Export all slides.
   - *Current slide:* Export only the one slide currently displayed in Edit view.
   - *Selection:* Export all selected slides.
   - *Slides:* Enter the numbers of the slides you want to export.

7.   Enter the header and footer text that you want printed on the top and bottom of each page.

8.   Select the **Include hidden slides** option to include the hidden slides in the output (or deselect this option to omit the hidden slides).

9.   Click **Publish** to create a Word file.

10. A confirmation dialog displays. Click **View Output** to open Microsoft Word and display the step-by-step file.
11. You can edit any of the components in the Word document, including editing text captions and deleting slides if necessary, as well as editing the header and footer.

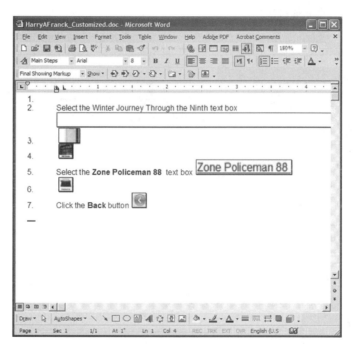

FIGURE 14-15   **The step-by-step file has one line per interactive slide.**

Printing Slides as Storyboards

This function creates a Microsoft Word file that contains page for each slide in the movie (such as buttons or click boxes.

To publish a Captivate movie as a storyboard reference, follow these steps:

1. From the **File** menu, select **Publish** to display the Publish window.
2. Click the **Print** icon to display the print options.

3.   From the Type drop-down list, choose **Storyboard** to display the storyboard options, as shown in Figure 14-16.

FIGURE 14-16   **Publish slides as a storyboard.**

4.   The Project Title text box defaults to the name you entered for the project file. You can keep this or type a new name. It isn't necessary to include the file extension—Captivate will add .doc to the finished filename.

5.   The Folder text box defaults to the folder that stores the project files. You can leave this as is, type a new folder location, or click the **Browse** button to browse to the output location.

6.   Specify which of the slides you want to export by entering an export range. Choose one of the following:

- *All:* Export all slides.
- *Current slide:* Export only the one slide currently displayed in Edit view.
- *Selection:* Export all selected slides.
- *Slides:* Enter the numbers of the slides you want to export.

7.   Enter the header and footer text that you want to be printed on the top and bottom of each storyboard page and select the options you want to be included in the output.

TABLE 14-8 Options for printed storyboard.

Select this option:	For this result:
Include hidden slides	Exports the hidden slides. If you don't want the hidden slides on your storyboard, make sure this option is not selected.
Include quiz question slides	Exports the question slides (and includes the answers at the end of the storyboard file).
Include question pool slides	Includes the question pool slides in the storyboard. Note that this option is only available if you checked the Include quiz question slides option.

8. Click **Publish** to create a Word file that contains your slides along with any selected options.

9. A confirmation dialog displays. Click **View Output** to open Microsoft Word and display the storyboard file. The first section includes a summary of the movie, and the second section includes one page for each slide.

FIGURE 14-17 The storyboard summary includes information about the entire movie.

10. You can edit any of the components in the Word document, including editing text captions and deleting slides if necessary, as well as editing the header and footer.

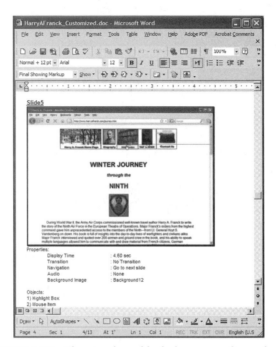

FIGURE 14-18   **The storyboard includes a page for each slide.**

ABOUT ACCESSIBILITY

Accessibility is the term that many people use to indicate that a product, such as a Flash movie or HTML page, can be read (or accessed) by people with a variety of limitations. For example, people with limited or no vision may use screen reader software to read printed text aloud. Or people with limited manual dexterity may prefer to use assistive devices with a keyboard instead of a mouse.

Many countries have adopted accessibility standards based on the Web Content Accessibility Guidelines from the World Wide Web Consortium (W3C). For information about the Web Accessibility Initiative, see the W3C website at http://www.w3.org/WAI.

The United States government has mandated that all federal agencies' electronic and information technology be accessible to people with disabilities. This regulation, often referred to as Section 508, includes a detailed set of standards that many companies find useful even if they aren't selling to the U.S. government. For more information about the United States government regulation Section 508, see http://www.section508.gov.

When talking about accessibility, there are three areas to consider:

- If people with various degrees of deafness watch your movie, they may not be able to hear your audio elements. It is important that you manually check each audio file to ensure that any important information contained in the audio file is also available in a visual element. For example, if your audio simply contains background music, you don't need to do anything. If your audio includes instructions to the viewer, those instructions should also be printed on the slide (in any of the different text captions or even as part of the background). If you use audio to indicate success (such as applause) or failure (such as a buzzer), then there must also be a visual distinction between these two caption types.

TIP

To test your movie to see if your audio is compliant, you can turn the audio off (in the Properties window) and then publish and view your movie. Or you could simply view your movie with your computer sound system turned all the way down.

- Screen reader software cannot read pictures, so you must enter a text description for slides that contain images. Captivate can help you do this through the Slide Accessibility button. You must also set the 508 compliance check box to allow the screen reader to access these elements.

- In order for screen readers to read elements such as buttons, controls, and question slides, you must ensure that the information required by the screen readers is included in your Properties window. You must also set the 508 compliance check box to allow the screen reader to access these elements.

For more information about Captivate and accessibility, see http://www.adobe.com/accessibility/products/captivate/.

Entering Text Descriptions of Visual Elements

For each slide, you can enter descriptive text that will be read by screen reader software. You can enter brief text as a slide label, or you can enter more descriptive text in the accessibility text area (or you can do both).

To enter text descriptions, follow these steps:

1. Do one of the following to display the Slide Properties window:

    - From Edit view, double-click on the slide background.
    - From Storyboard view or the filmstrip in Edit view, right-click on a slide and choose **Properties**.
    - In any view, from the **Slide** menu, choose **Properties**.

FIGURE 14-19   **Accessibility options are accessed from the Slide Properties window.**

2. Enter a label for the slide in the Label field.
3. Click the **Accessibility** button to display the Slide Accessibility Text entry window.

FIGURE 14-20   **Enter slide accessibility text.**

4. Enter the text in any combination of the following approaches:
   - Click the **Insert slide text** button to automatically insert the text from all captions on the current slide. This is most useful if you have only one caption, and it is fairly descriptive. Note that this button is only active if the current slide contains at least one text caption.
   - Click the **Insert slide notes** button to automatically insert the text from the slide notes. Note that this button is only active if the current slide contains slide notes.
   - Click the **Insert Closed Captioning Text** button to automatically insert the text from all audio elements on the current slide. Note that this button is only active if the current slide contains at least one audio closed caption.
   - Begin typing new text.

5.   When the text is displayed the way you want it, click **OK** to close the Slide Accessibility Text window.

6.   Click **OK** to close the Slide Properties window.

7.   Publish the movie as described in earlier sections of this chapter.

Entering Additional Information for Screen Readers

In addition to the text for each slide, a screen reader can read a variety of elements as long as you've got them entered and turned on within the movie.

TABLE 14-9 Accessible movie information.

For this element:	See this section and chapter:
Movie name	"Displaying Movie Information," Chapter 13
Movie description	"Displaying Movie Information," Chapter 13
Buttons	"Adding and Editing Interactive Elements," Chapter 9
Playback controls	"Changing Playback Controls," Chapter 13
Password protection prompt, if any	"Movie Start Options," Chapter 13
Question slides and all the elements on them	All sections, Chapter 10

SUMMARY

This chapter discussed ways to publish your movie and the variety of output options available to you. In addition to creating Flash movies, you can also publish Word documents based on your movie project. This chapter also described some of the considerations to keep in mind when publishing accessible content.

Glossary

AICC: Aviation Industry CBT Committee (where CBT stands for computer-based training) is an international association of technology-based training professionals. The AICC has been developing guidelines for CBT and related training technologies since 1988. For more information about AICC and its guidelines, see www.aicc.org.

AVI: Audio Video Interleaved format files. Movie files with the .avi extension are generally compatible across multiple platforms and can be imported into Captivate files as either new movies or as animations within slides.

bandwidth: The amount of data that is transmitted from one computer to another, usually given in megabits (Mbit) per second. A larger file will require a larger bandwidth for transmission.

bit rate: The number of bits that are transferred per second, generally expressed as kilobits per second (kbps), megabits per second (Mbit), or gigabits per second (Gbit). A higher number here represents a faster transmission (or quicker download).

BMP: Microsoft Windows bitmap format for graphics.

branching: The mechanism by which you can display different slides depending on whether or not the viewer answers a question correctly. This is often used with e-learning applications to control the display based on student progress through a learning activity.

caption: A caption is simply a piece of text that highlights or points to a portion of the screen. Captivate contains a variety of caption types that display at different times depending on the viewer input. For example, a text caption might instruct the viewer to click on a certain icon. If the viewer performs the task as instructed, a success caption displays. If the viewer doesn't click the right area, you may choose to display either a retry caption or a failure caption.

CBT: Computer-based training; a catchall phrase that covers any type of instruction that is delivered via computer.

click box: A click box indicates an area on the screen that the viewer should click with the mouse. You can emulate the functionality of buttons or links within a Captivate movie by creating a click box over the button and specifying a destination file that will be displayed when the viewer clicks the click box.

compression: A method of reducing the size of a file using an algorithm to remove unneeded bits. Compression reduces file size, but can also reduce file quality.

.cp: The extension used for Captivate project files.

e-learning: Short for electronic learning, this is a growing field that encompasses distance learning, computer-based training, web-based training, and a variety of other education delivery mechanisms. Instructor input is minimal or nonexistent at the time the learner is actually taking the training, and thus must be integrated up front during design and development phases. e-learning also usually has an electronic or automated grading or evaluation component.

EMF: Enhanced Metafile format for Microsoft Windows graphics. EXE: An executable file that runs a program or performs an action.

filmstrip: A representation of all of the slides in the movie that displays along one edge of the screen in Edit view.

Flash: A multimedia authoring program from Adobe that creates animations and movies. This term is also used to refer to the output of the Flash software or any other output that is compatible with the Flash Player (such as Captivate movies).

frames: In movie jargon, a frame is a single image that, when combined and played with other images, creates the illusion of movement on a screen. In Captivate, each slide is a frame that has additional functionality such as animations, click boxes, timing components, etc.

FTP: File transfer protocol that allows you to transfer information from one computer to another over a TCP/IP network.

GIF: Graphics interchange format for graphics, often used for web **delivery because of its compression and small file size.**

highlight box: A graphic on a slide that highlights a particular area, usually with colored borders and a partially transparent fill color.

HQX: Macintosh Projector file where the data is converted to ASCII format for better portability between systems.

HTML: Hypertext Markup Language uses tags and special encoding to create files that can be posted and displayed on the web and read by web browsers.

.ico: File extension used by files that display as icons on PC systems.

image: An image in Captivate can be any graphic or picture that you use in your movie. Valid image formats are JPG, JPEG, GIF , PNG, BMP, ICO, EMF , and WMF.

JPG or JPEG: Joint Photographic Experts Group format for images. This format is often used for web-based graphics.

LMS: Learning management system. A learning management system is software used to plan, implement, and assess learning processes. Different commercial LMS implementations will have different components (such as monitoring student progress, discussion lists, or even video conferencing).

Macintosh Projector file: Captivate creates this type of file with the .hqx extension so that it can be played on Macintosh systems, even though it was created on a Windows-based system.

MP3: MPEG format audio file using a compression scheme called audio layer 3.

pass rate: In e-learning applications, the total of correct answers required to "pass" a course. In Captivate, this can be expressed as a percentage or a raw number.

PENS: Package Exchange Notification Services, a type of update notification protocol standard created by the AICC (Aviation Industry CBT Committee) and used by many learning management systems.

PNG: Portable Network Graphic, a highly transportable image format. POT: PowerPoint Template format.

PowerPoint: A widely used presentation software program from Microsoft.

Questionmark Perception: A web-based assessment delivery system widely used for computer-assisted evaluation of courses.

quiz: Within Captivate, a quiz is defined as all of the questions and click boxes in a single movie. You can exclude any of the questions or click boxes from the quiz as needed.

recording: In Captivate, recording is the process of capturing screens and storing audio and mouse movement elements for use in Captivate projects.

resolution (screen): Screen resolution is the number of pixels that can be displayed on a monitor, expressed as the number of horizontal pixels times the number of vertical pixels. For example, a standard screen size might be 1024 x 768.

scoring: The mechanism of determining how well a student does on a quiz. You can keep track of the number of questions the viewer gets right, or you can attach relative weights (or importance factors) to each question. You can also calculate a score and integrate it into an LMS.

SCORM: Sharable Content Object Reference Model is a specification created by the Advanced Distance Learning group and the United States Department of Defense to standardize the transfer of information between learning management systems. For more information on SCORM, see http://www.adlnet.org/.

storyboard: A storyboard is a planning device for movies that consists of a rough representation of both the visual and audio components, usually in paper format.

transition: In Captivate, a transition is the way a movie changes from one slide to the next.

transparency: The percentage of the background behind an image that shows through the image. A high transparency means that a lot of the background shows through the image, and 100% transparent means the image is invisible. A low transparency means that the image is quite dense, and very little of the background shows through.

weighting: A mechanism that attaches more importance to some quiz elements than others when calculating the final score. For example, introductory questions may be worth less than advanced questions. The advanced questions would have a higher weight.

WMF: Windows Metafile graphic format.

ADDITIONAL
RESOURCES

As you work with Adobe® Captivate® software, your movies are likely to get more sophisticated. There are a number of resources available on the Web that can help you get the most out of Captivate software as it evolves, as well as help you keep up with the latest in e-learning and Flash development. All URLs are accurate as of the time of this printing.

Captivate and Flash Resources

Flash Player download—You'll need this and the viewers of your movies will need this: http://get.adobe.com/flashplayer/.

Adobe Resource Center for Captivate—Lots of useful information including tech notes and release notes as they come out (http://www.adobe.com/support/captivate/).

Adobe Resource Center for Flash—For more detailed information on the Flash output format (http://www.adobe.com/support/flash/).

Accessible Flash lessons—Discussion of how to ensure that your Flash files (however you create them) are accessible to all (http://www.webaim.org/techniques/flash/).

e-learning

e-learning guru site—Loads of terrific articles, tools, white papers, and links (http://www.e-learningguru.com/).

The E-Learning Guild—An organization for managers and creators of e-learning (http://www.elearningguild.com/).

American Society for Training Development—An organization for trainers of all types (http://www.astd.org/astd).

Society for Technical Communication (STC) Instructional Design and Learning (IDL) Special Interest Group (SIG)—Lots of good resources, including a directory of service providers (http://www.stcidlsig.org)

CAPTIVATE SHORTCUT KEYS

Captivate software often gives you many ways to perform the same task, such as choosing from a menu, clicking a link, or pressing a combination of keys on your keyboard. The following table lists the shortcut keys in order by the keys used.

To use shortcut key combinations, hold down the first key while pressing the second (and third, if any).

Shortcut Key	Action
F1	Open Adobe Captivate Help (To access dialog-level help, click the Help button on individual dialog boxes.)
F3	Test view current slide (Edit view only)
F4	Preview project
F5	Record audio
F6	Import audio
F7	Spelling and grammar check
F8	Preview project from current slide
F9	Show the Advanced interaction dialog box

Shortcut Key	Action
F1 0	Preview current slide and following n slides
F11	View Adobe Captivate in full screen
F12	Preview project in web browser
Ctrl+A	Select all
Ctrl+C	Copy (slide in Storyboard view or filmstrip, and selected object in Edit view)
Ctrl+D	Duplicate (slide in Storyboard view or filmstrip, and selected object in Edit view)
Ctrl+E	Extend length of object display time to end of slide on Timeline (Edit view only)
Ctrl+F	Open the Find and Replace dialog box
Ctrl+G	Change slide to optimized quality
Ctrl+H	Change slide to high quality
Ctrl+I	Increase indent (selected object in Edit view)
Ctrl+J	Change slide to JPEG quality
Ctrl+K	Lock the slide
Ctrl+L	Sync selected object to the playhead
Ctrl+M	Merge the selected object with background
Ctrl+N	Move to Slide Notes pane
Ctrl+O	Open project
Ctrl+P	Align selected object with playhead on Timeline (Edit view only)
Ctrl+Q	Insert Random Question Slide
Ctrl+R	Print the project (through the Publish dialog box)
Ctrl+S	Save
Ctrl+T	Change slide to standard quality
Ctrl+U	Edit with (in project Library)
Ctrl+V	Paste what is on the clipboard (e.g., slide, image, object, etc.)
Ctrl+X	Cut (selected object in Edit view)
Ctrl+Y	Redo
Ctrl+Z	Undo
Ctrl+=	Zoom in
Ctrl+-	Zoom out

Shortcut Key	Action
Ctrl+Tab	To shift between Storyboard, Edit, and Branching view
Ctrl+Alt+B	Show Thumbnails (Edit view only)
Ctrl+Alt+D	Update Library
Ctrl+Alt+F	Find in Library
Ctrl+Alt+L	Show Library (Edit view only)
Ctrl+Alt+N	Show Slide Notes (Edit view only)
Ctrl+Alt+O	Record additional slides
Ctrl+Alt+R	Reset to original size
Ctrl+Alt+T	Show Timeline (Edit view only)
Ctrl+Alt+U	Library usage
Shift+Ctrl+A	Add animation object (Edit and Storyboard views only)
Shift+Ctrl+B	Add new button (Edit and Storyboard views only)
Shift+Ctrl+C	Add new caption (Edit and Storyboard views only)
Shift+Ctrl+D	View slide properties
Shift+Ctrl+E	Insert new zoom area (Edit and Storyboard views only)
Shift+Ctrl+F	Insert Flash Video (Edit and Storyboard views only)
Shift+Ctrl+G	Show the Go to Slide dialog box
Shift+Ctrl+H	Hide/Show slide
Shift+Ctrl+I	Decrease indent (selected object in Edit view)
Shift+Ctrl+J	Insert blank slide (Edit and Storyboard views only)
Shift+Ctrl+K	Add new click box (Edit and Storyboard views only)
Shift+Ctrl+M	Add new image
Shift+Ctrl+N	Add new animation slide
Shift+Ctrl+O	Add new rollover image
Shift+Ctrl+P	Publish file
Shift+Ctrl+Q	Insert question slide
Shift+Ctrl+R	Insert rollover caption
Shift+Ctrl+S	Insert image slide
Shift+Ctrl+T	Insert text entry box
Shift+Ctrl+U	Insert mouse
Shift+Ctrl+V	Paste as background

Shortcut Key	Action
Shift+Ctrl+W	Insert PowerPoint slide
Shift+Ctrl+X	Insert text animation
Shift+Ctrl+Y	Copy background
Shift+Ctrl+Z	**Insert hover area**

Index